ESPECIALLY FOR

....

FROM

....

DATE

....

RADICAL WISDOM

A DAILY JOURNEY FOR LEADERS

BY

REGI CAMPBELL

RADICAL WISDOM

This book is dedicated to Miriam, the bride of my youth and my wife of 49 years. Mimi, if it weren't for your grace, commitment, and love, there would be no Radical Wisdom to share. Thanks for helping me "be accurate."

. . . and to one of my youngest friends, Jackson Beetler. JB, were it not for your brains, your consistency, and your heart for Jesus, these principles would never have seen the light of day. You raise the bar for every other millennial.

INTRODUCTION

Over the course of the sixty-five years I've been awake and conscious, I've been a collector of principles. Even before I became a Jesus follower I picked up "work smart and not so hard" from my boss at the grocery store and "least said is easiest mended" from my mom. These are principles I remember and can say out loud. We can all recite a few of these.

But others lie beneath the surface . . . things we think but never say, things like "losers never win," "trust no one," and "look out for yourself." We develop a lot of these subconsciously as we live life, get hurt, and try to figure out how to protect ourselves.

Principles are how we navigate life. We have dreams and goals and visions for our futures, but we navigate life one day at a time. One decision at a time. One relational interaction at a time. When we're confronted with decisions and new situations, our brains look for shortcuts. Its first stop is the memory bank. "If I open that barbeque grill with the temperature at 650 degrees, I will singe my eyebrows off." I know that because I did it last time I grilled, and I looked pretty ugly for a while. All pretty straightforward.

But when the facts are more vague and outcomes less predictable, our minds quickly turn to the principles embedded in our minds. We reach for wisdom . . . for solid guidance on what to do next. It's not always obvious. "Experience is the best teacher," yet sometimes we find ourselves making the same mistakes over and over again.

Wisdom comes from *examined* experience. That's what we're looking for. And not just our own, but also that of others who have been examining their experiences and converting their wisdom into useful principles.

Leaders are hungry for wisdom. They're like sponges . . . soaking up every tidbit of useful information they can find. So whether you're leading a large organization or simply leading yourself, my goal is to share the wisdom I've accumulated over a lifetime.

One more thing before I let you get started. It's about the word "Radical" on the cover. To me, what makes something radical is either how different it is or how intensely it's applied. My hope is that over the next twelve months, you'll discover and internalize a few principles that will *radically* change your life and your leadership forever.

THE "ONE YEAR TO LIVE" EXERCISE

A good friend showed me all the stuff he was involved in. He was already stretched in a hundred directions, and now, he had two more incredible opportunities in front of him.

We all have different capacities, and most of us don't operate anywhere near full. But somehow we have to sort out what to take on and when to pass up an opportunity.

"What would you do if you had just one year to live?" I asked. As soon as I uttered the words, they flew back and hit me in the face.

As I've pondered the question, here's what I figured out:

1. I want to spend more time with individuals and less with institutions. Institutions will sustain themselves, with or without me. But I have this precious little smidgen of time to walk on this earth with people I love and want to help.

2. I want to spend more time with the One who's going to usher me from this life to the next. He's familiar with where I'll be going. He not only knows the way there—He built the place.

3. Finally, I want to pursue "my art." Seth Godin talks about doing what you're good at . . . what you love. He points us toward our unique abilities and passions and says, "That's your art."

There is a Thoreau quote we often hear half of: "Men lead quiet lives of desperation."

The other half? ". . . and go to the grave with the song still in them."

What's your song? If the year ahead were your last one here, what would you do? What would you not do?

QUESTION

Will this be the year you start to "sing the song" that's in you?

FACTS ARE FRIENDLY

I've probably said it a thousand times: facts are friendly. And every time I say it, my wife disagrees. It's become a point of debate, not just with us but with our friends as well. Let me stake out the point/counterpoint.

Point: I need to know the facts. Don't spin it, don't sugarcoat it. Give me the straight up. It may hurt, but if I embrace ironclad truth, I can adapt. If I live in self-deception, only getting fed half-truths or false impressions, I can't respond effectively. Imagine a doctor trying to prescribe meds to save someone's life based on incorrect blood work.

Over time, the facts are my friends because they are authentic. Real. They're not buddies, floaters who just make you feel good for the moment but vanish when it's tough. Facts are friendly because they're true. I can depend on them. I can build good decisions on them. I can build a good life on them. The truth sets us free, right?

"Then you will know the *truth*, and the *truth* will set you free," says John 8:32.

Counterpoint: Facts are hurtful, painful, and not always friendly. In fact, they're more often your enemy than your friend. They hurt your feelings, cause pain, disturb your peace, and create worry and disillusion. Few facts add value and warmth to your life. And few relationships are enhanced when one person decides to share "just the facts."

Galatians 4:16 asks, "Have I now become your enemy by telling you the *truth*?"

Since I'm the one writing, I say facts *are* friendly. But we must always be kind and remember that maturity involves not saying everything you know.

CHALLENGE

**Will you parse for truth or
just assume facts are friendly?**

A WIFE WITH NO VOICE

One of the most helpless feelings in the world is hearing your wife say, "I feel like I have no voice!" Especially after you've just explained a situation or decision to her for the third time and you're sure you've listened to her input. I can't tell you how deeply it hurts to make the effort to give her the extra detail she always wants and then to have it thrown back in your face and be criticized.

A few months ago, a friend made this statement to me. I feel like I should carve it on a stone tablet.

> A wife who feels she "has no voice" is one whose husband has talked about the *issue* but failed to connect with her *feelings*.

A while back, a friend and his wife were at each other's throats over the new car they needed. His wife explained why she wanted a minivan—why it fit her needs and her personality at this stage of life (two small kids and lots of activities = "Mom's taxi"). My friend found a deal on a huge, safe SUV and bought it without any real conversation with his wife. She couldn't get past it.

But when he learned this principle, he went to her and let her unpack her feelings about both the car choice and about the lack of connection to her feelings. He "fell on his sword," and now they're on the same page again.

It's a powerful principle. Connect with her feelings first, then talk about the facts. You'll get a different reception.

SCRIPTURE

"Likewise, husbands, live with your wives in an understanding way." (1 Peter 3:7, ESV)

TRANSPARENCY VS. VULNERABILITY

More and more, I run into men who are willing to "tell it all." Almost like a badge of courage, they'll spill their guts about their pasts—about their extra-marital shenanigans, their divorces, their past lack of honesty, excessive drinking and other screwups. "God's forgiven me for all that. Isn't He great?" they'll say.

He *is* great, don't get me wrong.

But transparency carries with it a blood brother named vulnerability. Much of our sin (to use an old word) is a symptom of a much more onerous disease. Many of the men I've mentored struggle with vulnerability, with looking way back and way deep into the wounds that drive our "I've got to be successful and accepted" behavior.

One definition of vulnerability is the willingness to give and take meaningful feedback. Vulnerability says, "I'm going to let a counselor, a mentor, or a trusted friend into all my ugly stuff to help me interpret it accurately. When I can do that, I can accept God's grace and His forgiveness. I start to see myself the way God sees me."

We behave out of what we believe. As we start to see ourselves as God sees us, it's easier for us to behave the way He wants us to.

Transparency says, "Look inside my life. I'm not hiding anything."

"Vulnerability says, "Look inside my life *with me*. I want God to change me and make me more like Jesus."

QUESTION

Will you be vulnerable with a trusted friend? With your Heavenly Father?

STRONGER, CLOSER, TOGETHER

One common question in church is, "Don't we need to go deeper?" "Are we 'fast food church,' looking to make following Jesus quick serve, high calorie, low cost, low value?" "Are people going to become deeply rooted in Jesus through our church?"

I looked in Scripture for the words "deeply rooted." I found firm roots (Psalm 1:3), old roots (Job 14:7), and rotted roots (Isaiah 5:24). In Revelation 22:16, Jesus called Himself "the Root." But none of those are quite what I was looking for.

Finally, I found something called the Montgomery New Testament, which translates Ephesians 3:17 to include the words "deeply rooted." Maybe the parable of the sower, where Jesus talks about "good soil," makes us think the best roots are deep roots.

But consider the redwood trees of America's Pacific Coast. Many of these redwoods exceed 300 feet, with the tallest tree clocking in at 379 feet, taller than the Statue of Liberty!

These gigantic trees have very shallow root systems. Their roots extend more than 100 feet from the base, intertwining with the roots of other redwoods. This interconnectedness is the secret to their stability and strength.

Being *rooted* in Jesus means having a solid faith. The best way to survive and thrive in that faith is by becoming a part of a community of interconnected people who share faith in Christ, who are being changed by Christ, and who are joined together in the mission of Christ.

Are you interconnected to such a community? If not, seek until you find it.

SCRIPTURE

"That Christ may make his home in your hearts through your faith; that you may be so deeply rooted and so firmly grounded in love."
(Ephesians 3:17, MNT)

DECISION-MAKING . . . THINK ABOUT IT

All decisions, in the moment, from the perspective of the decision-maker, are between the greater of two goods or the lesser of two evils. There are no right or wrong decisions.

When I heard this principal from Robert McKee's book on story, I was repulsed, "Of course there's a right or wrong decision. If it violates Scripture, it's wrong. This is bull!"

And from an outcomes point of view, a decision to violate God's law is always wrong.

But as I've worked through it and I think about the decision, *from the perspective of the decision-maker, in the moment,* I've come to believe that he's right. The decision is between the greater of two goods or the lesser of two evils.

Let's say I have to decide between stopping to help a stranded motorist or getting to a meeting on time. Which is the greater good? In the moment, from my personal perspective, there is no right or wrong per se. I have to choose between the greater of two goods: be on time or be the good Samaritan. As a Christian, I better pray and obey.

But let's go the other way. I'm traveling, in a hotel room and I'm as lonely as can be. Do I spin up a porn flick on the TV? Or do I wallow in my loneliness and try to go to sleep? My choices are between the lesser of two evils: loneliness or outright sin. Hopefully I'll choose loneliness, the lesser of the two evils.

CHALLENGE

**When you have a decision to make, ask
"What are the two goods I'm choosing between
here?" or "What are the two evils?" It might
be clarifying for you as you navigate life.**

INTENTIONALITY AND THE "LYLE SYNDROME"

Our son had the best dog that ever lapped water from the face of the earth. Lyle was a black lab with more sense and sensitivity than you can imagine. We would have a conversation about food, then come back later and discover he had retrieved a bag of Ramen from the shelf. Unopened of course, because he wouldn't want to upset us. It was like he knew what we were talking about. He was amazing.

But intentionality wasn't Lyle's strong suit. When you let him out to pee, he'd walk a few feet, sniff, and change direction, before relieving himself somewhere. Then he'd sniff again and be off to wherever. Another sniff, another change of direction. You could call him, but never interrupt him. He was off on a totally unplanned adventure that had been determined, not by any thought or plan, but by the next whiff of something desirable that came his way.

A lot of us are living our lives that way. We go wherever our "nose" takes us. Our direction is determined by whatever feels the best, pays the best, looks the best on our resume, or seems the best to our friends.

Just like Lyle, we need a master. Someone who will come after us when we've gotten lost. Someone to help us hold back from things that can hurt us. And someone to lead us to the things that will truly satisfy and give our lives meaning.

Have you experienced the "Lyle Syndrome"? Have you "wandered off the farm" and found yourself far from where you intended to be?

SCRIPTURE

**"Trust in the Lord with all your heart; do
not depend on your own understanding.
Seek his will in all you do, and he will show
you which path to take." (Proverbs 3:5-6, NLT)**

JANUARY 8

SELFISH INTEREST

"The one human quality you can always depend on is selfish interest." The first time I heard that I bristled. "Wow, what a nasty outlook on people. Are we really that bad?" Then the real question . . .

"Am *I* that way?"

The answer is yes, I am. And you are, too. And what's really cool is God made us that way.

Let's make it simple. There is me, and there's everybody else.

Me? All the way back to Maslow, we've known that self-preservation is the most basic human need. We can't help others if we don't survive ourselves, so we have this innate desire to stay alive . . . to protect ourselves . . . to look out for number one.

Everybody else? Once I realize that *everybody else* has this same desire to survive and protect themselves, I can see through all the posing and positioning and remember that first and foremost, their need is to look out for themselves.

How does this help in my day-to-day interactions?

I do better if I perceive without judging. In every situation, every relationship, ask, "What does he need?" "What's her selfish interest here?" It's there, whether or not it's recognized or acknowledged. The quicker and more accurately I can assess the other person's selfish interests, the quicker I can decide if I can help them get what they want, or at least assess whether what I'm asking of them threatens what *they* want or need.

SCRIPTURE

**"We who are strong must be considerate of those
who are sensitive about things like this. We must
not just please ourselves." (Romans 15:1, NLT)**

"YOU WILL ALWAYS HAVE THE POOR AMONG YOU"

These words of Jesus almost take away the urgency to help, don't they?

Jesus was teaching His disciples the difference between the temporal and the eternal, between the practical and the divine.

We've taken His words out of context and used them to set ourselves free from taking the needs of the poor personally. Helping people directly is messy, and the line between showing mercy and creating dependency is vague. So we institutionalize helping the poor, writing checks so we can avoid being personally involved.

What if, for every dollar we spend on ourselves for things we want (but do not need), we spend a dollar to help the "least of these?"

After all, the Bible says, "Love your neighbor as yourself." If I love myself enough to buy something I want that costs $200, couldn't I choose to love my (poor or or-phaned) neighbor to the tune of $200?

Imagine how the poor would be helped, how the world would be changed, how God would be glorified, if we stepped up to a dollar-for-dollar commitment.

The poor will always be with us. But let's not miss out on the chance God has given us to help.

SCRIPTURE

"Religion that God our Father accepts as pure and faultless is this: to look after orphans and widows in their distress and to keep oneself from being polluted by the world." (James 1:27)

TRUTH TELLING

Isn't it weird how we lie? How we spin stories to make them represent the people we wish we were instead of who we are? Or sit quietly and let an untruth be perpetuated when we know it's a lie? And we'll do it with people we've known for years as much as with total strangers.

Jeremiah 27 tells us our hearts are deceptive, incurably so, but it seems ridiculous how much we struggle with telling the simple truth. Often the lie is not overt; it's not telling something untrue, it's failing to correct something that's not true or accurate.

My theory is that we have multiple versions of ourselves stored away in our minds. The athlete version of me ran a mile in under six minutes in high school. That never happened. The musician version of me opened for Marvin Gaye back in the sixties. The story gets told and retold, but it's fantasy.

We create these versions of ourselves so we'll measure up—so we'll be acceptable, admired, and respected.

Most people hear these stories and know they're lies. How? Because they have their own drawer full of stories they tell about themselves for the same reasons. So they'll be accepted. Admired. Respected.

Here's the real kicker: Maintaining all those fantasies makes us feel worse about ourselves, not better. It's called living a lie.

As believers, God has already found us totally acceptable (through Christ) *without* all that stuff. Grabbing hold of that and believing it changes your life.

CHALLENGE

Next time you find yourself on the cusp of bending the truth, perpetuating a deception from the past, or about to say something that isn't true, don't. Decide to speak truth instead.

LOVE IS NOT A HOLE YOU FALL INTO

It's a choice you make. And it's not always an easy choice. Often, I just don't feel like loving my wife, especially when she disagrees with me. Or when she's failed to do things I've asked her to do. Or when she's got stuff for me to do that I'm not motivated to do.

I'd much rather have a wife who meets my exact desire at the exact right time. I want her to wear a beautiful dress and makeup when we're going to be around people I care about. I want the best possible recipes prepared like Martha Stewart when we entertain. And of course, I want her to be sultry and sexy at bedtime, especially when the mood is right.

The problem is, all this is fantasy. *My* fantasy.

My wife can never meet all these expectations. Heck, I can't even verbalize some of them.

My wife is an individual who has the right to be herself. I must choose to love her *just as she is!* If I consistently show her my love, there's a chance she'll want to do things that please me at times. But that has to be from God's grace, not from a trade.

Face it: your wife is going to disappoint you. The question is:

>How will you respond?

Will you let your disappointment breed anger? Or will you *choose* to love her? Volitionally. Intentionally. Regardless of how you feel.

The fact is, you love your wife and you committed to her for life. Don't be distracted by how you feel. Choose to love her. Then do something that demonstrates your love. It'll change your heart. And hers, too.

CHALLENGE

**If you *really believe* that love is an act of
the will, not just a fluffy feeling, then act!**

EXCLUSIVE VS. INCLUSIVE

Carl Sandburg was a legendary American writer and poet. In an interview, he was once asked, "You are such a master of words . . . what is your least favorite word?"

His answer was the word "exclusive."

I get it. No one likes to be excluded, to be put on the outside, to be dissed.

The odd thing about Christianity in today's culture is that it's perceived to be exclusive. Since there's "only one way to God through Jesus Christ," Christianity excludes every other religious persuasion. It even excludes good people who aren't religious at all.

But the opposite is true as well.

Christianity is totally inclusive. One doesn't have to have Christian parents or a certain name or surname. Christianity doesn't require a person to go through a process to "convert," doesn't make them *do* anything. One simply has to believe the truth of Jesus' life, death, resurrection, and forgiveness of their sins, and they are Christians. Little baby Christians, but Christians all the same.

We make it so hard for those who don't believe. We talk about "giving your life to Jesus." But that's not in the Bible. The gospel is Jesus Christ crucified to provide forgiveness, acceptance, and a relationship with our Heavenly Father. Simple. Inclusive. Available to everyone.

If something is true, it's true. No one is excluded from gravity, right? Jesus is true. He's as real as gravity. And His love excludes no one. It just has to be received.

QUESTION

Does your attitude toward those who don't believe draw them to Jesus? Or does it feel like rejection and push them away?

ARE YOU ARROGANT?

It's the Saturday night bonfire at the men's retreat.

"Write on this card the issue in your life you haven't turned over to God."

The card gets nailed to a cross, then the cross gets burned in the fire.

Moving. Convicting. Healing.

I've done this before. Normally I write "busyness." It's been my besetting sin forever. This time, I pray and quickly write a word on the card. But when I look down, I am startled to see . . .

Arrogance.

"Lord, what do you mean?" I ask.

"You rush out in the morning and walk right by the place where you pray. Are you about serving Me? Yes. But you assume I want you to do what you did yesterday. You don't ask for new instructions. When you don't ask what I might have you do, that's arrogance, not humility."

A friend of mine got up one day and asked, "Lord, what would you have me do today?" His sister's name came to mind, along with a sense that he needed to call her. They had drifted apart because of a deep disagreement, but he called her anyway. She told him she was pregnant and had an appointment with an abortion doctor that morning. He asked if she would meet him instead.

She did. They talked. They prayed. She kept the baby, and he's now a thriving little boy. God used my friend to save a life, all because he stopped to ask God for His "orders" for the day and then acted.

QUESTION

**Do you meet with God every
day to seek new instructions?**

JANUARY 14

HUMAN BEING OR HUMAN DOING?

I recently had it handed to me by a good friend. He said, "When I see someone running as hard as you, I wonder who he's trying to please." He didn't even ask, "*Is* he trying to please someone?" He knew that answer. The question was *who*?

Most of us start out trying to please our dads. For some, that's the *who* for all our lives, whether we realize it or not. For years, each time I'd get a promotion or a raise, I'd call my dad before I called my wife. I never thought about what that really said about the most significant *who* in my life.

But after surrendering to God and replacing my earthly father with my Heavenly Father, things changed. I released my earthly dad of all my expectations; from all the things I wished he had been and done. I forgave him and accepted him just as he was for the rest of his life. But before long, I was driving just as hard as a sold-out Christian as I was before.

Why?

Because I made God my work. Many of us do it. We make Him something we do. The church *loves* it because we fill the volunteer jobs, the seats, and the offering plates.

But when we identify ourselves by what we do versus who we are, we miss what God really wants. He wants a relationship with us. He wants communion, engagement, worship, gratitude, and love. These things flow from the Holy Spirit living in our hearts when we stop being human *doings* and become human *beings*.

QUESTION

As you reflect on the past week, have you been a human doing or a human being?

TWO-WAY RELATIONSHIPS

Once you *get* the essence of Christianity (it's not about you, but about God and others) you find yourself really busy. You're immersed in church stuff: ministries, Bible studies, small groups, and the like. You step it up with your wife and kids, working to become the leader they need you to be. But before you know it, you're alone.

Alone, because loving others is easier than letting others love you.

Yes, you're all give and no get. But no one knows you. No one knows what you think, how you think, what you're afraid of, what you dream about. Because you're going so fast, seem so strong, and are "in God's will," no one is going to chase you down and ask, "How are you doing? I mean, *really* doing?"

Imagine you have a good friend, maybe someone you've been investing in and helping, who stops you and asks—who truly expresses an interest. "How are you doing, man? I mean *really*!"

Dilemma.

Do you tell him? Do you confess your struggles? Do you admit your loneliness? Does he really care about you and your stuff, or is he just being nice?

You won't ever know until you trust him with your true self. As a recent beneficiary of "two-way relationships," I can say unequivocally, *tell him the truth.* Open up. Let your friend love you. Express your need for help.

This is hard for men because we are prideful by nature. Christ was the opposite. He was "gentle and humble in heart." He took His closest friends with Him. He asked them to be there in His hour of need. He told them *everything*.

QUESTION

**Do you have a friend who knows
everything about you? If not, why?**

WHAT'S DOWN IN THE WELL COMES UP IN THE BUCKET

One of my young executives taught me a principle years ago that I've never forgotten. It was cathartic for me as a leader and as a husband.

He said, "When something one of your employees does bothers you, confront them with it before that day ends. No matter how petty, how trivial, how embarrassing, confront it. Don't go home and don't let them go home, without talking it out."

For years, I harbored grudges against my wife. "She's not *this*," "She doesn't do *that*." I let all those little things build up until they were destroying our marriage. What would have happened if I had dealt with all that stuff along the way? What if I had sought counsel about my feelings and judgments? What if I'd talked those things out with her *immediately* when I started to feel them?

The reality is that it took her leaving for a while to wake me up to the junk I had hidden down in my "well." Like a splinter buried deep in the sole of your foot, it has to come out, or it's going to lead to real problems.

God created us for relationships. He taught us to keep short accounts—"before dark" short. When we man up and deal with what's lodged in our hearts, we'll be healthier, lighter, and more lovable.

SCRIPTURE

"In your anger do not sin: Do not let the sun go down while you are still angry." (Ephesians 4:26)

DESERVE: MY LEAST FAVORITE WORD

There are few words in the English language that stop me cold. Hearing the Lord's name used in vain does it. But about the only other word that has same effect is the word, "deserve." Every time I hear it, I want to explode.

Deserve means "to be worthy of." What am I worthy of without Jesus?

He gives me every breath I breathe. He gives me every heartbeat, every bite of food, every sight I see . . . it all comes from Him. Every ounce of love I feel comes from someone He put (and kept) in my life. He owes me nothing. It's all grace, an undeserved blessing.

"Deserve" and "grace" are children of comparison and contrast. We feel like we deserve something because we compare what we did with the consequence that ensues. "He deserved that heart attack. He didn't exercise and looked like the Michelin man." "He deserved that promotion. He worked his butt off."

In our performance-based, risk-reward, pay-for-play world, we reduce everything to an equation—a yin for a yang, a tit for a tat. Or worse, we feel entitled. "I deserve, because I am . . ."

Selfish people want what they deserve. Grateful people are grateful for what they are given.

CHALLENGE

**Be thoughtful before you say, "I deserve."
Remember, what we deserve is eternal life
separated from God and our loved ones.
But because of God's grace and Jesus'
sacrifice, we have peace, love, joy, patience,
kindness, goodness, faithfulness, gentleness,
and self-control in this life, followed by
heaven with Him and the family of God.**

WHY GUYS LIKE GOLF

Guys talk about how tough the game of golf is—how frustrating, how unforgiving, how you can never quite conquer it, never master it.

But they keep going back to play thousands of times each year.

Could it be the occasional shot you make; the one that leaves your club with that sweet sound, arcs perfectly toward the target, and lands just where it's supposed to? It's a flash of affirmation that says, "Hey, I *may* actually have it in me. Maybe I *do* measure up! Maybe I do have what it takes!"

Then the next shot dribbles off the tee and the ball sinks into the pond. Your playing partners smile, maybe even laugh.

You feel shame. You want to disappear like your ball just did.

That's why I think golf is about shame and affirmation.

In the blissful moment of an awesome golf shot, your shame is replaced by affirmation. It doesn't matter that your score is the highest or that you're the worst golfer in the group. You feel the affirmation when you see the ball going straight at the pin and you know you're the one who hit it.

Men who have chosen to love Jesus and let Jesus love them have no basis for self-doubt or shame. We have complete, total, and constant affirmation from our Heavenly Father whether we are good golfers or not.

QUESTION

Are you willing to listen as He says, "I love you, man. Just as you are. I made you to be *you*. You have what it takes because you're My adopted son."

GOD DON'T WASTE NOTHIN'

Years ago, Patrick Morley described visiting with an elderly saint he knew. He wanted to pose a question only a saint could answer, so he asked her to explain Romans 8:28: "And we know that in all things God works for the good of those who love him, who have been called according to his purpose."

She thought for a minute, then said, "Well I guess it's just that God don't waste nothin'."

I've never forgotten her words. They explain a lot.

Maybe the most basic of questions, the one that follows, "Is there a God?" is this: "Why does God do what He does?"

The answer is simple yet incredibly complex. *For His glory.*

The most vivid example of this is when Jesus' friend Lazarus died.

Two days after he died, Lazarus was brought back to life. His sisters and friends got to see God's glory in real time. We can imagine they celebrated and praised Jesus big time.

God didn't waste nothin' in Lazarus's death. He got the praise He deserved. And everything was restored for Lazarus and his family in the end. They just had to wait in order to understand and receive it.

The same is true for us. The same Jesus who prevailed for Lazarus will prevail for us in the end. It may not be experienced in this life, but the outcome will be good because our God is good.

SCRIPTURE

"But when Jesus heard about it he said, 'Lazarus's sickness will not end in death. No, it happened for the glory of God so that the Son of God will receive glory from this.'" (John 11:4, NLT)

SO, WHAT IS FAITH ANYWAY?

We're Christians because we have faith in the life, death, and resurrection of Jesus Christ. That seems sort of easy when it doesn't cause us personal pain.

It's harder to have faith when God allows a man to get hit by a car while he's biking with his son. Or when God tolerates an innocent child being sold into the sex trade. Or when God seemingly doesn't answer when we cry out for mercy for one of His most committed servants to be relieved of constant, debilitating pain.

There are two elements in God's perspective that are missing from ours—two things we have to grasp and embrace *by faith* if we're going to make sense of pain and tragedy in this world:

1. **The long view**—God sees timelessly. We think right now; He thinks in terms of eternity. What feels like tragedy to us in the short-term is grace and mercy in the long-term.

2. **The broad view**—God is always doing multiple things in multiple people's lives at the same time. We have no idea how our momentary pain or overwhelming tragedy is being used to challenge someone; to break down a hard heart or to raise up compassion.

When Romans 8:28 starts with, "We know . . ." it means we *know in advance*. We know God loves us, and He's in charge. In faith, we surrender. We yield our demands for a certain outcome. We trust that He knows what's best.

In faith, we *choose* to believe that God has a plan and that our pain is going to be used sometime for good somewhere for someone.

SCRIPTURE

"Faith is confidence in what we hope for and assurance about what we do not see." (Hebrews 11:1)

JANUARY 21

SACRED SELFISHNESS

My CFO used to say, "There are two kinds of people in this world. The kind who say 'there are two kinds of people', and those who don't." I guess I do believe there are two kinds of people: those who are focused on themselves and those who care about others.

Consider the things we hear Christians say . . .

I have my faith.
I have eternal life.
I have the Bible.
I have peace.

I have my church.
I have the Holy Spirit.
I have my small group.

How many times did you hear "I"? Without thinking, we devolve into a faith that's all about us. It's *sacred selfishness*. And it's not what Jesus modeled and talked about.

Jesus gave His life away for others. He was *others-focused* and never *I-focused*. He revealed His purpose statement in John 10:10: ". . . I have come that they may have life, and have it to the full." He was telling us that the abundant life . . . the *full life* . . . begins when we turn our attention to the needs of others.

In our culture of silo living, where work, church, neighborhoods, and friends are so segmented from each other, it's easy to withdraw into the safety of our families and the people we *have* to serve.

Generally speaking, I can't be the answer to my own prayer. But I might be used by God to be the answer to someone else's.

CHALLENGE

Ask God to bring someone into your life who needs something . . . food, financial help, counseling, or maybe just a friend who will listen. He might just answer your prayer! And you might get a taste of the joy that comes from focusing on the needs of others instead of yourself.

A LIFE OF MEANING . . .

How can we live a life of meaning? A lot has been written about purpose, but less about meaning.

Let's define it first. Meaning is implied or explicit significance.

There are three arenas in which meaning is displayed:

1. **Self-actualization**—becoming all God intended you to be.
2. **Others**—giving yourself away to help others.
3. **God**—loving, worshiping, and obeying God.

So which area of life provides the most meaning?

I believe it's the trifecta. It's realizing that you're right where you're supposed to be. You're on a mission from God, and He is holding you up. Every encounter, every activity is *real*; it's you, the person you're serving, and God. You are God's hands and feet.

God doesn't necessarily call the prepared; He prepares the called. And when we are "called according to His purpose," He prepares, provides, sustains, encourages, and blesses.

Meaning is experienced when you see your efforts make a difference to the people you're serving, *and* you know you've exercised your God-given talents and gifts. You see the impact on others, and that gives you a lot of joy. But you know God was behind it all.

Meaning is doing something that matters. It matters to you, it matters to others, and it matters to God. It's all three.

SCRIPTURE

"And we know that in all things God works for the good of those who love him, who have been called according to his purpose." (Romans 8:28)

REST FOR YOUR SOUL

Do you feel like you're being bounced around like a BB in a boxcar? Maybe you got a surprise tax bill. Or perhaps a friend says you make him feel like an "object." Did a neighbor announce a surprise decision that affects your property without so much as a heads up? Or did a leader you've trusted say some things that surprised you? Maybe your doctor visit didn't go quite like you hoped.

Driven to your knees, you say, "Lord, this was a tough week." You pause and you hear God, in His soundless but familiar voice, say, "I love you." You smile, recognizing His voice and His smile. Your next thought?

> "Come to me, all you who are weary and burdened, and I
> will give you rest. Take my yoke upon you and learn from
> me, for I am gentle and humble in heart, and you will find
> rest for your souls." (Matthew 11:28-29)

God is inviting us in. He has what we need, even if it's not what we want. We want things to change. We want those things to have not happened. We want to feel good. To win at life. To have no worries. To be free.

But what we *need* is rest.

He's telling us to *come to Him.* We have to initiate. He's not saying, "Come to bed," "Come to counseling," "Come for a walk," "Come for a massage," "Come and have a drink." He's saying, *"Come to Me."* And if we will, He promises rest for our souls.

QUESTION

**When was the last time you chose to go
to the Father to get rest for your soul?**

GOAL-ACHIEVING OR TENSION-RELIEVING?

From a practical standpoint, everything we do is goal-achieving or tension-relieving.

A goal is a vision of what can be. Once we've embraced a goal, we've created tension between what is and what can be. This positive tension motivates us, and drives us toward achieving the goal. We may never put the goal in writing, but it certainly gets logged in our minds.

When we focus on relieving tension, we are pointed toward what *was* versus what *is*. It often arises from a desire to return to a pleasant place from the past or to protect the status quo. We may work just as hard to relieve tension as to achieve goals.

We all have some goal-achieving and some tension-relieving impulses in us. And there's a time for each. Goal-achieving actions are usually harder. They create a challenge. They require taking risk. Tension-relieving tasks are usually easier. They're familiar. Low risk. Safe.

But which seems more like Jesus? Which leads us to a deeper relationship with God and more dependence on Him?

When you sit down at your desk today, you have a choice. Will you relieve tension by straightening up, organizing, making lists, and restoring the order of the past? Or will you look at the things you can do that will change things . . . that will make a difference . . . that will add value to your organization, employees, customers, vendors, superiors, or friends?

QUESTION

**When you pray today, will you ask God
for what's easy? Or will you ask Him for
what makes a difference?**

. . . A DIME A DAY

One of my mentors credited his grandfather with this principle . . .

> "Give a man a dime a day for thirty days, then stop. He'll resent you for the rest of his life."

He was right. When we see someone with a need and we meet it, we feel good about our-selves. And after all, aren't we instructed in Scripture to help? Doesn't 1 John 3:17 say, "If anyone has material possessions and sees a brother or sister in need but has no pity on them, how can the love of God be in that person?" That's mercy.

I'm talking about something different. I'm talking about help that leads to dependence, help that weakens, help that absolves people of taking personal responsibility.

There are two places it's most obvious, at least to me.

First, with our children. The fact that 28 percent of all college kids become boomerangs, moving back home with college degrees in hand, shows that moms and dads are increasingly "helping" their kids become more depen-dent and less self-reliant.

The other place we see dependence is in missions. My friend tells of a village in Kenya that desperately needed chicken houses. An organization worked with local leadership to get the plans and building materials delivered there. Almost two years later, the chicken houses still aren't built. Why? Because the locals are waiting for the Americans to come on a "mission trip" and build them! They've been trained to expect it. That's what we do.

Invest with compassion. Give from mercy. But try to avoid the unintended consequence of repeated mercy: dependence.

QUESTION

**Where are you creating unhealthy dependency
through repetitive mercy?**

BITTER OR BETTER?

They say that life will make you bitter or better.

I'll never forget watching in disbelief as TV cameras captured the anger of people being asked to leave the free government housing provided after the Katrina disaster. They felt like *their* homes were being stolen from them, even though they knew the units had been provided as temporary shelter to get them through the recovery and cleanup.

We shouldn't be shocked. It's always been that way with people. Noah and his family were spared, yet his immediate act after leaving the boat was to get naked and drunk. Aaron walked with Moses and saw the hand of God every day. But left alone for just a little while, his gratitude turned to idol worship.

And then there are the ten lepers Jesus healed. Only one came back to say thank you.

Gratitude doesn't happen by accident. It's fleeting. It doesn't come easy. It's not natural in our selfish, self-absorbed skin.

But it's a choice we can make. Choose gratitude and watch your bitterness diminish. Think about what you've been given and watch your appetite for what you *don't* have fade.

The movie *Courageous* explored one of the most painful things we can experience: the loss of a child. The main character in the movie is overwhelmed with bitterness and anger until he finally decides to be grateful for the eleven years he had with his daughter instead of angry over what he wouldn't have. Easier said than done, but a far better choice.

The only sure cure for anxiety, bitterness, and anger is a grateful heart.

QUESTION

Has something you've lost made you bitter? Will you choose gratitude and let God make your life better?

THE JOY OF GIVING LIFE

I'm overwhelmed with joy when I watch a man go all-in for Jesus Christ and then see God redeem his marriage, his children, his business, his relationships.

That's life for me.

This quote from Nate Larkin's book *Samson & the Pirate Monks* has stuck with me:

> "When we make another man's progress our concern, giving him a listening ear and a caring heart and opening ourselves as a conduit for God's grace, we find our own walk propelled to a whole new level. We are truly helped by helping, taught by teaching, and encouraged by encouraging."

My real life began when I embraced Christ and accepted His call to be an ambassador for Him. I started to invest in the lives of others for Kingdom purposes—first my own children, then younger men in my church, then at work and through a ministry.

Little by little, I took more and more risk with people who were further and further away from the safety of my holy huddle. Now I show up for the first night of my new Radical Mentoring groups and meet most of the guys I'll invest in for the first time.

I've also learned that the best antidote for selfishness is giving, not just money, but time and emotional energy. Lots of people give their money. That's easier because time is an even more limited commodity. Give of your time and watch how God changes you and your world.

CHALLENGE

Isn't now the time to start moving away from just writing checks and truly invest in others? We can trust God to cover gaps in your work and families.

DANCING WITH THE STARS

After I surrendered to Christ years ago, my wife said, "You're not dancing anymore!" She had seen me constantly striving for the approval of my superiors at work; always seeking the affirmation of our friends; always moving, never still, never content, always driving for something.

All my life, I wanted to matter. I was always seeking affirmation. I vibrated, constantly working, schmoozing, smiling, cajoling, kissing butt, whatever it took to *matter*.

But to whom? Who was keeping score? Whom was I trying to impress?

I later learned I was subconsciously trying to please my father. At thirty-three, I was still trying to *matter* to my dad. When I replaced him with my Heavenly Father, I stopped dancing. God closed out the scorecard and signed it. Through Jesus' work on the cross, God gave me a perfect score as a son—no handicap and nothing to prove to my earthly father nor to anyone else. I was affirmed. Accepted. Loved. Forever.

That acceptance gave me peace for the first time in my life.

I still have those behavior patterns. I'm still hyperactive, still tempted to seek the affirmation of people, especially those I admire. But in my heart of hearts, I know I'm OK, I can relax. I can revel in God's love. I know I can depend on His affirmation.

My Heavenly Father loves and accepts me, and that's all that matters in this life—and even more thirty seconds after I die.

SCRIPTURE

"In him we have redemption through his blood, the forgiveness of sins, in accordance with the riches of God's grace that he lavished on us with all wisdom and understanding." (Ephesians 1:7-8)

YOU GET WHAT YOU GLORIFY

Have you ever watched as a young girl is "made up" by her mom, being introduced to makeup, rouge, eyeliner, and lipstick while still a child? Then she's told how beautiful she is, not because she is, but because she (or her mom) is trying so hard.

Have you been to a little league game and watched as the dad screams with delight over his son's base hit or home run? High-fives everywhere as he slides in and scores.

I've lived long enough to see some of those young boys and girls become men and women, and I've come to see that *you get what you glorify!*

When we spend countless hours and dollars dressing our children and adolescents to the nines, we're going to get "clotheshorses" when they grow up. When the only thing our sons get glory for is sports performance, we're going to get jocks when they get older.

There is nothing wrong with clothes or makeup, and nothing wrong with sports.

But be aware of what you're glorifying in your kids.

In my lexicon, the word "glorify" is interchangeable with the word "praise." What you praise in your kids is what they'll pursue for themselves as they grow up.

Consider glorifying your child's kindness for others. Catch them doing something for a brother or sister. Praise them for it. Glorify them for praying, reading the Bible, asking about Jesus, and giving money to the church, to charities, or to the poor.

Remember, you're always leading. The question is to where.

SCRIPTURE

"Start children off on the way they should go, and even when they are old they will not turn from it." (Proverbs 22:6)

DIVINE INTERVENTION?

Does God intervene in our circumstances? I don't know, but here's my best shot at an answer . . .

Perspective–God sees everything in series, while we see everything in sequence. We don't know when His intervention is active, meaning when He *does* something; or passive, when He (apparently) doesn't do anything.

Relationships–God is working on and in multiple people's lives during a crisis. He may be using disruption to wake someone up from spiritual death, to reawaken someone else who has drifted, or to encourage someone else with His love for them shown through others.

Timing–We want what we want when we want it . . . which is now. We can deal with waiting if there is certainty in the outcome at the end of the wait, but this side of heaven we don't get that very often. Death and life after death is at the top of the list of things where God's perspective on time and ours is way, way different.

Goodness–God is good. Do you believe that? If not, you're going to have a long, confusing journey through life. It wasn't His idea for death, disease, evil, and pain to come into the world. He created life, joy, beauty, and love. Believing God is good, no matter how bad the circumstances, gives us hope.

Love–God loves us enough to give us free will, which required Him to tolerate death, evil, and suffering. Through Christ's death and resurrection, we know how He loves us and expect the next life to be pain-free, death-free, and spectacular.

Lean on the fact that God is *with* you today no matter your circumstances.

SCRIPTURE

**"Be strong and courageous. Do not be afraid
or terrified because of them, for the Lord your
God goes with you; he will never leave you
nor forsake you." (Deuteronomy 31:6)**

SELFLESSNESS SHINES

Almost everything we do has a quid pro quo. There are very few things we do that are absolutely, unequivocally selfless.

The most vivid illustration is in marriage.

We trade all the time. . .

We empty and load the dishwasher to gain the freedom to watch football. We trade a little patience and understanding for sex. We trade taking care of the kids for the freedom to play a round of guilt-free golf.

But consider Christ's death on the cross. That was no trade. He got *nothing* in return for that. It was totally selfless on His part. He deserved no punishment, but took *all* of ours and got nothing in return.

When I read Ephesians 5:25, "Husbands, love your wives, just as Christ loved the church and gave himself up for her," I'm reminded of my calling as a husband. I am called to love my wife and "give myself up" for her—to give up my selfish desires, selfish habits, selfish goals and to put her above myself. When I do, she loves me to death. Without even knowing it, she's loving the Jesus living in me. And God gets the glory.

CHALLENGE

Try selflessness for one day. Live a completely selfless marriage existence for twenty-four hours. Put her first. Listen. Anticipate her needs. Do more than your part. You'll catch a glimpse of what Jesus wants for us in all our relationships: "to consider others above yourself."

SHEEPDOG OR SHEPHERD?

When I visited New Zealand a few years ago, I saw a demonstration of the well-trained working sheepdogs who daily move sheep from place to place.

Incredibly quick and extremely tenacious, the dogs reminded me of some of the bosses I've had and, unfortunately, of some of my own leadership early on. I thought I was leading, but I was simply barking, manipulating, scaring, and irritating those under my care.

Dallas Willard, in his book *Hearing God,* says, "The sheepdog forcibly maneuvers the sheep, whereas the biblical shepherd simply calls as he calmly walks ahead of the sheep." I really like that picture. Leading by doing. Influence over authority. Calling to your followers, to your family, "Come with me. Do what I do, and we'll be fine."

Is that how you're leading your wife? Your kids? Your family? Your employees?

Our leadership isn't being cut down by axes and chainsaws; it's dying through thousands of paper cuts. Small lies, inconsistencies, compromises, and hard-heartedness that we excuse because we're so busy. In reality, it's easier to be a sheepdog leader, to bark loud and continually wear ourselves out running around the herd, confusing activity with accomplishment.

But if we do the opposite, if we're shepherd leaders who earn the right to lead and who call as we calmly walk ahead, we'll look behind and find willing followers drawing their strength and confidence from walking in our steps.

QUESTION

**Are you going first, living and demonstrating
humility, consistency, discipline, and compassion?**

FEBRUARY 2

WHY RECEIVING IS GOOD

1. It reminds you that you're not in charge

2. It keeps you humble

3. You allow others the opportunity to feel the pleasure of giving

4. You get to experience gratitude

5. You develop a realistic self-image

6. You create space for others to shine

7. You begin to understand what strength really is

8. You become a more well-rounded person

9. Your relationships become richer

QUESTION

What can you receive today?

SET A GIVING GOAL

Over the first thirty-three years of my life, I probably gave less than $2,000 to the church and charity . . . total!

But when God showed up in my life, I quickly realized He owned everything—my career, my wife, my kids, my health. Everything.

As I started to read the Bible, I was hit with verses like "Everything in the heavens and on earth is yours, O Lord" (1 Chronicles 29:11, NLT). I wanted God, my boss, and everyone else to be generous *with* me, but I hadn't ever been generous to them.

I had a problem. A selfishness problem.

I believe that you don't solve problems; you set goals. So I sat down and set a giving goal. I set a tithe based on my projected income, then I built our family budget. Total expected income, minus tithe, minus saving, minus living expenses, equals surplus.

And here's where I made the big change. I looked at the surplus number and decided to set a giving goal—a hard number just for that year. I prayed about it, talked to my wife and got her support, and then I wrote it down. The income happened, the gifts were made, and my faith became stronger.

I've set a giving goal every year since. In fact, while I've missed almost all my exercise and weight loss goals, I've never missed a giving goal.

Instead of hoping for generosity, plan for it. Be intentional. Set a goal, work towards it, and watch God move.

SCRIPTURE

"Give, and it will be given to you. A good
measure, pressed down, shaken together
and running over, will be poured into your
lap. For with the measure you use, it
will be measured to you." (Luke 6:38)

FEBRUARY 4

GOD IS GOOD

"God is great, God is good. Let us thank Him for our food."

Maybe the secret to surviving tough things in life is hidden in the middle of this children's blessing: *God is good.*

I reminded God of my frustration in praying so hard for a friend (one of the most sold-out servants of the poor I know) who is in excruciating pain all the time. I, along with a thousand others, prayed every day for thirty days for this man's chronic pain to get better. Nothing changed.

"So why pray?" I asked.

"It's how I change *you*," He said.

I'd heard that before. "Prayer changes things," but also, "Prayer changes me." I thought, *I don't want me to be changed; I'm not talking to God about me. I want this situation changed. I want this outcome changed.*

Then I realized just what a miracle it was when He changed me, or at least started the process. Reaching down into my human mind and heart and changing it is no less supernatural than curing cancer, or opening a blocked artery, or making chronic pain go away.

But I still wasn't peaceful. I still couldn't understand what my problem was with prayer. So I asked Him, "Lord, what am I missing here?"

Here's what I wrote in my journal . . .

> *"You're* wanting to decide what's good. That's not your place. I am good. And I know what good looks like. You only see what you see. I see it all. Trust me. I love you. I am good. That's all you need to know."

SCRIPTURE

**"Give thanks to the Lord, for he is good.
His love endures forever." (Psalm 136:1)**

FEBRUARY 5

WHAT DO YOU WANT?

Storytelling and screenwriting begin with the question, "Who is he and what does he want?" The main character has to want something if it's going to be an interesting story. For it to be an epic story, he has to want something big and important and be willing to take extraordinary risk or pay an incredible price to get it.

Deciding what we want seems easy when we're young. "I want a beautiful wife," or "I want my college degree," or "I want a good job," or "We want a child." Concrete, specific wants.

As these things come, we check them off our list. And we're grateful.

But as we mature, the things we want become less concrete, more ethereal. We want to be happy. We want fulfillment. Meaning. Significance. We want to belong. To love and be loved.

And as these wants get harder to define, they get harder to measure. How do you check *fulfilled* off your list? Without God in your life, they get harder to obtain, too.

You see, God is about people. He told us to love Him first and foremost, but then after that, love others just as much as we love ourselves. I'll argue that loving God, in real terms, is best done by loving others. Jesus said, "whatever you did for one of the least of these . . . you did for me" (Matthew 25:40).

When we love people—truly love and serve them—we're honoring God. When we want what He wants—when we love and serve people, we're happier, more fulfilled, and content.

QUESTION

One definition of love is meeting a need. Will you focus on meeting someone's need today, someone other than yourself and your family?

FEBRUARY 6

A NEW NAME

The longer I live, the more I *know* the importance of identity. One dictionary defines identity as, "the fact of being who a person is." It sounds reasonable at first glance. But think about it: "the fact of being who you are."

Who is deciding the *fact* of your identity? Get kidnapped in another country and your identity would be determined by someone looking at your passport. Die in a plane crash and your identity might be determined by someone looking at your dental records. Commit a dastardly crime and your identity might be determined by someone decoding your DNA.

Get it? Our identity is determined by *someone*. And it's a huge deal.

Unfortunately, many of our parents (and grandparents, teachers, coaches, etc.) didn't realize how important this was. Some of us received identities like, "fat boy," "troublemaker," "jock," "bookworm," "sissy," "Romeo," or "klutz." Others got branded with "spoiled," "loser," "black sheep," and "never going to amount to anything."

Subconsciously, we buy into these identities, letting them define us our entire lives.

When Jesus came into the world, He became the new Identifier. Jesus told us to look at God as our Father and at ourselves as adopted sons and daughters. That means He loves us regardless of what we do, and we can't be "unadopted."

Our identity is *always* ascribed to us by someone other than ourselves, but it's up to us to *own* that identity and live out of it. "Jesus follower" is a great identity, but "beloved adopted son or daughter of my Heavenly Father" is even better.

Grasp who you are in His eyes, and it'll change everything.

SCRIPTURE

"So in Christ Jesus you are all children of God through faith." (Galatians 3:26)

THE FEAR OF NOT HAVING ENOUGH

The enemy of love isn't hate, it's *fear*. And all these years I thought it was apathy! Just when I think I've heard it all, along comes this new thought about the issues plaguing us every day.

Sometimes I think my son invented the acronym "FOMO." He was sixteen when he infected us with the *fear of missing out*. FOMO is really the fear of not getting more, of not having enough. (I tried "FONHE," but I don't think it's going to catch on like FOMO!).

God guarantees *provision*, not necessarily *prosperity*. This is different from the "prosperity gospel" and the way many TV preachers and hucksters misinterpret Scripture.

A few key points about fear . . .

- **Fear is selfishness**–It makes us think of ourselves, whereas love makes us think of others.

- **Fear is about self-protection**–Fear keeps us hiding and keeps us from being fully known by others. But love makes us vulnerable and more apt to be known, loved, and helped.

- **Fear keeps us from trusting God**–We have ideas about what God should do and we're afraid He won't deliver. Grasping how much God loves us drives out fear and gives us peace and confidence.

To overcome our fear, we must assess our capacity, entrust everything we have to Him, let Jesus shape us through life's challenges, and live in community with Him and with like-hearted people who trust and follow Him.

When I think about what holds me back from doing more, giving more, serving more, and being bolder, it's fear.

SCRIPTURE

"For God has not given us a spirit of fear, but of power and of love and of a sound mind." (2 Timothy 1:7, NKJV)

WHAT'S YOUR "WATTS"?

Walk into a dark room and flip the light switch. Darkness is replaced by light. In fact, darkness isn't really a thing in and of itself; it just happens when there's no light.

Genesis 1:4 recounts the creation of light: "God saw that the light was good, and he separated the light from the darkness." Sometimes we think of someone as *bright*. Every now and then, we'll run into a Jesus follower whose spirit *shines*. In the church world, we want people to *plug in*. We compare spirituality to electricity because both are invisible and somewhat hard to understand.

The reality is, some people seem to be "15-watt" people; others are "60-watt" and a few naturally glow like "100-watt" bulbs. If you're one of the latter, you're going to attract people (and moths!). But what if you're a "15-watt" person? Or "30-watt"? Maybe you're diligent about your faith but kind of private and quiet. How can you increase your "wattage"?

Through prayer. I've told people about the strength and confidence I felt go-ing in for my lung transplant. It was supernatural! I truly believe James 5:16b, which says . . .

> "The prayer of a righteous person is powerful and effective."

It's true, whether that prayer is from you, a few, or a multitude. I'm convinced that the more people who pray and the more fervently they pray, the higher the "wattage" of the person being prayed for.

So pray for each other, but don't forget to pray for *yourself* too.

PRAYER

**Ask God to raise your "wattage" . . . for your good,
the good of those around you, and His glory.**

CHRISTIAN OR DISCIPLE?

About 173 million Americans identify themselves as Christians. If you're reading this, odds are that you're one of them.

The word "Christian" has certainly become a brand in today's culture, with Christian movies, Christian music, and Christian food (that'd be Chick-Fil-A!). Is Christianity a value system that guides a lifestyle? Or could it be a "tribe" of people who salute the same ideals?

Oddly enough, the word "Christian" only appears three times in the Bible. And each time it shows up, it's used in reference to Jesus' disciples.

But the word "disciple" shows up 269 times in the Scriptures. Clearly, God's Word puts a lot of weight on being a disciple of Jesus.

Somewhere back in time, I was told that a disciple is a *learner* and *follower* of Christ. For me, that means first *learning* everything I can about Jesus, His life, His message, and His Father.

But *following* Jesus may be more important than learning about Him. We need to be changed by Christ. A disciple is a learner, but not just a *head* learner. He's a *heart* learner, opening himself up so God can change him from the inside out. It means transparency *and* vulnerability. It means introspection, repentance, a continuous pursuit of godliness and living out the platinum rule—loving others the way God loves us.

Are you a Christian or a disciple? Do you *believe* but live unaffected by a meaningful faith?

Your children will imitate your way of living and the faith they see you live out. Get it right and make every day count.

SCRIPTURE

"Remember your leaders, who spoke the word of God to you. Consider the outcome of their way of life and imitate their faith." (Hebrews 13:7)

NINETY-NINE PERCENT

Unless you were living alone in a cave, you know about the rare coast-to-coast total eclipse that happened in America in 2017. My daughter's family lives smack-dab in the middle of "the area of totality." My son's family lives in Athens, GA, about thirty-two miles from where the area of totality began. Athens was predicted to see 99 percent of the eclipse, so he thought, "that's close enough" and avoided the forty-one-minute drive to watch a two-minute phenomenon.

The eclipse turned out to be a strangely majestic experience. In the run-up to totality, the heat went out of the sun's rays (because of their diminished density). The temperature dropped. It got quiet. It was amazing, like nothing I'd ever experienced.

But over in Athens, it never got *really* dark. The crickets never chirped. The glasses stayed on. All the reports of this amazing phenomenon came from people who experienced it, not people who heard about it.

The point?

There's a *huge* difference between 99 percent and 100 percent.

Think about trust. You either trust or you don't. If there's a shred of doubt, trust is nonexistent. When we 99 percent trust God, it's like we don't trust Him at all. There's an obvious difference between 99 percent faith and *no* faith, but in reality, the contrast between 99 percent and 100 percent is *just as big!*

Ninety-nine percent faith isn't close enough. Giving ourselves over 100 percent to the Lord is the only path to peace in this life . . . and the next.

SCRIPTURE

"May your hearts be fully committed to the Lord our God, to live by his decrees and obey his commands, as at this time." (1 Kings 8:61)

GRATITUDE: THE ONLY SURE CURE FOR ANXIETY

We're all supposed to be grateful, right? Those who see the glass half full find it easier. They're grateful they've been spared the downside. They know how bad things could be and are grateful for their good fortune.

The half-empty people compare their "what is" to "what could have been" and to "what *should* be."

"Will they do what I expect?" "Will my dream come true?" "Will I get what I hope for?" Half-empty people are usually disappointed and struggle to be grateful.

When there's an absence of gratitude, there's an abundance of anxiety. **Anxiety comes from unmet expectations.** When we expect things from our wives, kids, extended families, circumstances, the government, our employers, the church—from anyone or anything—we set ourselves up to be anxious.

Logic says there are two ways to solve our anxiety: lower expectations or raise performance.

But there's another option, a better one: **Choose to be grateful.** Think about what you've been given instead of what you haven't. About what you have versus what you don't. Reflect on the good places you've been instead of those you haven't.

When we appreciate what we have, we realize that the only sure cure for anxiety is a grateful heart.

SCRIPTURE

"Do not be anxious about anything, but in every situation, by prayer and petition, with thanksgiving, present your requests to God." (Philippians 4:6)

WHAT MEN WANT

If you're a married man with kids, I'm going to go way out on a limb and tell you what you want.

1. **Emotional connection with your wife.** You may think you want sex, companionship, cooperation, respect, admiration, and even submission, but what you really want is *emotional connection*. You want her to track with you emotionally and stay close physically.

2. **Adult children who like you.** The goal of parenting isn't to raise good kids . . . it's to raise good adults. You want your adult children to *want* to spend time with you when they don't have to.

3. **To have eldership ascribed to you by your church and community.** I'm not talking about the church job; I'm talking about men whose wisdom is valued and whose voice is heard. Eldership as I'm describing it here is *aspired to* through faithful living, lifelong learning, generosity with time and treasure, consistent humility, and a servant heart.

What about career achievement? Fitness and appearance? Financial success?

Yes, all that matters.

But it pales in comparison to our desire to have a wife who truly loves us, children who like us, and a community that respects us.

Men can have these three things by following Jesus and living a Christ-centered life. Think about the men you know who have fabulous marriages—the men whose kids come back and hang out with them. Look around at the older, wiser men you most respect in your church and community. You'll see Jesus in them.

QUESTION

Are you thinking long-term and living intentionally toward your marriage, family, and the people in your church and community?

WWJD REVISITED

Back in the nineties, "What would Jesus do?" was all the rage. WWJD caught on with young people, and thousands of bracelets and bumper stickers were sold.

Although I never wore a bracelet, I loved the WWJD movement.

But as my kids got older and sometimes acted out, there weren't specifics as to what Jesus would do as a parent. He didn't have kids. Same with marriage. Same with dealing with aging parents, since Jesus didn't have an earthly father, and He died before Mary got old.

I learned an alternative approach: to ask God directly.

"Lord, what would you have me know about this situation?"

Amazingly, He's often ready to answer. What He shows me is about the heart, either mine or the person I'm asking about. What they want. What's bothering them. What the real issue is. Then I'll ask:

"Lord, what would you have me do with what you've shown me?"

Often that little prayer gets answered with an unction, a leading, a next step. Every time I obey, my faith gets stronger, and often it brings a "God-sized" blessing.

I believe this is what we mean when we talk about walking with God. Following Jesus is pausing, asking, listening, and obeying. Minute-by-minute. Decision-by-decision.

Will you involve Jesus in your life decisions? Will you move from religion to a dialogue with your Heavenly Father?

SCRIPTURE

"So I say to you: Ask and it will be given to you; seek and you will find; knock and the door will be opened to you." (Luke 11:9)

RADICAL EMPATHY

Here's a useful definition of empathy:

> Empathy—to pause your thoughts and feelings long enough to engage with the thoughts and feelings of another person.

Simple to say, hard to do. For starters, we live in our own world. We're constantly thinking and feeling. We can't help it. We're "me-focused," looking out for ourselves, making plans for our next meeting, snack, phone call, whatever.

Focus is fleeting, and after the first few seconds of a conversation, our minds slip back to *our* agenda, to *our* thoughts and feelings. The other person felt loved for a second, but our attention left as quickly as it came.

An empathetic person *pauses*. Stops. Focuses. Actually pays attention. Actually *engages,* listening to the other person and connecting with what they're saying and feeling.

This requires *selflessness*. It requires *patience*. It requires *love*. In our ultra-busy lives, *listening is loving*. When we pause and truly listen to another person, when we take the time to care by engaging with their lives, they feel that love, and our relationship gets stronger.

Try it! With every person and in every conversation this week, put the other person first. When you feel the urge to talk about you, ask a follow-up question about something they said. Stay with *their* thoughts and feelings, rather than switching back to yourself. This is moment-by-moment loving your neighbor.

SCRIPTURE

**"The second is this: 'Love your neighbor
as yourself.' There is no commandment
greater than these." (Mark 12:31)**

WILL YOU BECOME AN INCLUDER?

A friend was talking about Thanksgiving dinner growing up. "There was always someone there we didn't know," she said. "Mom would always call up someone she thought would be alone that day and include them at our family table."

I remember the school cafeteria and the kids who were never included at tables with other kids. Many of us had relatives who never included us in things their families did. Few things feel *worse* than feeling excluded and few things *better* than feeling included.

The enemy of inclusion is selfishness. "I just want *my* people." We know them. It takes less effort to be around them. It's work to include people who aren't like us—who might be emotionally needy, have little or no faith, have irritating habits, or talk too much about things we don't care about.

As Jesus followers, we're charged with loving others as God loves us, and that's about as inclusive as it gets. When we exclude, when we stay in our holy huddles, we unintentionally communicate self-righteousness.

In our everyday relationships with our families, friends, and coworkers, we don't see a lot to gain though new relationships. We're not selling anything. We're not trying to build databases or email lists. We're simply trying to make our way through an overworked world where time is at a premium.

Being an includer takes time and is messier and less comfortable than sticking with our exclusive circle of people who think, look, and act in ways that make us comfortable.

PRAYER

Ask God to remind you of someone who might feel left out . . . someone He wants you to include somehow. Then send an email, make a call, send a text. Do *one thing* to include that person.

WHAT STORY WILL YOU TELL?

Imagine you're eighty-five years old. You're in a nursing home, and your health is failing. Your grandson has always had a special place in his heart for you, but he's busy finishing college, or getting married, or starting his family. One day, out of the blue, he calls and asks to come visit. "I want to talk to you about *real life*, Papa," he says. "I wanna hear *your* story."

What story will you tell?

It's easy to tell him your **career story.** Success, failure, growth, retirement. He won't care.

Of course, you can tell him your **family story**. Your parents, your siblings, and how you grew up. How you met your wife, the divorce, his dad or mom's birth, his uncles and aunts. This story is a little harder to tell. He might be mildly interested.

If you're a church person, you can tell him your **faith story**. How you were baptized (or not), how you came to believe, the churches you attended, and so on. His attention span will depend on his *own* faith story.

But what your grandson *really* wants to hear is your **life story.** He wants to hear about *your heart*. Sure, you want to tell him about your successes and the things you're proud of. But he'll be much more attentive as you tell him about your failures, your bad decisions, your regrets.

Which story will you tell? Which story will be most helpful to him?

Most importantly, which story do you want to focus on in the days you have left?

SCRIPTURE

**"Even when I am old and gray, do not forsake
me, my God, till I declare your power to the
next generation, your mighty acts to all who
are to come." (Psalms 71:18)**

FEBRUARY 17

A BELIEVER WITH NO FAITH

Raised in the church, I was taught Christianity. I knew the rules, the characters and stories of the Bible. Even at ten years old when I was baptized, I could have passed a quiz on the basics.

But why did all that knowledge have no effect on how I thought or behaved *for years*?

I had no faith.

The Oxford English Dictionary defines faith as "complete trust or confidence in someone or something." Hebrews 11:1 defines faith as "confidence in what we hope for and assurance about what we do not see." So, here's what I deduce about faith . . .

Faith is complete trust and confidence. Before I knew Jesus personally, I had neither. I had no confidence, even in myself. After I found and began to follow Jesus, I realized I could *trust Him with outcomes*.

Faith is in someone or something. Here's a major problem. Mankind has always turned God into a set of rules. God is a *Someone*, not a something.

Faith is in what we hope for. Until I was thirty-three, heaven and hell didn't register with me because I thought I was going to live forever. Once I realized that God was real, He loved me, and I could trust Him with everything, I began to hope for different things–godly things that mattered.

Faith is assurance about what we do not see. Jesus followers commit their lives to emulating a man they've never seen to bring glory to a God they've never seen. We lean into the future we can't see, living a different way because we're following Jesus and His teachings, trusting *in faith* that His way is the best way.

QUESTION

Can you be a Christian with no faith? Will you ask God *right now* to give you more faith?

OBEDIENCE IS FAITH EXERCISED

There's a word nobody uses much anymore. In a world of freedom, positive reinforcement, and behavior modification, this word seems old school and out of touch. The word is **obedience.**

> "And I will put my Spirit in you and move you to follow my decrees and be careful to keep my laws." (Ezekiel 36:27)

Every believer has the Spirit giving us information on right and wrong. But if we want *more* of the Holy Spirit living in us, for His "still small voice" to become a more prominent one, for our faith to grow from that of a mustard seed to faith that can move mountains and endure hardship, it only happens through **obedience.**

When God the Father gives an order, He takes responsibility for the outcome. He knows the result will *always* be good if we obey. The commands of God in Scripture—commands like the Ten Commandments—are for all of us.

One night, I was mad at my wife and left to sleep on the couch. In frustration, I asked, "Lord, what would you have me do with my anger *right now?*" His still small voice said, "Get up, go back in the bedroom, and apologize." I chose to obey. We made up immediately.

This was an *individual* command for me to obey . . . or not. When we hear His voice and obey, we mature. We grow in our faith. Future boldness grows on the shoulders of past obedience. But it's not easy. It takes willingness, faith, and consistent obedience to His voice.

QUESTION

Will you lean into obedience as a way of life?

FEBRUARY 19

WE ARE COMPLETE

Every year my church has "Man Night." It's quite a production, with camp-fires, bacon snacks, brownies and milk, film clips—you know, real guy stuff. One year, at the end of the main talk, six truths about *identity* were put up on the screen along with this question: "Which of these do you struggle to accept and believe about yourself?"

Here are the six . . .

I am forgiven.   I am not alone.
I am chosen.   I am complete in Christ.
I am significant.   I am loved.

Now, I've been walking with God for a long time, so I assumed nothing they could throw up there would trip me up. But my eyes locked on this one:

"I am complete in Christ."

Do I really believe that? What happened to "I'm a work in progress"? Isn't this arrogance? What about sanctification? Growing in holiness? If I start believing I'm complete, won't I get lazy?

This big idea of being complete comes from Colossians 2:10 (NLT), which says, "you also are complete through your union with Christ." Through Jesus, I am complete. I can't be *more* complete than complete.

Believing that "I am complete in Christ" means shutting down any doubt about my salvation or my status as an adopted son of the King of kings. It means cranking up *growing in my faith* and not being duped into believing I have to *perform for my faith*. We pursue Christian service and good works not because we are incomplete, but as a result of our completeness in Christ.

I can't think of a more freeing reality.

CHALLENGE

**Say this as a prayer ten times today. Say
it out loud . . . "I am complete in Christ."**

IDENTITY IS ASCRIBED

Identity was Dictionary.com's 2015 Word of the Year. Millions are ordering DNA profiles on themselves. *What's my race? My nationality of origin? Who am I . . . really?*

Why do we care?

Because we don't know who we are and we want someone with credibility to tell us.

Beginning in early childhood, our parents started to ascribe our identity. "You're a **good boy**!" "You're going to be a **good big brother**." "See how **smart** he is? "Watch how **fast** he can run!" Those who had great dads heard, "You are **my son**!"

In school, teachers and coaches ascribed our identities. "He's not very **athletic**." "He's quite a **ladies' man**." "She's one of the **popular girls**."

At work, at home, at the club, at church, all kinds of people ascribe versions of our identity. "He's a **CEO**." "He's a **great dad**." "She's been **married before**." "He must be a **loser**, since he's been **laid off** three times in three years." "He's an **old retired** guy."

Jesus followers, our identity is ascribed by our creator God. And it was ascribed to us the day we accepted God's invitation to be adopted into His family. From that day forward, we've been a child of the King of kings! If we choose to live in our ultimate, true identity as **beloved sons and daughters of the Living God**, all the other identities ascribed to us by others don't matter so much.

SCRIPTURE

"Yet to all who did receive him, to those who believed in his name, he gave the right to become children of God—children born not of natural descent, nor of human decision or a husband's will, but born of God." (John 1:12-13)

RULES ARE DECISIONS MADE IN ADVANCE

Think about it. When the sign says, "No Parking," someone made that decision for me in advance of my arrival. They looked out for my safety, someone else's green grass, the usual traffic pattern, whatever. They said to me, "You're not going to park here!"

Here's the thing about rules: They're intended to *protect*. God gave us the ultimate rules (e.g., commandments), things like loving Him, honoring His name and His day, and not making anything else more important than Him. He made those rules to protect us from ourselves.

Right out of the shoot, the first generation of humans decided they wanted to make their own rules, and look what that got them (and us)—sin, death, pain in childbirth, and work that's really hard.

God gave us all these rules for our protection because He loves us! Here's a radical question:

What rules should we make for ourselves *to protect ourselves?*

Here's one of mine: Tell the truth about everything, no matter how ugly or embarrassing. Another one: Don't loan money to people. If you're their friend or family and they have a valid need, give rather than lend.

Don't get too carried away with this "making rules" thing. That's how the Pharisees screwed up. They made rules to keep people from breaking rules and ended up with a morass of 613 rules *nobody* could follow.

QUESTION

**What personal rules should you make to
protect yourself from sin, temptation, and pain?**

FEBRUARY 22

PERCEPTION IS REALITY?

There's an old saying: "Perception is reality." And it's true . . . to a point. We act on what we *perceive* to be real and true. That's *functional reality*, but often it's not *true reality*.

The world has always been round, but for thousands of years it was perceived to be flat. Was it ever flat? Nope. Did people *live like it* was flat? Absolutely. For centuries, people were afraid that if they went too far from shore, they could sail over the edge.

The first theories of a spherical world showed up in Greek philosophy in the sixth century BC from Pythagoras and later from Aristotle in 330 BC. But only the "around the world and back again" voyage of Magellan in 1521 *proved* the reality of a round earth.

Let's bring this principle a little closer to home.

Perceived reality: "My wife just doesn't love me anymore."

Once we get that "reality" into our heads, we're constantly looking for evidence to prove we're right. The truth might be that they don't love us *the way we want to be loved*. Their acts of love don't register with our desires for how we want to be loved. They're giving us love in pesos when we want it in dollar bills. We don't value their pesos and are too busy, lazy, and insensitive to learn the exchange rate. So, while the *true reality* is we're being loved, we don't perceive it.

The next time you find yourself thinking, "It is what it is," think again. Maybe it's just what you *perceive it to be*.

QUESTION

**Is it time to talk with your Heavenly Father
and get a divine perspective on your reality?**

DEATH BLOWS TO DOUBT

Life happens. Our circumstances often cause us to question what we believe, creating doubt in our hearts about everything we thought was true. It happens to all of us.

But what matters most is how we respond to doubt when it arises. Here are four truths to lean into when it happens to you.

1. **God is real.** The apostle Paul answers this in Romans 1:20: "For since the creation of the world God's invisible qualities—his eternal power and divine nature—have been clearly seen, being understood from what has been made, so that people are without excuse."

   By faith, I *choose* to believe that God is real.

2. **God loves me.** When I had nowhere else to turn, I set aside my doubts, my pride, my ego, everything. I prayed "God, I need you. I need your forgiveness. I want to know you love me."

   By faith, I *choose* to believe God loves me.

3. **God can be trusted.** Because I know He loves me, I trust Him with every outcome. Whatever comes, I can relax, knowing it came through His hand. Did He *make it happen?* Did He *let it happen?* I don't know. I simply know He loves me.

   By faith, I *choose* to trust God.

4. **There is a life after this one.** Jesus proved it with His death, resurrection, and ascension. I don't know where, I don't know what it will be like. But I know that justice will ultimately be done, and that I'll be where Jesus is because I believed in Him and followed Him.

   By faith, I *choose* to believe in eternal life.

CHALLENGE

**The opposite of faith is fear, uncertainty,
and doubt. Choose faith.**

WHAT'S YOUR ONE THING?

I remember my daddy saying, "I'm a 'jack-of-all-trades' but master of none." I took that as gospel and have said it for years, especially after not being able to complete some home repair and making that shame-filled call to the handyman.

In *Garden City*, John Mark Comer says we use this quote to let ourselves off the hook for not being really good at one thing. In fact, he claims it's a misquote of Benjamin Franklin. He actually said, "jack-of-all-trades, master of *one*." That's a whole different message, isn't it?

So, what's your one thing? Maybe you've been afraid to commit to one thing for fear you *wouldn't* be good at it. Or that you wouldn't be good enough.

I know too many men aimlessly hoping to live a life of significance. They're constantly looking for the "new thing" that will finish their search. Yet they rarely look inward. They rarely try to discover what they're really good at. They rarely try to build on that gift and make it unstoppably strong.

Remember this: God made you really good at something so you might be a blessing to others, to make in impact on this earth by using your gifts to be a servant.

So find *your* one thing and focus on it. Bury the "jack-of-all-trades" excuse and focus on becoming the "master of one."

As Zig Ziglar said, "Don't be-come a wandering generality. Be a meaningful specific."

SCRIPTURE

"Whatever you do, work at it with all your heart, as working for the Lord, not for human masters, since you know that you will receive an inheritance from the Lord as a reward. It is the Lord Christ you are serving." (Colossians 3:23-24)

THE VOICE OF DAD

Ask guys about the first thing they remember, and there he'll be. Somewhere in the picture is their dad. In my first memory, I'm standing in front of the mirror wearing my brand-new white short-sleeved shirt with a big blue and red stripe across the front. First grade school pictures are today. My dad is combing my hair so it'll look right, like I'm cared for. That was a big deal for Daddy; everything he had was clean and well groomed.

If you saw the picture they took of me that day, in my cute white shirt and slicked down hair, you'd think, "Aww! How cute! How perfect!" But if you were me, or if you saw the video version, you'd remember the heat of the room, the stress of a man in a hurry doing something he didn't like to do. You'd remember the tone of his voice when he fussed, "WILL YOU STAND STILL?!?" "I AIN'T GOT ALL DAY!"

For most of us, that's the paradox called "Dad." "Daddy." "Pop."

Did he love you? Sure.

Did you *feel* it? Not so sure.

If you're a dad, choose to be kind. Always be kind, no matter what your kid says, or does, or doesn't do. What he'll remember won't be still shots, they'll be movies. Make sure your words and your tone *always* communicate kindness. How you talk to your young sons and daughters will have a profound impact on their lives. Make sure the soundtrack to their movie is one of kindness, not criticism.

SCRIPTURE

**"Fathers, do not exasperate your children;
instead, bring them up in the training and
instruction of the Lord." (Ephesians 6:4)**

PARENTECTOMY—CUTTING YOUR KID LOOSE (PART I)

Parentectomy: a slang term meaning removal of a parent (or both parents) from the child. It was coined by Dr. M. Murray Peshkin, the medical director of the Children's Asthma Research Institute and Hospital in Denver. He noticed that some of his most severe asthma patients improved markedly as soon as they were removed from their homes and hospitalized, before their treatments had a chance to work. They got better when they were removed from their parents.

We love our kids so much, we're blind to the consequences of our love and generosity. We make it easy for our kids to stay kids—to stay in the cocoon of "Parent-ville." In 1960, 77 percent of women and 65 percent of men completed all the major transitions into adulthood by age 30. These transitions include leaving home, finishing school, becoming financially in-dependent, getting married, and having a child. By 2000—in just forty years—only 46 percent of women and 31 percent of men had "grown up" by age thirty.

Why is this? Why aren't our kids cutting the cord like we did? How are we complicit in their extended adolescence? A few observations:

1. We don't want our kids to suffer.

2. We want our kids to like us.

3. We like being needed.

Are you trying to raise popular, cool, beautiful kids who hang around for the next ten years? Or good, healthy, independent adults who will follow Jesus, love others, and build a good life for themselves and their *own* families?

QUESTION

Be honest, is a "Parentectomy" in order?

FEBRUARY 27

THE TOTAL SURRENDER CONTRACT

I get nervous when preachers say, "Surrender your life to Jesus." Jesus talked about living "life to the full." What's this about?

When I think about surrendering, I picture the end of a war movie. The fight has dragged on. One side is surrounded. No way out. They hoist a white flag, yielding to the more powerful. The victors decide what happens next. The will of the losers has been yielded to the will of the victors.

I can relate to those losers. Why? Because I *was* one when I surrendered. After flailing around for years, trying to prove my significance through career success, I found myself alone. Broken. Out of options. I turned my eyes to the sky and surrendered. "Lord, I give up. I have totally screwed up my life. I know you've been waiting for this day for a long time. I accept your for-giveness. I'm yours. Whatever happens from here on out, it's up to you. I trust you. I know you love me. It's you and me Lord . . . you and me!"

That was the end of the life I knew—the one where I was in charge. Where I didn't think or care about anyone else. It was the beginning of a new life—one that matters. A life of peace, love, and meaning. The one that begins with *surrender*.

What does it really mean to surrender? To trust God with *everything*? My friend *Larry* taught me a lot about surrender. A few years back, he shared the Total Surrender Contract with me.

CHALLENGE

**Read the Total Surrender Contract. Read it again.
Pray. Pray more. Ask God to give you the courage
to sign it and honor its terms for the rest of
your life. Then, when you're ready, sign it.**

TOTAL SURRENDER CONTRACT

Dear Lord, I give myself to You, without reservation, and surrender to You my will, my mind, my emotions, my body, my plans, my hopes, and my dreams. I give You my home, my marriage, my spouse, my children, my geographical location, my recreation, my entertainment, my career. I commit into Your hands my successes, my failures, my habits, my finances, my problems, my time, my integrity, my character, my attitude, my business conduct and relationships, my Christian walk, and my response to authority.

I am relinquishing the following rights to You. My right to . . .

- my possessions
- my reputation
- acceptance from others
- success
- pleasant circumstances
- presume upon what your will may be for me
- beauty or strength
- friendships
- be heard

- take up offense
- be loved by others
- handle or control my addictions
- be right
- see results
- avoid reaping from what I have sown
- change others
- life itself
- _____

Lord, I give You permission to do anything You wish with me, to me, in me, or through me. I claimed the above once as mine. Now I acknowledge that they all belong to You and are under Your control. You can do with them as You please. I willingly make this commitment in the name and authority of the Lord Jesus Christ, and I recognize that this is an agreement with You that can never be broken. Now that I have surrendered ownership of my life to You, I understand that You will never give ownership back to me. I accept that I am not my own . . . that I am the temple of the Holy Spirit . . . and that I have been bought with a price (1 Corinthians 6:19-20). Amen.

_____   _____
Signature   Date

PARENTECTOMY–CUTTING YOURSELF LOOSE (PART II)

I'd always thought of the parentectomy as the child cutting the cord from the parent. Until recently, I'd never thought about the other side of the parentectomy–the need for the *parent* to cut the cord and let their adult children go free.

More than a few of the younger guys I've mentored come in with heavy burdens created by their parents and/or in-laws. They struggle with parents who continuously put expectations on their adult children.

If you're one of those parents, you need a parentectomy! You need to set your children free from your expectations and get a life of your own. I get it! After we've poured so much time, energy, effort, and prayer into our children, we want to keep being around them and hearing their voices. We still want to be *with* them emotionally.

But that's a problem. When they're married, they're supposed to be with *their* mates and their own kids. They wear the expectations of their own spouses, jobs, homes, plans, and friends. We, the parents who raised them, need to get our own lives. To insert ourselves into their lives, even if we are offering them good times and good things, might not be healthy. It works against them and it works against us.

Don't get me wrong. I'm not suggesting we cut ties with our kids. There will come a time when we'll desperately need them to love and care for us. I'm just saying we need to be gracious and sensitive and find a healthy balance.

SCRIPTURE

"Children are a heritage from the Lord, offspring a reward from him." (Psalm 127:3)

BORN STOIC, DIE EPICUREAN

Wil Durant is credited with coining this platitude:

> Nations are born stoic, but they die epicurean.

I believe this is true about organizations and even individuals. We start out fending for ourselves. We scratch and scrape, wasting little and stretching every dollar and minute for all we can get out of it. As we get more prosperous, we loosen up. We're a little less careful, a little more relaxed about our spending and how we use our time. We take up golf, or fishing, or photography. Our standards get higher and higher. We don't want McDonalds anymore; we like fine dining, white tablecloths, and to be served with excellence!

I've watched companies do this. The first office is a sublease with twenty-year-old furniture. Every customer is served like they're the only one. Every employee does multiple jobs. It's stoic, it's stripped-down. It's fantastic.

But as success comes, the company moves to "more appropriate" class-A office space. Everyone knows their single, specific job. Customers are handled by the appropriate department. And it's so boring.

We start out living small and end up living larger and larger. What we have in abundance, we're less careful with.

Only passionate leaders can slow this slide. It helps to recognize that we are stewards, not owners, and that our audience is God Himself, and our accountability is to Him.

Lead a life that loves people and uses things, not the reverse.

SCRIPTURE

"You have lived on earth in luxury and self-indulgence. You have fattened yourselves in the day of slaughter." (James 5:5)

MARCH 2

WHAT THE BEST NEGOTIATORS DO

Dad comes home from work and is greeted by two whiny kids. "Daddy, I need this orange for my school project, and Danny won't let me have it!" Dad looks at Danny, who screams, "But I need this orange for my science homework." Dad knows exactly what to do. He grabs the orange, walks to the kitchen, takes a big knife, and splits the orange, handing half to Danny and half to Eddie.

They both scream louder than ever. Without knowing it, Dad has ensured failure for *both* his kids. Why? Because Eddie needs the juice of *one entire orange*. And Danny needs the peel of *one entire orange*. Now neither can be successful because of Dad's failure as a negotiator.

Most people have heard about Solomon and how he wisely settled the dis-pute between two women who both claimed to be the mother of a certain child. His order to "split the baby" smoked out the fake mom. But we've convoluted the "split the baby" idea. Meeting halfway isn't always the answer.

Next time there's a conflict, ask questions and sort out what each side wants and needs *before* ruling on the case. Let them suggest compromises and trades to come to their own peace.

In other words, exercise wisdom. Don't waltz in looking to be the hero of the moment. Discover what's really going on and listen to what they're really saying.

SCRIPTURE

**"My dear brothers and sisters, take note of this:
Everyone should be quick to listen, slow to
speak and slow to become angry." (James 1:19)**

RAW SPOTS

When you're saying something and you feel a little twinge of, "I shouldn't be saying this," and you look at your wife and the temperature has dropped twenty degrees and the wind is now coming from the north . . . you've hit a raw spot.

For years, I ignored it. I just kept talking. But I'm learning that hitting a raw spot requires an immediate apology, not snow-plowing forward. "Can't you take a joke?" or "Just get over it!" doesn't cut it.

Here are three huge raw spots of the female gender:

1. **Criticism**—No one likes to be criticized. But women, because they're so relational and intuitive, have a keen sense for criticism. They can *feel* it, even when it's not spoken or mean-spirited.

2. **Appearance**—So many dads and granddads create raw spots in little girls with comments about their weight or body shape. Words like chubby, skinny, or heavy can haunt women all their lives.

3. **Value**—Our capitalistic culture assigns value to people who become rich, famous, or both. The most important voice a wife hears is the voice of her husband. It's critical he value her *and* what she does for him and the family.

If you really think about it, you already know what you do or say that bothers your wife. Write those things down. Talk to her about them. Let her confirm, deny, or correct what you do or say that hits a raw spot. Then, ask God to give you the wisdom and self-control to avoid them.

SCRIPTURE

**"Husbands, in the same way, treat your wives
with consideration as a delicate vessel, and
with honor as fellow heirs of the gracious
gift of life, so that your prayers will not
be hindered." (1 Peter 3:7, BSB)**

JUST YOUR EARTH SUIT

The other day, my wife and I counted eight people whose deaths we've been close to in the last few years–close family members and friends. Some sudden and tragic, some long, drawn out, and excruciating.

Years ago, I heard a speaker talk about our "earth suits." He asserted that God places our soul, our personality–who we are and were created to be –into an "earth suit" for our journey on earth. Scripture tells us that God knew us before we were formed–before we were put in our earth suit and incarnated as a little peep. Similarly, when we die, we continue to exist. We simply exit our "earth suit" and take on an "eternal body." as our soul goes on to be with God (or someplace else separated from Him if we spurn Jesus). Paul called our bodies tents and temples, but neither word picture has stayed with me like the earth suit.

My friend Jack was a little boy when his grandfather died. Jack's folks took him to the mortuary for the viewing even though he was very young. Jack vividly remembers being held up in his dad's arms so he could see his deceased grandfather in the coffin and then hearing his dad say emphatically, "Son, that is *not* your grandfather. He's no longer here." The certainty of his dad's words gave Jack great peace about death.

I am *not* my body, but I spend a lot of time, money, and energy taking care of it. Let's take care of our souls with the same diligence.

SCRIPTURE

"He who keeps the commandment keeps his soul, But he who is careless of conduct will die." (Proverbs 19:16, NASB)

ANTICHRIST? SERIOUSLY?

"This is how you can recognize the Spirit of God: Every spirit that acknowledges that Jesus Christ has come in the flesh is from God, but every spirit that does not acknowledge Jesus is not from God. This is the spirit of the antichrist, which you have heard is coming and even now is already in the world" (1 John 4:2-3).

I've always dreaded the day the Antichrist would show up. The description in the book of Revelation is scary, with graphic images of beasts, and dragons, and war, and tribulation, and Armageddon. But these verses remind me that it's not just then, it's now. The "spirit of the antichrist . . . is already in the world."

Boom.

The culture we're living in is dominated by voices of people who do not acknowledge that Jesus has come in the flesh and that He's from God. Some are overtly "anti-Christ," while others seem benign, simply being themselves.

This isn't a rant against culture so much as a call to create *new culture*. A new model for life, marriage, fatherhood, work life, and leadership—a light-on-a-hill kind of culture that will draw people toward Christ and away from antichrist beliefs.

Take the initiative. Make a new culture. Be creative, building a family and reputation that's all about Jesus and His righteousness. Be diligent, committed, and courageous, and don't believe there's a middle ground. It's Christ or it's anti-Christ.

SCRIPTURE

"Whoever is not with me is against me, and whoever does not gather with me scatters." (Matthew 12:30)

WE LIVE *FOR* THE LORD?

It's not hard to find someone who is *for* the Georgia Bulldogs. Or *for* the New England Patriots. Americans are *for* America. We relish our identity as Americans as we celebrate our independence each July 4th. When you're *for* something, you identify with it, you advocate for it, and you'll even set your priorities around it.

Merriam-Webster defines *for* as "the person or thing that something is sent or given to." What are we "given to" in our daily lives? What (or who) do we think about? Identify with? Advocate *for*? Set priorities around?

Our work and career? Our home? Lawn? Golf game? Favorite college team? Vacations and time off? Our family? Our church?

The list is endless.

When we think about the time and attention we give God every day versus what we spread to the things on the above list, it's almost comical. The creator God who invited us to call Him Father wants to be our best friend. Yet He only gets a few minutes each morning before we hit the gym. Then when we're under pressure or in a crisis, suddenly His piece of our energy, attention, and mindshare get really big.

So how do we change this? How do we know when we're living *for* the Lord?

When we're thinking about, praising, and thanking Him. When we're looking for opportunities to serve and show kindness to others. The best thing is, when we slow down and read His Book, bring Him into our decisions, ask for His guidance and listen to His voice, and live as He wants us to live, we feel His peace and His presence in our lives. That's what He wants *for* us.

SCRIPTURE

"If we live, we live for the Lord; and if we die, we die for the Lord. So, whether we live or die, we belong to the Lord." (Romans 14:8)

WHEN IS A MAN A REAL MAN?

When I hear someone say, "So I should *let* my wife do whatever she wants?" I think, "*Let* her?" Show me a marriage where the guy "*lets* his wife," and I'll show you one where the wife has her bags packed–psychologically if not physically.

Real men are in control, right? Not right. I confess, while I would have vehemently denied it, for years I tried to control my wife. I had expectations. But when I stopped expecting, coaching, counseling, criticizing, questioning, and trying to control, our marriage improved.

Being in control implies that one has authority. A lot of Christian men love the idea of having authority over their wives. They hang on the first seven words of Ephesians 5:22: "Wives should submit to their husbands in everything" without paying attention to Ephesians 5:25: "Husbands, love your wives, just as Christ loved the church and gave himself up for her."

No person can control another person, not really. And when I look at Jesus, I see the most powerful leader *ever* choosing to live as a gentle servant. He could have exerted control if He'd wanted to, but He chose to lead through influence.

As men, our identity comes from being an adopted son of God. If your identity is tied to being a "real man," e.g., the husband in control of his wife, that's a false identity, and it doesn't look anything like Jesus.

Encourage your wife, meaning "give her courage." Instead of more, "Wives should submit to their husbands" we need more, "Husbands, love your wives."

SCRIPTURE

"Do not let any unwholesome talk come out of your mouths, but only what is helpful for building others up according to their needs, that it may benefit those who listen." (Ephesians 4:29)

FIRE YOUR FATHER

Last Father's Day, you gave him a call, a dozen golf balls, or maybe lunch out with the family.

Now fire him. That's right, if you're an adult, you may need to fire your dad.

Hear me out. I *so* wanted to please my dad. When I got a raise or got promoted, I called my dad before I called my wife. Just like that little boy waiting for him after work, I was still trying to matter, still striving to please him.

But when I found Jesus, something incredible happened, something I didn't expect. I discovered a Father's love that was unconditional, not based on my behavior or performance. Grasping His love changed *everything* for me. I mattered to my (Heavenly) Father.

Once a counselor sat me in a room with a notepad, a pencil, and an empty chair. "Write down every single thing your dad *ever did* or *didn't do* that hurt you. Then, imagine he's sitting here. Read him your list . . . out loud. Tell him how it felt, what you wish he'd said. All of it. Then, forgive him. Tell him, 'Since God has forgiven me, I can't *not* forgive you!' Then wad up the paper and throw it away."

I read my whole list to the empty chair, forgave him, and then fired him.

From that day, I never looked at my dad the same. He was no longer my father; he was a friend. I was released from his expectations, and he was released from mine.

If you don't need to fire your dad, stop and thank God for that. But if you do need to be released from his expectations, don't wait another minute.

QUESTION

If you can't truly thank God for your earthly father, will you forgive him, fire him, and then let your Heavenly Father take his place?

PROTEST POLKA

A counselor friend loaned me a book about marriage relationships. Unlike most books focused on "fixing" people, Dr. Sue Johnson and Kenneth Sanderfer's *Created for Connection* is more about learning to dance together. It's been revolutionary for me.

Johnson says we all emerge from childhood and adolescence with certain "raw spots." When we touch our wife's raw spots, it hurts. Badly. The husband, maybe inadvertently, made a move on the dance floor and his wife made a countermove. The dance has begun; so has the argument.

There are several dances described in the book, but the one that best fit my wife and me is the "protest polka." Polka is a synchronized dance where one partner moves forward as the other steps back. One partner is sort of the aggressor, while the other pulls away in response. This is us.

Here I am wanting emotional connection, and, ironically, I'm the one ruining the connection because either I haven't studied my wife well enough to know her raw spots, or I'm so careless that I run over them without a thought. Couples who learn to navigate each other's raw spots have fewer arguments, deeper emotional connection, and more intimacy.

Here's some advice: Study your wife! With an open hand and heart, learn her coherent narrative. Through the stories of her life, try to figure out her raw spots. Confirm them, then discipline yourself to avoid them. You may see a big change in the intimacy and emotional connection you have as you stop rubbing against her raw spots.

SCRIPTURE

"Husbands, in the same way be considerate as you live with your wives, and treat them with respect as the weaker partner and as heirs with you of the gracious gift of life, so that nothing will hinder your prayers." (1 Peter 3:7)

SLOWING THE GAME DOWN

I watch no more than seven hockey games a year—the Stanley Cup Finals. The effort, quickness, and passion is captivating. And when the puck finally slips through that morass of players and sticks into the net, I never see it until the horns go off and the crowd goes wild. When they show the replay in slow motion—when they slow the game down—then I can see the short passes, the ricochets, the lightning-quick reactions.

We can all see it on the replay, but it's a trick to *slow the game down while it's under way*. Most men say they're busy, that everything feels out of control. They say, "When my kids get out on their own, I'll slow down," or, "As soon as I get promoted," or, "As soon as we sell the company," or, "When I get older."

We make the mistake of thinking life magically slows down on some mythical day, but it doesn't. The speed only changes when we do something new, focus on fewer things, and invest more time in those few things.

Slow your game down. Spend *more* time on *fewer* things. Start a daily gratitude journal and write down one new thing you saw or experienced and tell God thank you. Knowing you're going to write something down will help motivate you to look for His good gifts, forcing you to slow down and take it all in.

SCRIPTURE

**"Who of you by worrying can add a
single hour to your life?" (Luke 12:25)**

BLIND WILLIE

For almost twenty years, my wife and I have had a little fish pond beside our home. I feed the fish every morning. I throw the pellets in the same area every time, and all the fish hurry there and start chomping on fish food. All except one. This boy is orange, black, and butt-ugly. His eyes are white and bulging.

While the others eat, this one floats, swims around in circles, and seems to have no interest in food. Eventually, we figured out he was totally blind. So I named him Blind Willie. I have started shaking the food cup as I approach the pond, signaling to Willie that it's time to eat. Even though he's always late to the party, he gets there. And no matter how much food I've provided, I'll throw in enough to make sure Blind Willie gets some.

I don't think fish do much thinking, but I do. And I can't help but think about the way God loves us. Sure, He feeds the superstars—the ones who *get it* and *got it* a long time ago. But He also keeps an eye out for guys like Blind Willie —guys who don't have eyes to see. He goes the extra mile, figuring out other ways to bring even His most blind children to His food.

QUESTION

**Is there someone in your sphere of influence
who is spiritually blind? Someone who's floating
or swimming around in circles, or has no interest
in spiritual food? Rest in the fact that your Heavenly
Father is rattling the cup, throwing little pellets of
spiritual food in their direction, and waiting patiently
for them to realize He's there and He loves them.**

IN THE MIDST OF YOUR CIRCUMSTANCES

No man can gain perspective in the midst of his circumstances.

Your perspective is the way you see something. *Perspective* has a Latin root meaning "look through" or "perceive." All definitions of *perspective* have something to do with looking.

Our perspective is often skewed by our vested interests and our ego. We want to brag about the things we get right and hide those that are going south. This is why you need another man in your life, someone *outside* your circumstances who walks in, looks around, and sees things you don't see. It's sort of like the clutter in your house. It's been there so long you no longer see it. But bring in a stager or someone focused on decluttering and "Boom! There it is!"

Why is it so hard for us to step outside our circumstances and objectively look back? What keeps us from inviting in a trusted friend or a counselor or a consultant?

Pride.

We don't want to be wrong. We don't want people to think we didn't see it for ourselves. We're afraid we're going to have to change.

As Jesus followers, we know we don't *own* anything. Our life is a steward-ship. Good stewards aren't afraid. Just look at the "ten-talent guy" in the Bible. He took *huge* risk, and he was handsomely rewarded.

QUESTION

Can we be great stewards without inviting fresh eyes in to help us gain and keep perspective?

MARCH 13

PURPOSE AND YOUR THIRD WORD

Have you ever thought about writing a life purpose statement? Purpose asks, "Why am I here?" Of course, the stock answer for Jesus followers is "to glorify God," and that's 100 percent true. But what do you do with that as a life purpose?

I'd like to throw out the idea of a third word. My theory is that all Jesus followers are called to *love* and *serve*. Those are givens. The life purpose statement of a Jesus follower would begin with "I, (your name here), exist to glorify God by loving and serving others and to (your third word here)."

My third word is *challenge*. I don't know how I got there, but it is what it is. I've been told that *challenge* is a combination of discernment and courage. Discernment leads me to form hypotheses about people and their motives. Courage enables me to lovingly confront them with what I see, sometimes leading them to different perspectives and decisions.

What's your third word? The third word is unique to you. It's what you do well and naturally. It's what you were *wired* to do from the beginning. I know guys who are problem solvers, planners, and administrators. When they're doing that thing—that *third word thing*, they're in the zone. They're fulfilled.

CHALLENGE

Come up with three to five "third words" that might fit you. Then get it down to just one. If you struggle, hand the list to your wife or closest friend and have them pick the word that most describes what you're wired for. Ask God to affirm it. Then ask Him to lead you into opportunities where your unique ability can be leveraged to build His Kingdom and bring Him glory.

INTERPRETERS

Kids come into the world without a clue, and as soon as they can talk, they start asking questions. "What's that, Daddy?" "What's that mean, Mama?" Parents use their knowledge, experience, and language to help kids interpret what's happening in the world around them. All along the way, kids are getting better and better at interpreting things for themselves.

Christian mentors help their protégés *interpret* what a Jesus follower does, what it means to be a Christian man, leader, husband, father, and friend. They model what it's like to be transparent and vulnerable and, in so doing, connect with other men and with God in a way they didn't know existed before. Mentors help people interpret God's Word, but also interpret their own stories.

Mentors are interpreters. They've been through a lot of life, misinterpreted all kinds of stuff and suffered the consequences. But they've learned from those experiences and want to help others avoid the mistakes they made. Maybe more importantly, their mentees are equipped to help those coming behind them to interpret their stories and make sense of their lives and the God who loves them so pervasively.

When a mentor's motive is to help create a disciple of Jesus, then he's a disciple-maker under the alias of mentor. When we love a brother and want to help him learn the "Jesus way of life," we're making disciples and disciple-makers.

God wired all of us to grow by developing relationships with each other, sharing with one another, and helping each other grow to be more like Jesus.

SCRIPTURE

**"God authorized and commanded me
to commission you: Go out and train
everyone you meet, far and near, in this
way of life." (Matthew 28:18, MSG)**

PLUS ONE

Every year when the NFL draft rolls around, the name Ryan Leaf comes up. An episode of *NFL Top 10* ranked him as the No. 1 draft bust in NFL history. Interpretation: The player who came into the draft with the most potential but went on to epically fail.

What went wrong? Leaf points to *isolation*. "Some of the most successful and talented people are some of the loneliest because they isolate so much," Leaf told ESPN.

Ryan Leaf's name is often mentioned in the same sentence with Peyton Manning. Manning was drafted number one, right before Leaf, and went on to a stellar career. Living in Manning's shadow and the image of what might have been adds even more shame and guilt to Leaf's story. But bringing his shame and guilt out of the dark and into the light has helped Leaf move beyond his past. "The more and more I talk about it," he says, "I think it takes away that power of shame and guilt."

Every guy needs a plus one—one other guy who knows *everything* about you and who will tell you the truth. One person you aren't isolated from. One person you can tell what you're thinking, what you're doing, and what you're thinking about doing.

Challenge

We have lots of acquaintances, but only a few friends. From those closest to you, is there one who knows all your dark corners? One whom you trust and who, knowing all your ugly stuff, will love you more, not less? That's your plus one. Go tell him. If you don't have one, go get one. Be purposeful . . . it's that important.

THANK YOU NOTES

Most people hate to write thank-you notes. We like to get 'em but hate to write 'em.

I got one from an eight-year-old once. His dad was in one of my mentoring groups and seemed to grow a lot through the experience. I assume he told his son about it, and the little boy wanted to say thanks for helping his dad. So he drew me a picture and sent the note, along with a cool little gift.

I couldn't help but think of the ten lepers Jesus healed. Only one came back to say thanks. I can almost picture him helping his little boy write a thankyou note to Jesus for helping his dad.

A good friend of mine got a thank-you note from the President of the United States—a real handwritten one. I'll *never* get one of those, but if I did, I still wouldn't treasure it like I do the one from my eight-year-old friend.

QUESTION

Will you take time today to thank someone who impacted your life or the life of someone you love? You never know how it may impact them.

USE IT OR LOSE

One of the things Jesus said has always seemed out of character to me. I've never understood why the ultimate embodiment of God's love would say, in Matthew 25:29, "For whoever has will be given more, and they will have an abundance. Whoever does not have, even what they have will be taken from them."

That doesn't sound like Jesus to me. What was He talking about?

Then I read John 6:63, where Jesus said, "The Spirit gives life; the flesh counts for nothing. The words I have spoken to you—they are full of the Spirit and life." He was talking about the Holy Spirit in us.

We receive a *seed* of the Holy Spirit when we first believe. It's like a starter kit of faith. That seed is the Spirit of Jesus, and it's planted in the *soil* of our souls. God's desire is for it to flourish and grow—for its abundance to fill our lives with the fruit of the Spirit.

So how do we keep this seed alive in us? How does it grow and prosper? By obedience.

When the disciples asked Jesus for more faith in Luke 17:5-9, He suggested they keep on obeying, just as a slave would obey his master. Faith is like fertilizer for the seed of the Holy Spirit within us.

The more we obey and follow Him, the more faith we have. The presence of the Holy Spirit becomes stronger. The less we obey and follow, the more calloused we become. Our spiritual ears and eyes get dull and dim and, for all practical purposes, are taken away.

SCRIPTURE

"For you know that when your faith is tested, your endurance has a chance to grow." (James 1:3, NLT)

SO . . . HOW DO *YOU* SEE GOD?

Judge? Police chief? Genie in a bottle? Loving? Cruel? Distant? Available? Smiling? Angry? Irrelevant? Powerless?

Be honest. How do you *really* see God in your mind?

When we're first confronted with this question as adults, our picture of God emerges from our subconscious childhood experience with our father or a father-figure. With so few dads resembling Jesus in what they do and say, it's no surprise that few of us have an accurate image of God. We piece together our idea of Him based on the prayers He didn't answer, the trage-dy He allowed, the opinions of our friends, the celebrities we admire, and maybe a little Scripture. Without intending to, we create a patchwork picture of God with little resemblance to His actual identity.

How we view God has *a lot* to do with whether we feel loved or not, whether we care for others or not, whether we turn to God often or just in a crisis, and even whether we want God in our lives or not.

Look no further than Jesus to find the answer. He modeled a perfect life. He defined God as Father. *A perfect Father.* Not the one we had, not the friend's father we always wished we'd had, but a totally perfect Dad.

QUESTION

**What might a perfect father look like for you?
Take a minute and jot down the characteristics
of a perfect father. Then compare them with
Jesus and the God of the New Testament. Start
to think of God as your Father, Jesus as your
best friend, the Holy Spirit as your Counselor
and guide. Three in one . . . the Triune God.**

BEFORE HONOR IS HUMILITY

Look around at the people you admire most and you'll find humility. When people strive to "be somebody," they're often trying to be somebody else.

Humility may be the most revered character trait from God's perspective. "Blessed are the poor in spirit: for theirs is the kingdom of heaven," said Jesus.

So how do we get humble? Two ways:

1. **Gratitude**—A grateful heart is a humble heart. A man who realizes his skills, his position, his opportunities, his relationships, his *everything* comes from God—that man is well on his way to a humble heart.

   The cool thing about gratitude is it's a *choice* you make.

2. **Brokenness**—This is the way most proud hearts become humble hearts. Few of us have the faith to humble ourselves and recognize God in His rightful place. It takes coming to a place where Jesus is all you have to appreciate that Jesus is all you need.

About two millennia ago, the only man who had no pride, the only man who ever lived without sin, the only man who didn't need to be humbled, *chose* to humble Himself. He *volunteered* to lay down and let them drive nails in His hands and feet, taking the capital punishment for crimes and sins He didn't commit. *The sins He took the punishment for were mine and yours.*

Learn from Jesus. Make a humble heart a volitional choice and avoid the brokenness and collateral damage from sin and selfishness. Take responsibility for your pride, arrogance, sin, and selfishness.

Thank Him for taking that junk to the cross for you. And believe Him when He says, "It is finished."

SCRIPTURE

"Before a downfall the heart is haughty, but humility comes before honor." (Proverbs 18:12)

SPLIT PERSONALITY

Ever feel like you don't know yourself? Someone cuts you off in traffic and words come out of your mouth that you'd never use in prayer. *Did I actually say that!?* Then you're at a funeral and feel tears well up as you hug the widow and pray for her. The tears are real. You ask, *Who am I? I mean, really? Who's in there?*

Well, if you've ever been *saved*, then you have a *split personality*.

In addition to *your* personality, there is another one living in you: the Holy Spirit. It's that *other voice* you hear, the one urging you to be humble and kind, to be patient, and to forgive.

Jesus followers have these two personalities—two voices speaking in their heads. When we listen to our own voice, we're critical of people, hold grudges, stereotype, and judge. That voice of our *flesh* reminds us of who we were.

But the voice of God is also speaking, almost whispering, suggesting, "Forgive her, like I forgave you!" And "Trust me, I'm with you. Everything's going to be alright." And "Drop that thought. It's not taking you to a good place. Pray. I'm here."

The key to the quality of your life depends on which voice you listen to and obey. You don't *talk* your way into righteous living; you have to *behave* your way there by obeying the voice of God in you.

All Jesus followers hear the two voices. It's which voice we *obey* that determines the quality of our lives and our usefulness to the Lord.

QUESTION

Which personality will you live out today?
Which voice will you listen to and obey?

March 21

JESUS' SPLIT PERSONALITY

Join me on a deep dive into the personality of Jesus. All my life, I've heard that He was fully man, fully God–100 percent human and 100 percent divine at exactly the same time. Isn't it interesting that we have both God and man living in us, too? A little different man though, a sinless man (Jesus) versus a sinful man (me or you).

From a human standpoint, Jesus was fully human. His mother was pregnant with Him and birthed Him the way mothers generally do. He grew up physically and aged the way humans do.

He had human emotions: crying when His friend Lazarus died, getting angry when Jerusalem wouldn't repent and especially when the money changers took over the Temple. Even from the cross, He did a couple of distinctly human things. He made arrangements for His mother to be taken care of, and He cried out to God asking, "Why have you forsaken me?" These are all evidences of His humanity.

But all along the way, Jesus prayed and talked with His Father in Heaven. He *never* acted alone. He *never* took credit for anything He did. He *always* sought and listened to the Father's voice. He *always* obeyed. He had choices just like we do, but He *never* gave in to sin. *He lived a perfect life as a human being!*

How did He do that? *By constantly seeking the Father and obeying what He led Him to do.*

His is the "still small voice" urging us to pray and to "seek first His Kingdom and His righteousness."

QUESTION

Will you pause, pray, listen, and obey today?

HOW BRIGHT IS YOUR LIGHT?

Whether you're a sports fan or not, if you live in America, you remember the name Tim Tebow.

In the late 2000s and early 2010s there were millions of opinions on why he was constantly in the spotlight. Yes, he won the Heisman trophy. Yes, he led some come-from-behind wins. Yes, he was an unconventional quarterback.

And yes, he was (and is) public about his Christian faith.

But Tebow isn't just public about his faith, he is genuine. His life matches his words . . . he walks the talk. His *light* for Jesus shines bright. That was new and different in the world of celebrity and fame.

There are things Tebow *does*. He goes on mission trips, helping the least of these in Jesus' name. He prays on the field. He gives credit to his Lord and Savior for everything. He is unashamed.

Then there are things Tim Tebow *doesn't do*. He is a virgin . . . saving himself for his future wife. He doesn't drink for fear he'll lead others astray. He doesn't brag or boast, always projecting gratitude and humility.

It's not Tebow's *talk* that distinguishes him, it's his *walk*. Decisions he's made and how he lives them out.

There's a lesson here for the rest of us. The brightness of our *light* isn't determined by how loud we talk but by how loud our behavior speaks—the consistency of our decisions, the depth of our commitment to follow Christ, and our obedience to God by doing the right thing regardless of what people think.

QUESTION

What are the things you don't do that speak loudly to those around you? What are the things that, if you stopped doing them out of love and obedience to your Savior, would make your light shine brighter?

ABUNDANCE VS. SCARCITY

Parenting is tough. It's one of the hardest jobs around. There's no manual, no established formula, and God throws curveballs by making every child different. Over time, you grab hold of any principle that makes sense; you try it, and if it works, it becomes yours.

So I'm going to propose one: create an abundance environment for your kids.

Kids need and want love. As with anything in this world, if it's in short supply, then it becomes more valuable and creates contention. If it's abundant, it's no big deal.

Take oil and salt as examples. Every country needs petroleum, so there's fierce competition for it. Prices are high and promise to go higher. We fight, we manipulate, we bribe, we sell our souls for oil.

On the other hand, salt is a necessity for human life, but it's plentiful. The price for a box of salt is a few pennies. It's abundant.

When dads fail to engage with their kids, when they stay so busy their kids never feel they *matter*, when dad's presence is minimal and he never *really* has time to hang out with them, that's a scarcity environment.

But when there's a consistent abundance of daddy's presence and an endless supply of his love, there'll be less competition, less manipulation, and more peace in the home. Daddy has to *be there* physically and emotionally.

An abundance environment doesn't come naturally, and it isn't easy.

But it's worth it.

QUESTION

Thrive vs. Strive?

Is your home an abundance environment or a scarcity environment? Kids thrive in environments of abundant love. They strive in environments of scarcity.

AUTHENTIC HUMILITY

When I'm asked what makes a great mentor, one of the first words that pops into my head is humility. Not false humility, but the real deal. The kind you can't fake.

Where does that kind of humility come from?

From a deep-seated belief that God is the *source* of your success—*all* your success. Humble men believe that whatever they're being praised for *wouldn't be* if it weren't for Him. Whether it's His hand in the events and circumstances, His hand in building godly character. Whatever is good in them, it's from Him.

If you really stop and think about what you'd be without God, it's not a stretch to give Him the credit. He either changed you or protected you. All by yourself, you'd be a lot less than you are with Him living inside you.

One of my favorite Proverbs (23:7, KJV) says, "As he thinketh in his heart, so is he." If you truly think in your heart that you deserve the credit, that it's really your tenacity, your brains, your personality that's making you success-ful, then you will never be humble.

God is the Creator of your success. He can end it in a heartbeat or allow a heart to stop its beat. Only with this realization will you be able to gain true humility.

So whenever praise comes your way, say thank you. It's rude to reject some-one's kind words. But look for a way to immediately deflect the credit to the One who really deserves it.

QUESTION

Are you authentically humble? Do you truly believe that *all* your success comes from God?

MARCH 25

HOW'S YOUR SPRING?

Men who take the time to invest in younger men are rare. Very rare.

Why is this?

I found the answer as I read John 4 and saw two words I'd overlooked. Jesus is talking to the woman at the well. He tells her about "living water," the kind that that once you drink it, you're never thirsty again. In verse 14, Jesus says, "But whoever drinks the water I give them will never thirst. Indeed, the water I give them will become in them a spring of water welling up to eternal life."

The water Jesus provides *for* us becomes a spring *in* us.

Where I grew up, there was a spring in the woods on the way to the community swimming pool. When they widened the road, the spring got filled in and the water was piped to a storm drain. Wasted. Useless. Forgotten.

When you came into authentic relationship with Jesus, something started bubbling deep inside of you—an exciting, perpetual energy and enthusiasm that has the potential to refill itself for the rest of your life.

When it wells up, it has to come out. You want to worship, pray, sing, love Him, and serve Him. And to serve Him the way He told us to, you'll serve people. Loving and serving others taps that spring like nothing else!

QUESTION

**Does this describe your spring? Have you widened your road
and let the dirt of busyness fill it in? Are you piping your water
into work, sports, or maybe even church work? Dig out your spring.
Reconnect with the Source and let the "living water" flow anew.**

. . . AND HUNGER TOO!

At the very time Jesus was telling the woman at the well about the spring of living water, His disciples were in town buying food. But when they returned and urged Him to eat, He wouldn't . . . or couldn't. They asked each other, "Has anyone else brought him something to eat?"

Jesus was so fired up about what He was doing that He couldn't eat. The woman at the well *got it*. She accepted Him as Messiah.

How did He know?

Not only did she go into town and tell everyone, she brought them out so they could see Jesus for themselves. She had become a mentor—a disciple-maker. And that got Jesus so fired up that He couldn't eat. He said, "My food is to do the will of him who sent me and to finish his work."

She rose to His challenge. "Many Samaritans from that town believed in him because of the woman's testimony." She paid it forward.

And Jesus *loved it*!

So much so that He stayed with them another two days. And remember, these are unclean, half-breed Samaritans we're talking about.

Do want to experience that exuberance? Do you want to be so excited about something you can't eat? Love those around you and engage them in real conversations. Challenge them to see themselves honestly and confront the truth about their lives. Cast a vision for them as true worshipers and followers of God.

When God does His work in them, you will have helped make a disciple!

SCRIPTURE

Reread this remarkable story in John 4.

WHERE'S HER HEART?

One time I was having lunch with one of my mentees. It was our "one-on-one" to get to know each other. He toured me around his office, introduced me to his partners, and totally blew me away with how smart and competent he was.

But at lunch, when we started talking about marriage, the conversation turned a little stiff. Finally, I asked him this question regarding his wife:

"Do you know where her heart is?"

A long silence followed.

Then it hit me. Do I know where *my* wife's heart is? I mean today. This week. Right now.

I like substituting the word "desire" whenever I read the word "heart;" it's very revealing. For instance, when I see Psalm 51:10, "Create in me a pure heart, O God, and renew a steadfast spirit within me," I read it, "Create in me pure *desires, O God."

It's clarifying. It helps me to be intentional in a more immediate way.

So the real question is, "Do I know where my wife's *desires* are?" That's a better question. How can I love my wife "as Christ loved the church" and not know where her *heart* is or what she really *desires*? Today. Right now. What does she *want* in her life that I'm not giving her . . . focused time, or help with the kids, or help around the house, or the support she needs as she deals with her sick mother or grandmother?

QUESTION

**Do you know where your spouse's
heart is? Do you know what she *desires*
from you? Find out. Fast.**

DENIAL IS NOT A RIVER IN EGYPT

We don't know how to deal with death, other people's or our own.

We all *know* we are going to die; death is a certainty for every single one of us. The mortality rate continues to hover around 100 percent! Yet, depending on which research you read, between 55 to 70 percent of Americans die without a will. We just don't want to deal with it. We don't believe it will actually happen to us . . . or at least not in the near future. We live in denial.

What am I saying?

Deal with it. Get yourself ready.

If you love your wife and kids, get your house in order. Talk, pray, seek counsel—whatever it takes to get on the same page. Prepare your wills. Cover all the eventualities. Think five years, not forever. Put it on your calendar and come back to it again when you're a little further down the road. Don't put it off—deal with it.

Over the years, I've had a number of close friends die with *no warning*. I've seen the aftermath. The personal loss, the pain, the grief, the anxiety of "if only we had . . ."

So be ready financially. Make sure your wills, your insurance, your 401K beneficiary designation, *everything* is ticked and tied.

Be ready relationally. Make every effort to repair any broken or damaged relationships. Leave a legacy of forgiveness, love, and grace toward your family and friends.

And be ready spiritually. Surrender to Him completely. Love. Obey. Serve.

SCRIPTURE

"There is a time for everything, and a season for every activity under the heavens: a time to be born and a time to die. . . ." (Ecclesiastes 3:1-2)

WHEN I (FINALLY) DROPPED TO MY KNEES . . .

It was early in my business career. Our start-up venture was a little over two years old. We opened our first expansion city office, and it was awful. Wrong market, wrong people, wrong location, wrong tactics, wrong everything!

On a flight with our chairman and our attorney, it became eminently clear that we were in trouble. After we landed and arrived at our hotel, I walked to my room with the weight of the world on my shoulders.

As the elevator climbed toward my floor, the thought crossed my mind, *You haven't had a quiet time in two weeks. You've been blowin' and goin' and have spent zero time with God.*

I walked into the dark room, laid down my suit bag, and without even turning on the lights, I dropped to my knees by the bed. I was ready to say, "I'm so sorry, Lord . . ." But before I could say anything, the following words appeared in my mind's eye: "You are in the center of My will for your life right now." God knew my heart; He already knew my need and my prayer!

I tried to pray, but it was useless. I had finally humbled myself before Him, and He had responded. I got up, brushed my teeth, and went to bed. I slept like a baby, and within a few days, God saved our company through a large refund and price reduction from our largest vendor. We were instantly cash flow positive, and I had *nothing to do with it!*

Good things happen—no, God-things happen—when we drop to our knees!

SCRIPTURE

**"Our God is in heaven; he does whatever
pleases him." (Psalm 115:3)**

MEMORIES OR MEANING?

A friend was telling me about going through his parents' things after his dad passed away. The pictures of places in the Holy Land, pictures from Italy and Greece, pictures from England and France—all thrown in the garbage.

Why? Because those pictures were only relevant to the person who took them. When they passed on to the next part of their existence, the pictures became irrelevant and useless. Memories are that way; they're only meaningful to the person who experienced the thing that created them. And when that brain is unplugged, they disappear.

We spend a lot of our time and money-making memories for ourselves and our loved ones. As we do, we are drawn further and further away from living lives of fulfillment.

Pursuing meaning in our lives doesn't exclude having great memories, but meaning matters in a deeper and a more long-lasting way.

Meaning says the activity you're involved with is really important.

Meaning says it matters at a deep level.

Meaning says the consequences of the activity will affect the people involved for a long time. Where there's meaning, there's a multiplier effect; future generations of people will benefit from things that have meaning.

Mentoring younger people gives life meaning. To influence a younger person to choose to become a volunteer leader with Young Life instead of becoming the local sports bar trivia champ, that is meaning. To watch someone you've mentored become an influential leader in his church, that is meaning. To watch a protégé lead his family through an incredible crisis in a godly way, that is meaning.

QUESTION

What have you experienced in life that has *more meaning* than being used of God in the life of another person?

DRIVEN OR CALLED?

Author Gordon MacDonald asks a profound question:

"Are you driven or called?"

Driven described me the first twelve years of my career. I had all the child-hood preparation for being driven—parents who rarely said "well done" for anything, a dad who worked a lot and modeled being driven, and an environment where I was criticized and shamed when I didn't measure up. I emerged laser-focused on being significant, no matter what. I was the epitome of driven.

What does a driven guy look like?

Addicted to progress, always wanting more, little regard for integrity, ab-normally busy, unnecessarily competitive, obsessed with symbols of success.

Sound familiar?

The answer for me, and ultimately for you as well, is to become a *called* person. Called men have decided to trust God with everything and to accept His will as their own. What does a called guy look like?

Called men know exactly who they are. Their identity is not synonymous with what they do. Instead, their identity is synonymous with who God says they are. Their identity is grounded in something greater than themselves, and they live each day with an unshakable belief in who they truly are.

Called men have a work ethic equal to driven men, but there's one major difference: Called men live, work, and breathe every moment in light of eternity.

QUESTION

**Are you called or driven? How do you
walk yourself back from the drivenness
that stands ready to take over again?**

THE HEAVY WATER OF TRUST

In a nuclear power plant, "heavy water" keeps the reactor cool as it burns the fuel which creates the steam that turns the turbines that generate electricity. Heavy water is actually deuterium oxide, which is like water but about 11 percent more dense. (There's your physics lesson for today!)

The catastrophes (and near catastrophes) at nuclear power plants come from failures in these heavy-water cooling systems. Each time, for different reasons, the amount of heavy water has declined, allowing the heat level to rise and get out of control.

In relationships, *trust* is the heavy water.

When your wife has an incredibly high level of trust in you, that trust cools all kinds of "heat" when it comes. You show up late from a business trip? She's fine because she trusts you. There's money gone from the checking account? No problem because she trusts you. She assumes a good answer to the mystery (like your plane was delayed, or you forgot to write down a check, or tell her about some expense you had to take care of).

But if the level of heavy water in the reactor goes down, whether it leaks a little at a time or it bursts out all at once, the entire deal is at risk because the heat rises above heavy water's ability to cool it. That's called a meltdown!

Marriages have meltdowns. And they are very, very hard to recover from. When the heavy water of trust leaks down in a marriage, suspicion replaces trust. Suspicion brings defensiveness and more suspicion. Tempers flare. Things heat up, and sometimes, they melt down.

Protect her trust. It's precious and very hard to rebuild.

CHALLENGE

Be constantly aware of the trust level in your marriage. Overcommunicate, deliver on your promises, anticipate her needs, and keep her connected to your world.

IS IT FOR REAL?

We can't *know*, completely and totally, what's real until we die.

That's why it's called faith. We have to park what we don't know and not let those issues derail us.

Peace comes from resolving what you can know and what you can't know, then spending all your time on the things you can know.

It's the serenity prayer, but with a few words changed:

> God, grant me the serenity to accept the things I cannot *know*, the courage to *learn* the things I can, and the wisdom to know the difference.

As I said earlier, you can't know for absolute certain that Christianity is true until thirty seconds after you die.

But what I *know* is this: Since accepting Christ on faith, I have a running conversation with God, and that conversation is real. I know He tells me He loves me. He answers my questions—not all of them, but a lot of them. He "kicks me in the conscience" when I do wrong by Him or any of His children. I see His involvement in the circumstances and relationships in my life. These things I *know*.

It ultimately comes down to what the blind man said to the Pharisees when they were trying to pin him down on the details of his healing and on the man who healed him. He said, (and I'm paraphrasing), "Look, all I can tell you for sure is that I was blind, and now I can see."

Is God real, or just some perception in the minds of weak people?

All I know is, "I was blind, and now I can see."

QUESTION

Do you struggle with the unanswerable questions? Ask the Lord directly. You might be shocked at how He answers.

THE MOST IMPORTANT PERSON

Have you ever caught yourself "self-referencing"? That's when you take the topic of conversation and make it about *you*. Some people do this on *every* topic of conversation *every* time. It's exhausting.

Here's how it goes. If I say something like, "We had a great service at church on Sunday," the self-referencing person says, "My church is doing a building campaign. They asked me to be on the committee, but I'm not sure I have time." No matter the subject, they take it to *their* life, *their* health, *their* kids, *their* history, *their* frame of reference. They shut down real conversation.

If you want to improve your conversational skills, practice "others-referencing." When you hear, "We had a great church service on Sunday," say "Wow, that's awesome. What made it great?" The person will know you're listening, and asking another question about what *they* care about demonstrates love. It's staying in *their* frame of reference.

Check out this quote from Leo Tolstoy:

> "Remember that there is only one important time and it is Now. The present moment is the only time over which we have dominion. The most important person is always the person with whom you are, who is right before you, for who knows if you will have dealings with any other person in the future? The most important pursuit is making that person, the one standing at your side, happy, for that alone is the pursuit of life."

QUESTION

Will you attempt to be fully present and love people by really listening to them?

APRIL 4

SURPRISE! SURPRISE!

Have you ever been completely surprised by the abrupt resignation of someone on your team?

People get better jobs; people move on. That's understood and accepted. But unexpected decisions can blindside us. We wonder, *Why was I not included in their deliberations? Do they not trust me? Are they afraid of me? What should I do differently?*

Answer: We have to know our people's hearts and let them know ours.

As leaders, we have to study our people—know what's important to them and what makes them tick. We do this when we hire them, but after a while, we forget and start taking them for granted. We're busy; they're busy. It stops productivity for us to sit down and talk . . . I mean just talk.

But those conversations are the only way we can stay connected to a person's heart, know what's going on with them, and get invited to participate in their decisions instead of being blindsided.

It's true at work, and even more true at home. If we want a family that's open, honest, and doesn't surprise each other with the unexpected (except on birthdays, of course), then we need intentional time to know our loved ones and be known by them.

It's a process that never stops. People change over time. That's OK. It's our responsibility to discover where their heart is, find out who they really are, and use that insight to love them better.

QUESTION

**Who do you need to spend time with
so you really know their heart?**

APRIL 5

GUNNERS

Gunners are the hyper-aggressive leaders who make things happen.

I'm a gunner. I didn't realize it until my son described one of the gunners in his med-school class. "She is on a mission, man. She knows the answers to every question, she's always there, always early, and always focused. She hardly knows anyone's name in the class, but she knows every faculty member, and they all know her."

We've all met gunners; even now you can think of someone who fits the name *gunner*. (Advice to some of you: Don't look in the mirror; you might see one looking back at you!)

If a gunner is to develop, mature, and become more balanced, it'll be in one of three ways:

1. **Voluntary engagement**—Through intense, ruthless self-examination, they decide they don't want to be a gunner anymore. They surrender their ambition to God. They humble themselves.

2. **Pattern of failure**—People won't submit to being used or abused for long. Employees will leave, kids will stay away, and the gunner's spouse will find a life of their own, either in this marriage or a new one. The solution is the same. Surrender. Selflessness. Humility. Faith.

3. **Harsh discipline of reality**—If multiple relational failures don't get the gunner's attention, he's ultimately going to hit the wall. It will take a loving God to get him through. Same solution, but unnecessary pain for himself and those he loves!

A friend put it this way: "God starts with a whisper. If we don't listen, He loves us enough to yell. And if we still don't listen, look out, because He also loves us enough to get out the hammer!"

QUESTION

Are you a gunner?

WORKING WITH A DIFFICULT PERSON

So, you work with someone who's difficult. Maybe they're a gunner, maybe they think they're an expert in everything, maybe they're always distracting from the goal, or maybe they're just rude. What do you do?

Well you can't minister to someone you don't love, and praying is one of the greatest acts of love we can do. Furthermore, God does His best work when we pray.

Why? Because prayer is how God changes *your* heart.

You can only manage you. Only God can change *them*. You will be part of the problem or part of the solution *based on how you manage you*—how you respond.

The key is acceptance. We Christ followers talk about love all the time, but we rarely talk about acceptance. That's the first step. Accept them as a person, just as they are. And then communicate your acceptance. Don't judge, criticize, placate, or try to schmooze.

People are drawn to acceptance and run from rejection. To have influence, you'll have to accept them *just as Jesus accepted you* when He first saved you. People can sense when they're accepted. Over time, they warm up to those who accept them.

Accepting others will make you stand out, because most people run, or hide, or wear a mask. Or they go negative, becoming critical and cynical and ruining their opportunity for influence.

If you continually pray for the difficult people in your life and choose to accept them even when everything in you says "run," you may just be the person God uses to help them find a better way of living.

QUESTION

**Are you praying for the difficult people in your life?
Do they feel your acceptance? Might God have a divine
appointment waiting for you and them sometime in the future?**

APRIL 7

ARE YOU ANGRY?

Anxiety comes from unmet expectations. When people, or God, or circumstances don't do what I think they should, I become anxious, unhappy, frustrated, sad, or maybe even a little depressed.

But when I *really expect* something, when I *demand* it and it doesn't happen, then I get angry.

Most of the angry people I know have been angry for a long time. There's an undercurrent. I walk on eggshells around them because I never know when something's going to trip the switch and set them off. Somewhere in their past, they made a demand on God (or someone), and they didn't come through. They've never gotten over it . . . not really.

So how *should* we deal with anxiety and anger?

The answer is found in managing our expectations and dropping our demands. We can't make people or God do what we want, so we have to recognize the expectations and demands we're setting and learn to manage them.

All meaningful relationships are interdependent. They're built and fueled by need. It's healthy to express our needs–to God (that's called prayer) and to others (that's called friendship).

Once we learn to express our needs to God and to others, then our tact has to be to trust God and accept what comes.

Having expectations is natural. But identifying them for what they are, processing them to sort out what's reasonable, what's selfish, and what's totally over the top–that's where maturity starts to kick in. And when we can relinquish those expectations and accept what God wants us to have, then we can start to experience peace and contentment.

QUESTION

What demands have you made that led you to anger?
Will you trust God to give you what you need?

APRIL 8

ZONE VS. MAN-TO-MAN

It's rare that I have a BGI (Blinding Guiding Insight). Here's one:

> We've gone "zone." Jesus played "man-to-man."

When you play zone defense, you're responsible for an area. Anyone who comes into your zone is your responsibility.

In man-to-man, you've got a guy to track. A person. A face. You can study him. You can prepare for him. In the game, you know where he is and what he's up to. He never gets out of your sight.

Too often we play zone. Work, home, family, church, small group, Sunday school. I cover these zones well. If someone comes to my zone I'm ready, but I'm not looking to go out of my way to reach someone.

Jesus played man-to-man. He broke all kinds of social mores by connecting with people one-on-one. The woman at the well, the rich young ruler, Zacchaeus, Matthew, on and on. Jesus didn't just show up in His zone. Jesus didn't just go teach His Sunday school class or lead His small group. He initiated. He *connected* with people the Father led Him to. He went man-to-man.

I had lunch with the senior pastor of a megachurch. Thousands of people, hundreds of staff, millions of dollars. For forty-five years, this man has mentored a group of guys toward growth in their faith. He said, "If I had to choose between preaching on Sunday (zone) or doing these groups (man-to-man), I'd give up preaching!"

Personally, I went man-to-man a number of years ago, and no other decision I've made has been more richly rewarded.

QUESTION

Are you willing to go man-to-man? Ask God to show who He wants you to engage with and to give you the courage to initiate.

APRIL 9

INCONVENIENT

Here's a test for you. Think about something you could do—some role you could play in helping others in Jesus' name. Stop right now and think.

Now, think about how you might *actually move forward* with your idea.

I'll bet you a dollar that within thirty seconds, your mind ran to how inconvenient it would be to take it on. Convenience is virtually sacred in America, and it's taking the place of true involvement and heartfelt commitment to doing what Jesus called us to do.

I'll make up a few hypotheticals. See if your thought pattern is like mine.

Idea: "I could lead a Bible study at the nursing home for the elderly and the abandoned."

> **Inconvenience:** "I don't have that kind of time."
> **Interpretation:** I don't really care that much.

Idea: "Our friends are going through a rough patch in their marriage right now. We should invite them over for dinner and love on them a little. Heck, we might even be able to help."

> **Inconvenience:** "We are *so* busy. That's just one more thing."
> **Interpretation:** I don't care enough to be inconvenienced.

Don't get me wrong. I'm not saying we should say yes to everything we're invited to do or that comes to our minds. But I am suggesting we start being more honest with ourselves and ask this question:

> Is my hesitance to step out and serve coming from a lack of calling or a lack of convenience?

QUESTION

**How about you? Will you at least ask the "
convenience question" before you say no
to what God may be calling you to do?**

THE BIBLE IS "SO TWO THOUSAND YEARS AGO"

Why do so few people read the Bible?

I'm not talking about a random verse pulled out to make a point; I'm talking about the book itself, the entity, this thing that's integral to our faith.

God's Word is eternal. It'll last beyond the Internet, the iPhone, the Final Four, everything. In heaven, we'll recognize the words, the wisdom, and the authors, and we'll never tire of learning what it all means.

God's Word has been around—unchanged for hundreds, if not thousands of years—and a lot of the world's population believes its essence. Isn't it smarter to build your life on a time-tested plan? The Biblical approach to life is wise, effective, stable, unchanging, and true.

When I read the Bible and ask, "God, what are you teaching me here?" or, "Lord, what would you have me do?" and then listen, He often gives me wisdom that I'm just not smart enough to have thought up on my own. I do it. I also write it down in my journal, because I don't want to forget. Much of what's in this book has been discovered that way.

Read your Bible, and chat with the Author as you read. Pray. Ask questions. Listen to His answers and instructions.

SCRIPTURE

"For the word of God is alive and active. Sharper than any double-edged sword, it penetrates even to dividing soul and spirit, joints and marrow; it judges the thoughts and attitudes of the heart." (Hebrews 4:12)

WHAT WILL YOUR NEXT-GENERATION LEGACY BE?

"What a dad pursues with fervor, his kids will pursue in moderation. What a dad pursues in moderation, his children will ignore. And you won't know how you did until you see what your grandchildren do!"

When I first heard a speaker say this, I bristled. It can't be true, not always. But then he used countless examples from Scripture.

Abraham. Sold out. Obedient. Invented the word *faith*. Isaac his son? Definitely a godly man, but there was this thing with going against God's instructions and heading down to Egypt. And then there was that time he passed off his wife as his sister, a sin his father modeled for him years before.

Does the speaker's theory hold up when you check out their children's children?

Isaac's kids, Jacob and Esau were godly. But what about the deception Jacob used to gain the birthright? And Esau's impulsiveness to swap it for a bowl of stew?

The point is that we dads *must* pursue God with *fervor*, not *mediocrity*. Our kids are subconsciously deciding how important their faith will be *to them* by watching how important our faith is *to us*.

Don't take any chances. Go all-in. Make the decision to be a public, sold out, no-holes-barred, praying, tithing, loving, grace-filled follower of Jesus.

You can know, at least from this day forward, that you were fervent in your pursuit of God. Let no one call you moderate ever again.

And maybe your grandchildren will have a chance!

QUESTION

Would your kids describe you as
***fervent* in your love for Jesus?**

REHEARSING THE LAST ACT

When you're twenty, you think you're invincible. Death happens to other people, not to you. If you're under forty, you still don't think you're going to die . . . not really. You *know* it'll happen, but you don't really *believe* it.

But eventually the day comes when you or someone close to you has a health issue. Or an accident. Death is now a possibility. No, it's a reality. You rehearse your death in your mind. You visualize how it will go down, who will be there, what you will say, what others will say. After enough rehearsals and with a strong faith, you put it aside.

There will come a time—the time. *This is the real deal*! The performance to end a lifetime. No do-overs. No take two. And with a real live audience, too. Our family. Friends. Neighbors. Coworkers. We'll be center stage. The main character. The star of the show.

In that moment, we'll find out if we are real, if our faith is real, if we actually live it out in the most pressure-packed moments of life.

If our faith is real—if Christ lives in us—there's no difference between who we are and the character we've played in life. Our "mask" and our face are the same. We *are* the person we wanted others to think we were. Like an onion, we are the same on the inside as the outside, only stronger!

When Jesus reached that moment, He said, "Father, into your hands I commit my spirit!"

That's the way I want to leave the stage of life. Full of faith. Peace. Anticipation. Hope.

QUESTION

**When you rehearse your passing,
do you tighten up or relax?**

CAN YOU DEFEND CHRISTIANITY?

Donald Miller shares this story in *Blue Like Jazz* . . .

> "Defend Christianity," demanded the radio jock.
>
> "I can't," replied Miller.
>
> In disbelief, the host asked again, "What do you mean? You write Christian books and stuff. You can't even defend what you write about?"

Miller went on to explain that today Christianity means too many different things to people. All around, people who wear the brand name, "Christian," often repulse those who aren't believers. Rarely do they compel them.

When I first committed myself to Christ years ago, I was dangerous. I wanted to *save* everybody. I telephoned every adult in my family to confront them about their faith. I amused friends with my insensitive zeal. The net result of all my talking? Zero new Christians.

The *secret sauce* of Christianity is Jesus. Yes, Jesus! Even the name is just plain hard to process. Yet we need to recognize that Jesus has no physical presence on this earth except people like us.

Own the fact that you can communicate the love and acceptance of Jesus to all you meet. You get to be His light in a dark world. You get to be His hands and feet as you go throughout your day.

QUESTION

Will you be Jesus to someone today?

THERE IS NO HEAVIER BURDEN THAN A GREAT OPPORTUNITY

Years ago, someone bought several billboards on the interstate. With no reference to a company or a cause, they simply said,

"There is no heavier burden than a great opportunity."

That struck me.

What is my "heavy burden"? I don't want to miss out on my great opportunity. What could it be? What am I missing?

Most of us drift into our career paths. Only a fraction of us end up in fields we were formally educated for. Most of us go out looking for a job and take the best offer. After we've done that a few times, we end up far from where we thought we would. Chemistry majors sell plumbing supplies. Industrial engineers teach chemistry.

But for Christ followers, there is a hand directing our steps. When we trust that hand—His hand—we can release our anxiety and relax into the role and responsibility we've been given. I love Psalm 16:5-6:

"Lord, you alone are my portion and my cup; you make my lot secure.

The boundary lines have fallen for me in pleasant places; surely I have a delightful inheritance."

It's easy to think back on your path and think you chickened out on some great opportunity, some chance of a lifetime. But we believe in an omnipotent, omniscient God who never makes mistakes. You are where you are for a reason. You didn't miss out; He had other plans for you. And He still does.

SCRIPTURE

"In their hearts humans plan their course, but the Lord establishes their steps." (Proverbs 16:9)

REMOVE THE "D WORD" FROM YOUR MARRIAGE VOCABULARY

"If you *ever* consider divorce you will *always* have to consider divorce," my first mentor told me. He said, "Take it off the table. Remove it as an option. Don't use the word. Don't even acknowledge it as a possibility."

Being a car guy, I came up with this analogy.

What if the car you have *right now* were the *only* car you could ever have? What if there was a law saying you could never swap your car for another one? Ever.

How much time would you spend on the Internet looking at other people's cars? Why would you envy the shiny new models? It would do nothing but frustrate you.

And how would you treat your current, for-the-rest-of-your-life car? Wouldn't you be a little more inclined to make the sacrifice and service it? To give it what it needs? To really take care of it? You might even find yourself being pretty proud of it after a few years. You could have a classic, if you'll just nurture it and give it TLC!

Cars made forty or fifty years ago were pretty homogeneous when they rolled off the assembly line, like brides and grooms on their wedding day.

But years later, precious few of those cars remain intact. Those that are cared for and preserved become more and more unique as the years go by. And their owners feel happier each year they didn't yield to the temptation to "trade 'er in."

CHALLENGE

Forgive. Whatever it is, forgive. Repeatedly, forgive. Forget about the "D word" and make your marriage work!

APRIL 16

PARTICIPATION WITHOUT INVOLVEMENT BREEDS CYNICISM

Here's a principle: Participation without involvement breeds cynicism.

I discovered this in church. We'd been involved in our church for years, but little by little, we'd moved on from *this* ministry and rotated off *that* committee. We found ourselves being cynical about the very things we used to be involved with. When we were involved, when we had a stake in the decision-making, it was all good. As we slid into passive participation, our hearts were lost, and we became cynical. We found a new church.

The principle comes from Matthew 6:21: "For where your treasure is, there your heart will be also." Our treasure is our energy—our caring and concern for our church, business, or organization. When we invest the treasure of our energy, our hearts follow.

Involvement says, "I'm in." "This is partly my deal." "I care about this." "I'm going above and beyond." "I have pride of ownership."

Participation says, "I'll probably be there." "I hope it's good, but if it's not, so what? I don't have a dog in this fight."

Next time you find yourself sour and cynical about something, check your level of involvement. Maybe putting in a little more of your treasure will bring a change in your heart!

QUESTION

What are you participating in that you should either quit or become more involved in?

UNSOLICITED ADVICE

When we volunteer our opinions about someone's "thing," be it their children, work, decisions, art, whatever, we set ourselves up as judge. We convey, "I know what this could or should be, and here's what you should do to fix it."

Relationally, being right or wrong is irrelevant. When your assessment, opinion, or advice is different from what the owner or creator of the "thing" hoped for, they'll feel criticized. That may have been the last thing you intended when you opened your mouth (or sent that email), but that is how it's *received*.

They may not tell you they felt criticized. Most people stuff it and move on. But believe me, it's there, and it's not forgotten. My wife remembers vividly the first thing I ever said to her decades ago. I made a joke about how she set her feet during her cheerleading routines. I was trying to be funny and break the ice with the prettiest girl in the school. She thought I was criticizing. Not *deep* criticism, but criticism all the same.

Being aware is most of the battle. Catch yourself before you start. "Do I *truly* have something valuable to offer here?" "Will the world be a better place if I provide my two cents?" "Will the recipient be grateful or defensive?"

Remember, just as beauty is in the eye of the beholder, criticism is in the eye of the receiver.

And unsolicited advice is almost always received as criticism.

CHALLENGE

Be intentional about improving your relationships today. Maturity is *not* saying everything you think. Will you think but resist the urge to "say"?

PAYING COMPLIMENTS

What makes for the best compliment? When should we speak, and when should we keep our mouths shut? Here are five principles to consider:

1. **Don't tell them directly**—The highest compliment you'll ever receive is one not intended for your ears. If you've observed something special about someone, tell their husband, wife, or best friend. It means much more coming from a third party whose only agenda is to build them up.

2. **Compliment character**—Bragging about someone's performance, looks, or even their skill will encourage them at a surface level. But if the behavior that's impressed you emanates from a character quality you can identify, the impact is at least doubled.

3. **Be intentional when you pay a compliment**—Think about what you're going to say and why you're going to say it. *Am I trying to be liked? Or am I about encouraging (giving courage to) someone?* Compliments are, in a sense, rewards. And what is rewarded is repeated. Think about what you want repeated before you pay compliments.

4. **Don't dilute the value of your compliments**—Paying too many compliments devalues each one. When someone is constantly gushing praise, it's hard to take them seriously. In fact, you might even question the very thing they're complimenting you about.

5. **Connect your compliment to something they did**—When you can validate your compliment with an action the person took, it's more meaningful. Praising someone for being generous means more when it's tied to a recent and observable act of generosity.

Paying good compliments takes intentionality, focus, and time. But meaningful compliments are rare gifts people remember all their lives.

QUESTION

How are you at dishing out praise?

RECEIVING COMPLIMENTS

I once played acoustic guitar for a future Miss America contestant who sang in our high school assembly. No one knew I could play, so when the assembly was over, several people came up and complimented me, including Tommy Caldwell, the bass player for what later became the Marshall Tucker Band.

"Hey, man, that was great. I didn't even know you could pick," he said.

"Oh, I'm not any good. That's really the only song I know."

Tommy grabbed me. He squared up my shoulders, looked straight into my eyes, and said, "Listen. There are tons of people who will criticize you and cut you to pieces. But when someone pays you a compliment, say thank you and shut up!"

Why is it so hard for us to take compliments? Should we accept them? Aren't we humble sinners, saved by grace through no works of our own? Isn't it prideful to revel in the praise of men?

Receiving praise is hard because we're stuck in this tension between the flesh and the Spirit, between the visible and the invisible. On one hand, *you* did the work, *you* made the presentation, *you* swung the bat, *you* performed the song. But on the other hand, *God* gave you the health, the energy, the intelligence, the talent, and the opportunity.

The best option is what Tommy said: Smile and say thank you. The words honor the Giver. The smile is for you.

QUESTION

**When someone compliments you,
will you smile and say thank you?**

HOW MUCH IS ENOUGH?

"How much is enough?" is a difficult question everyone must answer.

For two or three generations, parents pounded the success mantra into their kids (that would be us baby boomers). "Go to school so you can get a good job and be successful." "Marry well, have kids, buy a house, take great vacations, and you've got success"

That was the plan.

But look at what happened. We got the jobs, the houses, the families, and the trips, but we're still striving for more. We're never content. We mindlessly press on for bigger titles, higher salaries, larger houses, and more of everything.

So how much is enough?

Somebody told me to look at it backwards.

Start with the end in mind. Think about what it will take for your kids' college and weddings, for retirement and other expenses. You'll probably come up with numbers that seem impossible, but at least you'll have a picture of what *enough* looks like.

Knowing how much is enough can change how you live. It may lead you to save more, spend less, and think longer term. It can create a surprising shift in your thinking. When you know how much is enough, you might decide to stop chasing the god of more. And it can remind you how much you need God.

At the very least, you'll know what to pray for!

For enough.

SCRIPTURE

"And my God will meet all your needs according to the riches of his glory in Christ Jesus." (Philippians 4:19)

WHERE DOES YOUR SIGNIFICANCE COME FROM?

I spent the first twelve years of my career trying to please *them*. *They* thought I should get an MBA. *They* wanted me to take a new job and move.

They were a combination of my dad, my peers, and my wife. Getting ahead, making a lot of money, having a nice house and nice cars showed *them* I measured up—that I had what it takes. I wanted affirmation so badly, and I could get it by having more and achieving more. And more.

When I was thirty-three, my life blew up. Career blew up. Marriage blew up. I found myself totally alone with God. In the first real conversation I ever had with Him, He let me know I was significant *to Him*. He let me know He loved me with or without success.

For the first time in my life, I *knew* I was significant. And it wasn't because of anything I did. It was because He offered to adopt me into His family, and I finally accepted. In an instant, we connected.

Isn't it amazing that God would reach into a world with billions of people and choose *me* to be an adopted son? Could anything top that?

Try to be significant by being successful, smart, famous, rich, strong, popular, or handsome, and there's always someone *more* successful, *more* famous, *more* rich, *more* popular, *more* handsome. If your significance is defined in comparison with others, you'll always wonder if you're *really* there.

But when God defines you as significant, *you're significant!*

Accept it. Embrace it. Relax in it. Appreciate it.

SCRIPTURE

"God decided in advance to adopt us into his own family by bringing us to himself through Jesus Christ. This is what he wanted to do, and it gave him great pleasure." (Ephesians 1:5, NLT)

THE MORE YOU HAVE, THE LESS YOU CARE

Comedian Jeff Foxworthy volunteers at a homeless shelter in Atlanta. One year, he gave each of the men $50. Then he placed a bucket on the floor and offered the guys a chance to donate to people who were in even deeper need. By the time it was over, the bucket had more money in it than he'd given the men in the first place.

Conversely, as those who accumulate wealth get more, they tend to give a smaller and smaller percentage to help others. There's a principle at work here:

> The more you have, the less you care.

Meet my need, and I'll be grateful. I might even share what I get with others in need. Give me more than I need, and I'll be less grateful and less sensitive to the needs of others. I think it's human nature, but it's not what Jesus taught.

Look at the story of the rich young ruler. He had it all, and he knew it, which is why he came to Jesus asking about perfection.

How did Jesus respond?

> "If you want to be perfect, go, sell your possessions and give to the poor, and you will have treasure in heaven. Then come, follow me." (Matthew 19:21)

Jesus reminded the guy that there are two kinds of treasure—the kind on his net-worth statement and the kind that matters long-term: "treasure in heaven."

Jesus held up a mirror and helped him see his lack of compassion. But then as always, Jesus offered him compassion. He said, "Then come, follow me," offering the guy the opportunity to be His disciple once he got his priorities straight. Jesus didn't slam the door shut; He opened it wide.

QUESTION

Is Jesus holding up a mirror? Have you gotten so much you've lost your compassion?

DILUTION IS THE SOLUTION TO POLLUTION

When 172 million gallons of oil spilled into the Gulf of Mexico a few years ago, one environmental expert said, "Dilution is the solution to pollution."

The reverse is true too, and it can help us understand yesterday's principle: "The more you have, the less you care."

When people struggle to stay alive, not much else matters. They're focused, resourceful, and, yes, generous. People have great empathy for others facing the same circumstances, and they'll do just about anything to help. But as we climb out of poverty and move beyond survival, we start to think more about ourselves. And that's the beginning of selfishness.

Here's a sobering thought:

> All the resources needed to feed, cloth, shelter, and heal the world's population are in the world *right now*.

We may believe that on a macro level, but what can we do about it?

We can do something on a micro level. We can pick a child, pick a ministry, pick a country. We can connect, consider, and then commit. We can do for a few what we wish we could do for a bunch. Don't just write a check and move on; get connected and stay committed for the long-term.

Our problem isn't a lack of resources; it's a lack of willingness to sacrificially use our resources for others. When we become so accustomed to having an abundance, we become numb to opportunities to serve.

QUESTION

**Will you do for one what you wish
you could do for everyone?**

THE THING VS. THE IDEA OF THE THING

For years, I kept my eye out for a '66 yellow GTO like the one I had as a kid. One day, I saw it. It jumped out of my browser and grabbed me.

The idea of my old GTO, with its black vinyl top, 8-track player, mag wheels, and loud mufflers, was all there in my mind. All I had to do was bid on it.

The delivery guy rolled the car off the truck and the fun began. I turned the key, and it started . . . but the engine sounded like it had whooping cough. The 8-track player? It sounded like an AM radio station just before you go out of range. I wanted to throw up.

We get an idea in our mind, and we visualize "the thing" in its best possible light. The problems get ignored or suppressed because we don't want to be talked out of our dream. Then, when we get the thing, the stuff we ignored hits us in the face.

The *idea of the thing* is usually connected to our expectations—the *thing* to reality. Resentment ultimately comes from the difference in the two. Instead of thoughtfully and prayerfully considering *the thing itself*, we buy into the *idea of the thing* and set ourselves up to resent the very thing we wanted so badly.

CHALLENGE

Think hard about what you're about to buy, who you're about to befriend, or what you're signing up to do. Are you considering the thing? Or the *idea* of the thing?

APRIL 25

THE THREE QUESTIONS ALWAYS ASKED IN RELATIONSHIPS

Years ago, someone gave me a recording of Lou Holtz giving a motivational speech to a bunch of salespeople. What he said has never left me.

He said, "People always ask three questions before they buy from you. They want to know . . .

1. Can I trust him?
2. Does he know what he's talking about?
3. Does he care about me?"

When I heard this, I thought, *Heck, those are the questions I ask about my boss . . . and my next-door neighbor.* As I've mulled them over, I think they're the questions behind all our relationships.

Can I trust him? That's about *character*.

Does he know what he's talking about? That's about *competence*.

Does he care about me? That's about *compassion*.

As a dad, I can't think of better overarching goals for raising kids. We want our kids to be of good character, to grow up to be men and women with strong character and high integrity.

We want them to learn and be good at what they do, so we encourage them toward things they love. Eventually, they find something that fits them, and they take off.

And compassion, caring for others may be the hardest. Our world seems to reward those who think inwardly, but as Jesus followers, we are called to live a life of compassion for others.

QUESTION

**How would people answer these
three questions about you?**

THE LESSER OF TWO EVILS IS STILL EVIL

We talked a while back about how all decisions come down to the choice between the greater of two goods or the lesser of two evils. But here's another dimension: The lesser of two evils is still evil.

"I smoke, but at least I'm not gaining weight."

"Online porn is better than having an affair."

"I'm not doing anything to help anyone, but at least I'm not doing anything to hurt."

Christians, churches, the media, men—we've lost our willingness to call evil, evil. We dilute evil to a less onerous thing by pretending it isn't there. We lose the contrast between what's good and what's not. That makes us less aware of what's distinctively good and less grateful for the forgiveness we've been given through God's grace.

We don't struggle as much with the big ones. Culture still thinks murder is evil. Bearing false witness is wrong, especially if it's Bernie Madoff or a big-time CEO. It's a little less evil when it's writing a five on the scorecard when the three-putt really made it a six.

The further the sin is from the Ten Commandments, the less we seem to recognize it. Catholics talk about the seven deadly sins: wrath, greed, sloth, pride, lust, envy, and gluttony. Those are personal. I've never even thought about killing anyone, but I've done all seven of these multiple times, some daily.

QUESTION

Will you step up to be the leader God made you to be? We don't have to preach against evil, let's just live without it. Let's bring it into the light of truth, call it what it is, and protect our families from it.

LOVE PEOPLE, USE THINGS

We all have memories we wish we didn't. For me, there's the fuzzy memory of a face sitting at a desk in the back of my office at AT&T. I don't even remember her name. She was an older lady, and she was awful at her job.

I let her go.

It didn't matter that she was a few months from retirement or that she'd worked there virtually all her life. She didn't measure up. I was a thirty-year-old MBA who wanted to make his numbers and get promoted again. I had the wisdom of a goat. Before Jesus, I was all about achievement. People were just things I used to get what I *really* loved: success!

If you've walked with God any time at all, you've learned that He's all about people. People are His highest and best creation.

People and God's Word are the only two things that pass from this world to the next—that's how important people are to God.

After surrendering my life to Christ, I learned a whole different approach to firing people. I made it my job to help them find another job, one that fit them better and they could succeed at. If we couldn't find that job within the organization, we'd look outside. We weren't through until that person was in another job somewhere.

People feel good about themselves when they do the right thing. I felt a lot better about the people we "outplaced" than those we just let go. Yes, it takes more time. And yes, it's a lot of extra work and trouble. But at the end of the day, I did it because people matter.

QUESTION

**Do you love things and use people?
Or use things and love people?**

MAKE DECISIONS, NOT RULES

We all hate stupid rules.

Here's an example. A sign at the beach says, *"No dogs on the beach."*

Since the keepers of the beach can't be there to make an individual decision about every guy with a dog, they create a rule that *makes the decision for them*, and me, and everyone else. The problem is, it's a one-size-fits-all decision that takes individuals out of it.

A rule is a decision made in advance. It's made for each of us without knowledge of who we are and what we're about. And most rules are made necessary by the small number of people who don't take personal responsibility and screw everything up for the rest of us.

This rant about rules is really for rule-makers—for leaders who have authority and can make rules for others. Ask yourself this question before you make a new rule:

Am I making this rule so I won't have to make decisions?

Leaders are willing to make hard decisions. It's easier to make blanket rules so we can avoid making decisions with individual people. Life gets messy when we get involved personally. But if we're to lead as God intends, we have to face the mess and do our best.

Think hard before you make rules. For your kids, your household, your staff, or your clients. God gave us rules, but not very many of them. Most of the time, He wants us to honor Him, love people, consider the circumstances, and make a decision.

QUESTION

**Do you find it easier to make rules
than to make decisions?**

"I DON'T THINK I CAN TRUST YOU"

What do you do when someone says, "I don't think I can trust you"? When somebody lets you know your word isn't good because you said you were going to do something and didn't do it? Or you did something so out of character they couldn't square it up with who they *thought* you were?

Too often you won't hear it in so many words; you'll just feel it. Your kid won't look you in the eye. Your wife starts having whispery phone conversations with her back to you. A good friend just fades to black. The customer won't buy from you again. You wake up one day and realize people are missing, and you don't know why.

But when someone cares enough about you to call you out, it's perplexing. It's like being told to go stand in the corner of a round room. What do you do? You can't put the toothpaste back in the tube. You can't undo what you did or unsay what you said.

You can go into sales mode and plead, "Trust me!" But that doesn't work.

You can go into apology mode and tell them how sorry you are . . . how you didn't mean to do it and it'll never happen again. That may salve the wound, but it won't restore trust.

The truth is, you can't *talk* your way out of what you *behaved* your way into. You have to *behave* your way out of what you behaved your way into.

If you've breached a trust, make up your mind to say what you're going to do and then do it. After enough repetitions, you may be trusted again.

If there's another way to rebuild trust, I've never heard of it.

QUESTION

Is there someone important in your life who doesn't trust you? What are you going to do about it?

APRIL 30

SELECTIVE NEGLECT . . . WHAT NOT TO DO

There's the story of a young violinist, the youngest to ever play at Carnegie Hall. She rocked it, got a standing ovation, and was led giddy from the stage to the pressroom.

"How did you get so good on the violin at such a young age?" the reporter asked.

"Selective neglect," said the little girl. "I neglected everything else, everything but the violin."

Almost anyone who's good at something gets there through selective neglect. They *worship* (assign worth to) the thing they do and neglect everything else. This violin virtuoso neglected friends, sports, and free time. Grownups neglect spouses, friends, family, hobbies, exercise, sleep, kids, just to name a few.

The irony is that what's selectively neglected is often more valuable than what's worshiped. It doesn't matter how good you are; there'll always be someone better. Jesus said this:

> "What good will it be for someone to gain the whole world, yet forfeit their soul? Or what can anyone give in exchange for their soul?" (Matthew 16:26)

Our soul is our personality—our unique life on this earth. If your life were a dollar, what are you spending it on? Is it worth it? In the end, it's all about intentionality. We can't do it all. Either intentionally or by default, we're going to cheat somewhere. Cheat someone. The question is, who will it be?

There's wisdom in having a "not-to-do" list. Make one and be intentional in your selective neglect. In the end, when the things that don't matter get burned away, you'll have more eternal treasure to lay at the Master's feet. And you'll have a healthy, well-nourished soul along the way.

QUESTION

Are you selectively neglecting the right things?

MAY 1

"DON'T FIX ME, FEEL ME"

Bob Goff's book, *Love Does*, inspires me like few books have.

His book drives home a principle I've bantered around for years: *The only love that's real is love that's demonstrated.* You've gotta *do something* or love is just an idea. Just words.

I think there's another level to love. It's sort of "pre-love." It's empathy. It's feeling what another person feels. Right now. In the moment.

Feeling someone is more than acceptance. More than tolerance. It's choosing to care about them as a person and really listen to what they're saying *and* what they're feeling.

Feeling people is rare. We're in such a hurry. We text rather than talk. There is so much to do, so little time.

And it takes selflessness, at least for a few minutes. You can't be thinking about yourself and *feeling* someone else at the same time. You have to put yourself and your agenda on the side table and focus on the person you're with. Exclusively.

God doesn't need me to fix anybody. He wants me to *feel* them, one at a time.

CHALLENGE

For the next seven days, in every conversation you're in, *feel* the other person. Be fully present. Watch their eyes. Listen to their heart as well as their words. Don't be thinking about what you're going to say next. Don't think about how you can help them with their problem. Don't think about how to *fix* them. Just *feel* them.

MAY 2

LET YOUR "YES" BE YES; YOUR "NO," NO

Remember when Jesus was handed a Roman coin and asked if the Jews were to pay the onerous taxes imposed by their occupiers? Jesus said, "'Give back to Caesar what is Caesar's and to God what is God's.' And they were amazed at him" (Mark 12:17).

Why were they amazed? They probably wanted Him to start a revolution. But He didn't. He validated the fact that we're *all* under authority, then and now.

Don't you love the clarity of a "yes" or a "no"? When you're under authority and your authority says "yes," you've got a green light and you're off to the races. If it's "no," then it's no. There's peace in "no." There's certainty. Closure.

I wish I'd known Matthew 5:37 the first thirty-three years of my life. Here's how it goes:

> "All you need to say is simply 'Yes' or 'No'; anything beyond this comes from the evil one."

When you ask someone to help and you get a, "Yes, I'd be glad to," it's like a cool breeze on a hot day. Get a, "No, I can't do that," and it knocks you off balance for a second, but you recover quickly.

It's the gray area that causes problems.

". . . anything beyond this comes from the evil one." Amazing but true. Think about it. It's in the gray area that evil gets a foothold. It's living as close to sin as we can without sinning.

Seek clarity and give clarity everywhere you lead. Get to a "yes" or "no" and let people under your authority know what you decided. They'll thrive under the clarity of a decisive leader.

QUESTION

What's your instinctive reaction to authority?
As a Christ follower, what should it be?

THE OPPOSITE OF LONELINESS

There's an epidemic in our culture—loneliness. Especially among men. Busy schedules, work demands, and our tendency to be weak in relationship skills are a recipe for loneliness. What's the solution?

Richard Bach once said,

> "The opposite of loneliness isn't togetherness . . . it's intimacy."

Intimacy isn't easy to get. You can't buy it; you don't automatically get it by taking your wife away for a weekend or by playing golf with your buddy every Saturday. In marriage, you can turn on the charm, focus on your wife, listen to her, give nonsexual touches, and make her feel very, very loved—and still feel alone.

That's because intimacy is two-way. It happens when you love and when *you're loved*, when you listen and when *you're listened to*.

The biggest roadblock to intimacy is inadequate self-disclosure. We struggle with being open with our spouse and closest friends. We're so afraid of what they'll think of us.

It's easiest to be intimate with God. He's safe. He loves us unconditionally, He's forgiven us in advance for our screwups, and He'll listen to us and never laugh, roll His eyes, or remind of us of the last time we brought this up. We know He loves us.

But we need spouses and friends we can be intimate with, too. As usual, we see how God wants us to relate to each other in the way He relates to us.

So, what should we do? Be the kind of intimate friend God is to you. Tell those closest to you what you need.

And soon any loneliness you feel will be cured by true, godly intimacy.

QUESTION

**What keeps you from moving your marriage
and friendships from casual to intimate?**

NOURISH YOUR SOUL

Ever eat a good meal and feel nourished? Some lean chicken, steamed carrots and broccoli, a fresh salad with a little bit of dressing, and a piece of freshly baked homemade whole wheat bread. It's not the most filling or the fanciest, but it's what you're supposed to eat. It's what your body needs.

How do you find that kind of nourishment for your *soul*?

I'm talking about the person you are without the body. The person God knew (and loved) before He put skin on you. The person who will survive death and live forever somewhere.

There are two ways I know of to nourish your soul.

1. **Worship**—I can't explain it, but worship refreshes us. And singing is a huge part of worship. I'm drawn to songs sung *to* God rather than *about* God. I'm even less drawn to songs we sing telling each other how great God is. Why not tell Him?

2. **Serve**—When I forget about my to-do list and help someone, something changes inside me. Maybe it's because we feel good about ourselves when we do the right thing. Maybe it's because we're emulating Jesus.

   Maybe it's because we're doing what He told us to: "Consider others more important than yourself." I can't explain why, but it happens. When I serve someone—when I put their needs first—my soul gets nourished.

When you feel burned out and your soul feels tired, give it nourishment.

QUESTION

**Does your soul need nourishment? Will
you try worshiping or serving today?**

MAY 5

REDUCING STRESS

Dictionary.com defines stress as "mental, emotional, or physical strain or tension."

I get the strain and tension thing—the gap between what is and what could or should be. And no doubt, stress goes up when the stakes are high, when the outcome really matters. Unchecked stress can take a physical toll in addition to robbing our joy. Hypertension, insomnia, jaw and tooth pain, hair loss, intestinal problems, and even twitching can be stress related.

In every corner of my world, I see stress. Businesses and ministries stressed with growth or liquidation problems. Prodigal children. Marriage problems. Health issues. Guys who need to get help but won't.

But here's one thing I figured out. Time (specifically the lack of it) is a huge part of the stress equation, and often we can do something about it.

We stress because of deadlines imposed by others and ourselves. Some of us are addicted to progress. If you're a GTD (get things done) person who makes lists, sets goals, and self-imposes deadlines, you're doing it to yourself. Having deadlines put there by others is bad enough, but then we make matters worse by adding our own. Time does to stress what pressure does to cooking: accelerates and intensifies. Think about the stress in your life. If there were fewer deadlines, if there was more time, would your stress level go down?

CHALLENGE

Write down three things you're stressed about today. Now ask, "What would happen if I had a later deadline and more time?" If the deadline has been imposed by someone else, consider asking for an extension. If it's self-imposed, cut yourself some slack.

HUSTLE

If I didn't love hustle, I wouldn't love mentoring younger guys so much. In this staid and stoic stage of life, hustle is fun to see and be around.

Jon Acuff, a smart guy who has amassed a huge tribe in the digital world, defines hustle as, "doing important things others aren't willing to do."

Simple but profound.

Let's start with *doing*. That's different from analyzing, strategizing, collaborating, planning, and all that stuff. Doing means acting. My friend John said to me, "Action reveals options that analysis never will."

Next is *important things*. I didn't say *all things*. I didn't say *urgent things*. When is the last time you sat down and listed the ten most *important* things you could do to grow your business? Strengthen your marriage? Improve your health? Deepen your relationship with God?

Finally, *others aren't willing to do*. When my son Ross finished his medical training and decided to start his own practice, he got up early each day and delivered boxes of donuts to the offices of doctors who could refer patients to him. It was important for those potential referrers to know him. It took effort *and* humility on his part.

Doing something "below your station" that others might not be willing to do is hustle. Hustle has a lot of connection with the idea of working *heartily*, as in Colossians 3:23 (NASB):

> "Whatever you do, do your work heartily, as for the Lord rather than for men."

QUESTION

**Hustle is a lot about saying "yes." Are
you willing to say "yes" to a little hustle?**

GOOD CARE

"Take good care of your mother . . . and remember to be kind"
—Jackson Browne, *The Pretender*

Mother's Day is coming! (Hopefully) you'll make a phone call, send a card or flowers, buy lunch, or go for a visit. But that's one day. What about today? Next week? Every week? Once you're grown and gone, it's not usually your responsibility to take care of your mother.

But you have the *opportunity* to take *good care* of her. What's the difference? Taking care means responding to her needs, but taking good care requires intentionality. Good care means studying your mom. Understanding her. Loving her the way she wants to be loved.

I think mothers of adult children are some of the most misunderstood people on the planet. Mothers are certainly not all alike, but they want to know you're OK, they want to be valued, and they want to belong.

And here's something else: They want you to initiate the conversation, self-disclose (so they don't come across as nagging), and express appreciation.

I can hear the moans! "Yeah Regi, but you don't know *my mom!*" You're right, I don't. But try what I'm suggesting. Give it three months. Put it on your calendar so you won't forget. Only you can do this.

People feel good about themselves when they do the right thing. Initiating loving contact with your mom on a regular basis is the right thing to do to "take good care of your mother and . . . be kind."

SCRIPTURE

"Honor your father and your mother, as the Lord your God has commanded you, so that you may live long and that it may go well with you in the land the Lord your God is giving you." (Deuteronomy 5:16)

ENOUGH?

Appetites urge us to *more*. More sweets. More carbs. More money. More fun. More friends. More followers. More sales. More clothes. More square feet. More vacation. More family time. More everything. We act like more is always better. But it's not.

There's something special about enough. Put your K-cup in the Keurig, put your mug in place, push the button, and watch. It's perfect when just the right amount of jittery joe fills your cup. Too little and you feel cheated. Too much and it's wasted and messy. Just enough, that's the ticket.

The starting point is to define how much is enough for you and yours. We can always get by with less, but aside from that, what is *enough* for the key areas in life?

Money—How much money do you need to support your church, provide for your family, and live comfortably?

Family—How much time will you invest in your wife and kids?

Friends—Guys tend to have buddies but not friends. Start with one, just one. Who is (or might become) the one friend who knows and loves you?

Health—Do you have a plan for healthy eating and adequate exercise?

Time—Do you steward your time well? Or do you spend it recklessly, wondering why you can't seem to fit in a quiet time, family time, or anything else?

The antidote to *more* is *enough*. "Having it all" means having *enough* of all the *best stuff*. If you never define *enough*, you'll screw up your life mindlessly chasing *more*. You might end up exhausted, empty, and without.

CHALLENGE

**Define *enough* and you'll discover
contentment and peace like never before.**

POURING IN. POURING OUT.

Look around your community, and you'll find Jesus followers. The Bible calls these people *disciples*. They are learners and followers of Jesus.

Learners listen. They take notes. Some of them read. They get information about Jesus and what Christians should do. They show up in church and watch preachers on TV. Some might think they're the *backbone* of the organized church. I'm not so sure.

Followers are different. They learn, but then they actually try to live out what they've learned. To live like Jesus told them to. They try to model Jesus in their lives. Their faith isn't *out there*; it's *in here*. They initiate. They put principals into practice. They live examined lives and learn from their mistakes.

The church needs more learners to become followers.

Learners find it easy to become reservoirs and survive on the living water of Jesus. Followers are rivers that splash the love of Jesus over other people's faces.

For years, preachers have been pouring into learners. Authors, teachers, conference speakers, Bible study and small group leaders—all pouring in.

But when does one start to *pour out*?

Become a Jesus *follower* and you can't help but start pouring out.

"... for the mouth speaks what the heart is full of." (Luke 6:45)

CHALLENGE

Move from reservoir to river. From learner to follower. From selfish soaker to meaningful mentor. It all starts with a "yes" to making yourself available to people who are less mature in their lives and their faith—and a "no" to sitting with your remote control.

RELIGION AS A CATEGORY

When I venture outside my holy huddle of Christian friends, my words about Jesus are often synthesized into the category of religion.

Intellectuals have long put religion in a category. History, anthropology, archeology, comparative religion—all of these study how people process and document the human experience.

But putting Jesus in a category and leaving Him there is a huge mistake, the missed opportunity of a lifetime.

"She's started going to a new church, and she's really changed. It seems to be good for her, but I sure hope she doesn't get too far into religion." These are the words of a spectator, not a participant.

Religion was a category for me for thirty-three years. In reality, the category was irrelevant to my everyday life. Maybe I had an occasional twinge of guilt. A funny feeling arguing against stuff in the Bible. But for me, religion was noninvasive. I did whatever I wanted to and only used religion to project an image when I thought it would help me.

Then God hit me with reality like a ton of bricks: This category was manmade. My relationship with God should fill my entire life, not just a small box. Jesus impacts everything about us: work, family, time, language, you name it. Everything about us changes.

Do you relegate faith to a category? Is it something you do in private that doesn't impact much beyond Sunday, Christmas, or Easter?

Get to know Jesus. Discover His all-encompassing, life-changing message. Realize that a relationship with Him forever alters every facet of our lives, not just a few things in a category.

SCRIPTURE

**"Seek the Kingdom of God above all else,
and live righteously, and he will give you
everything you need." (Matthew 6:33, NLT)**

MAY 11

"THE GIFT OF THE LOVER"

If Twitter had been around in 1400 AD, Thomas à Kempis would have been a superstar. Here's what he might have tweeted today:

> "A wise lover regards not so much the gift of him who loves as the love of him who gives."

Thomas was (obviously) talking about God. Most of us first come to Him looking for a gift. We want His gift of forgiveness. We want His gift of healing from an accident or an illness or His gift of healing in a relationship with a wife, or a kid, or a boss.

As we get to know Jesus, we come to appreciate His love somewhat separate from His gifts. We trust His love even when the gifts aren't exactly what we asked for. We've matured when we can thank Him for these, too.

This principle carries over to our spouses. My friend John sees every stack of clean laundry as a gift from Martha. He knows there's love behind it.

I'll bet if you think for a minute, you can come up with a few things you and your wife do for each other that are outgrowths of your love but aren't commonly thought of as gifts. Most of us are moving so quickly we miss the love behind these gifts. And in the process, we miss the one who loved us.

CHALLENGE

Today, spend some time thinking about the *lover* behind the gift. Reflect on things she does that you take for granted. Thank God for her, and then find just the right time to thank her *specifically* for things she does for you and your family that are often overlooked.

HOPE IS NOT A STRATEGY

A lot of us dance on the edge of optimism and carelessness. "I'll figure something out," has come out of my mouth more times than I want to admit. Sometimes it's the only workable plan, but it's also a way to kick the can down the road and deal with stuff later.

"Hope is not a strategy," pops into my head when I see someone in a bad situation that is getting worse, yet they seem to have no clue. There's no initiative and no sense of urgency. They are whistling while Rome burns.

I'm not knocking hope. Lose hope and you've truly lost your way; eventually you may lose your life. Depression can spring from a lack of hope.

The word *hope* is used 133 times in the Bible. Of all the gifts God gives human beings, hope may be the best—hope for this life and for another one through Jesus Christ.

But in the context of living and leading day-by-day, hope is not enough. We need to get out of a hopeful mind-set and focus on action, on moving forward with what God tells us to do.

So, here's the question: *What do you hope for but refuse to face up to?*

God gives us brains, an amount of physical strength, and a degree of mental capacity. Then He embellishes what we've been given through His gifts of the Spirit, including patience and self-control. He reminds us that we "can do all things through Christ who strengthens us."

Act on those things you hope for. Decide on a step you can take today to move forward. You don't need a complete strategy or a sophisticated solution. Just do something. Now.

CHALLENGE

Stop hiding behind, "I'll figure something out."
Take a step that turns your hopes into reality.

A PROBLEM WITHOUT A SOLUTION IS A FACT

Former Israeli Prime Minister Shimon Peres once said:

> "If a problem has no solution, it may not be a problem, but a fact, not
> to be solved, but to be coped with over time."

I'm stunned by the clarity. Sort out problems from facts. If they're facts, deal with them. Digest. Absorb. Move forward from facts, both old and new.

Sure, we sometimes jump to conclusions, assuming *facts* to be true that aren't. But it may be more exhausting, frustrating, distracting, and wasteful trying to solve the unsolvable. A few examples . . .

- Something about your wife isn't exactly like you want it to be. Instead of accepting these things as facts, you ruin your marriage trying to solve these problems.

- There's a wound down deep inside of you, something that happened to you or something you did way back when. Forgive the one who did it, even if that someone is you. We can forgive anyone for anything because our Savior forgave us for everything.

- Something your father said you've never been able to put away. Some of our dads said mean, thoughtless, life-altering things to us growing up. That's a fact. You and I don't have to live up to them or live them down.

PRAYER

Holy Spirit, please help me see facts and
give me the courage to cope with them. I need
discernment so I don't waste my precious days
trying to solve problems that aren't problems.
Thank You for being my faithful guide to the
peace of Christ. Amen.

YOU DO WHAT YOU ARE

You are what you do, right? Think of how we label people: "I'm an investor." "I'm a doctor." "Lawyer." "Salesman." "Preacher." "Entrepreneur." "Mr. Mom." Most of the time we stop right there, calling on stereotypes to inform people of who they're talking to.

My brother was a soldier. He was, is, and will always be a soldier. His seven-year-old granddaughter asked him if his Army t-shirt ever gets dirty. (She's never seen him wearing anything else). He took her to his closet and showed her ten clean ones just like the one he had on. It's his identity.

The identity label is empty when you're younger, when you haven't done anything yet. "High schooler." "Teenager." "Kid." "College student." None of these tell anything about who we're talking to. More importantly, these labels don't tell their wearers anything about themselves. We want an *individual* identity, not a demographic category.

Maybe the answer comes from figuring out *who we are*. Grasping who God has already made us to be informs us about what He's calling us to do. Maybe our destiny begins with our design.

In other words, we should live with the labels God has given us . . .

Adopted
Forgiven
Child of God

Let's lose the labels of who we were before Christ. You're no longer a sinner, a liar, or a cheat. You are forgiven, redeemed, adopted, loved, and accepted.

PRAYER

**Father, help me to see myself as You see me.
Clear up the lies I've believed about myself.
Give me the courage and confidence to label
myself from my status in Your eyes and not
from my past. In Jesus' beautiful name, amen.**

THINK WITH YOUR HEAD

There's an old Native American saying, "Think with your head, not with your heart." I believe it to be true.

Almost nothing I've ever done out of raw, unfiltered emotion turned out well. The concept of "follow your heart" is crap. Following your heart lands you in the ditch. Listening to your heart, being aware of your emotions, taking your own feelings into account as data points, yes. But falling into "Yeah, but I don't care. I'm going to tell her what she's doing," or "I'm tired of this. I'm going to let him know how I feel," rarely works out well.

Responding is better than reacting. If you're in the hospital and you hear the nurses say, "He's having a *reaction* to the medication," that's not good. But if you hear, "He's *responding* to the medication," you probably feel better. Reacting is usually from the heart. Responding involves the head and the heart.

When you respond, you bring both your head *and* your heart to the game. Your head brings perspective. It takes everything into account, at least everything it can pull up in a split second. Adding your *head* to the *heart* brings strategy to your energy. And it brings a better outcome.

Take a moment and listen to the Word of God. Slow down and let Him work truth into your heart and your head.

SCRIPTURES

"Do you see someone who speaks in haste? There is more hope for a fool than for them." (Proverbs 29:20)

"Those who guard their mouths and their tongues keep themselves from calamity." (Proverbs 21:23)

"A person finds joy in giving an apt reply—and how good is a timely word!" (Proverbs 15:23)

THE SCRIPTWRITER

OK, I'm going to be really, really honest with you. What I'm going to say, I'd like to keep this between us, alright? I'm trusting you here . . .

I've had my doubts about prayer.

When I first hit my health issues, I didn't know whether to ask people to pray for my healing or not. On one hand, I read that, "Prayer doesn't change anything but *me*." On the other hand, I read Jesus' parable about the persistent widow, knocking and knocking and knocking until finally the master comes and gives her what she's asking for.

But then I read a C.S. Lewis devotional that blew my mind and answered this question for me. Consider this:

God is timeless. His timelessness is what we least understand about Him. It's what's most different between God and people.

God is the scriptwriter of all history. Before He formed me, He knew me. He knows how everything turns out because He writes the script!

When we pray, God hears our prayers and takes our prayers into account as He writes the script. So even though the script was written eons ago, every single prayer we utter enters into the mind and heart of the Scriptwriter.

As I pray, I know I'm speaking to the Scriptwriter. He listens to my prayers and takes them into consideration as He develops the characters, plots, and outcomes. No prayer is ever wasted. I should pray about everything that matters. He loves me, so if it matters to me, it matters to Him. After I pray, I have to trust His judgment.

QUESTION

**Aren't you glad you know the Scriptwriter?
Will you talk to Him today?**

MAY 17

WAITING FOR GOD

My wife and I had to make a big decision a while back. We've sensed God's direction and have been moving with Him, even though it seems risky, somewhat irrational, even painful, because it'll bring death to some things we're comfortable with.

Then one Sunday, we listened to a great sermon about obedience. "Life is only made possible when something dies," the preacher said. "Life always comes from obedience. The pain of obedience always leads to the promise of obedience."

That's a lot of pressure on obedience. That means we'd better hear Him right. Better know it's *His* voice we're hearing.

The next morning I prayed, "Lord, I need more than your permission. I need your instruction. I need a command. I need an order to obey!"

Here's what I wrote in my journal . . .

> *"Regi, I'm not going to take all the mystery out of this. Look at how your feelings have changed as you've talked with Me about this decision. Look at how Miriam's feelings have changed. Look at how your feelings have changed about other alternatives. Look at the peace you have. You have to trust Me."*

Often the mystery includes fear, which paralyzes, so we say things like, "I'm just waiting for God to give me direction," or, "I don't want to get ahead of God."

And yes, sometimes we *do* need to wait. But more often we simply need to take a step. We need to move forward, even if it's just a little bit. We may not know the whole path, and that's fine. But we should act on what we know He's called us to do.

QUESTION

Is there something He's called you to do?
Are you waiting, wasting, or walking?

MAY 18

GOD'S BEST

Growing up in the South, I was taken to a small church in the textile mill village near where we lived. There was lots of love, lots of food when people died, and lots of bad theology.

"You need to do what the Bible says, Regi. You want God's best for your life, not His second best."

God's second best? That seems like an oxymoron. Can you imagine our perfect God with a "runner-up will"?

I think God's second best is the natural order of things. It's life when you leave Him out. It's what you get when you go your own way. It's the way of life for people who don't know Jesus. It's the path to problems for those who do.

Our fulfillment in life, our joy, our peace is connected to how much of God we include in our lives. His best gets better the more we let Him in.

Is Jesus my best friend? Do I worship Him? Seek and obey His unique guidance every day? Do I love my wife as Christ loved the church? Do I love my kids and not exasperate them? Have I surrendered to His call to a unique role in His Kingdom? Have I collapsed into His will for my life and discovered my destiny?

This is where I find God's best—His peace in the big stuff and the little stuff, the stuff of eternity and the stuff of the next five minutes. When I'm remembering Him constantly, seeing His hand in my life, thanking Him for everything, praising Him silently, and obeying every unction He puts in my heart, that is God's best.

QUESTION

**Are you experiencing God's best
or the world's second best?**

SURRENDER TO WHOM?

As I've listened to people's stories over the years, I'm keen on the specifics of the "moment of surrender"–the event, the twenty-four hours before, and the twenty-four hours after one meets Jesus in an authentic way.

No one is ever the same after they surrender to Him. But it seems there are two ways surrender happens. I used to think everyone got there through a "Damascus road" kind of encounter–a surrender where you're a crumpled-up mess, a snot-ball laying at Jesus' feet, out of options, humbled, broken, and begging for mercy.

But I've learned that some people get to know Him more gradually and wake up to find themselves surrendered, in love with Him and, more importantly, aware that He's in love with them.

One of the ways that happens is through seeing a prayer answered. People think God is a distant, impersonal being at first. But when God responds in a supernatural way, that moment draws people closer. It builds their faith. They become more deeply committed to Him, surrendering more and more over time.

Think about Jesus' decision to surrender Himself to die. Through prayer and His knowledge of the prophecy of Scripture, He knew it was what the Father wanted Him to do. It was too difficult to imagine. No one understood His surrender.

But He knew who He was surrendering to. Jesus knew His Father, our Father. He knew God would come through for Him in the end.

Follow His example. Go all-in. Let Him be the center. Your Master. Your King. Your Ultimate. Your Father.

QUESTION

Do you believe that the God of the Bible is good? That He'll come through for you if you surrender?

COLLABORATING WITH GOD

Surrender is usually what you do when you have no other options. That's why it's so hard for us. We always have other options. We can always "tough it out," "work a little harder," or our default, "let's wait and see what happens."

Day in and day out, we're faced with decisions, usually only one at a time. If we've been in church or read the Bible much, we think, "What would Jesus have me do?" and we get an answer pretty quick.

But then the hard part comes, because, "What Jesus would have me do," is often different from what we want to do. It will be costly, difficult, and risky.

Jesus said, ". . . I have come that they may have life, and have it to the full" (John 10:10). "Having life" means eternal life. But the "life to the full" part is what I think most of us miss.

I believe that "life to the full" is obtained by living life in a collaborative way with God. You have "life to the full" by facing everything you do and every decision you make in threes, not twos.

Let me explain. It's not me and the decision about taking that new job; it's me, God, and that decision.

And that's where surrender comes in.

If we ask and He answers, then we have a decision to make. Will we do what we want to do? Or will we obey? Will we surrender? The Christian walk we've heard so much about is this collaborative approach to life, and not just in the big things, but even in things that seem trivial at the time.

CHALLENGE

Think about a decision you face today. Pray, seek God, and make the decision *with Him*!

THE REVERSE RIPPLE EFFECT

We are familiar with the metaphor of the ripple effect: a little thing with an impact radiating far beyond the intention. It's something we say when talking about evangelism. And it's something your high-school-friends-turned-multilevel-marketers know well.

The ripple of love spreads first to the person you're loving, and then through to other people here on earth. Our Heavenly Father beams. He's the one who stimulated you through the Holy Spirit; you simply did your part.

Recently I picked up three different devotionals, and each pointed to the same thing: "Give us this day our daily bread." Interpreted: Focus on today. The *right now*, not tomorrow and not yesterday.

When we put away the distractions and pay attention, we discover how we can leave a positive impression with the person in front of us. We'll not know this side of heaven how far our ripple went, but we'll find out in eternity when we meet those we affected.

Remember, as a Jesus follower, the ripple effect also works the other way: Everything we do ripples back to Him. Every single interaction with a coworker, a neighbor, our children, our wife, the kid in the drive-thru window. Imagine, every single "moment of truth" is an opportunity to create a *ripple* of praise back to the Father.

QUESTION

Will you focus today on giving love? Moment by moment?

ADVICE ON ADOLESCENTS

The adolescent years are hard for both teenagers and their parents. We strive to just get them through it, hoping they emerge as smart, responsible adults. Many kids walk through this season and become confused, conflicted, angry, and withdrawn. In a matter of months, we watch them go from happy, innocent, "full of themselves" children to sullen, quiet, burdened, beat-up adolescents.

Here are a few things I've learned, from my own experience and from friends.

1. **Teenagers are influenced almost exclusively by their friends.** If you want to have influence, you'd better make friends with them, and you'd better do it *before* they hit puberty.

2. **Authentic friendship is a two-way street.** Parents want their kids to be totally transparent and vulnerable with them, but they aren't that way to their kids at all.

3. **Balance truth and grace.** My friend John's formula for teenage parenting is "a clear set of inviolable, nonnegotiable rules that consistently connect with real consequences, coupled with buckets full of acceptance." It's truth and grace. Wash, rinse, and repeat.

4. **Use power wisely.** Wise parents subtly and cleverly steer their teens toward friends with positive character and away from those with negative or dangerous influence.

5. **Walk the talk.** As children move into adolescence, they shift from listening to watching parents. When they hear us *preach* but then see our behavior not match our words, they're out. Hypocrisy has no weight.

Getting your progeny through the teenage years is a day-at-a-time, situation at-a-time, decision-at-a-time thing.

CHALLENGE

Do the next right thing, take the next step, and don't be in a hurry. You'll look back someday and realize this short season was a precious one.

UNANSWERED PRAYER

So square this up. Jesus says in Mark 11:24, "I tell you, whatever you ask for in prayer, believe that you have received it, and it will be yours." But then we pray (granted, with varying amounts of faith) and nothing happens. Or it goes the other way.

Eighteenth century Scottish theologian P.T. Forsyth said, "We shall come one day to a heaven where we shall gratefully know that some of God's great refusals were sometimes the true answers to our truest prayer."

Sometimes our prayers are answered, but we lack eyes to see. God sees the deeper intent of our prayers and responds to the greater need, which, over time, solves our spoken need.

When I ask God for what I need instead of what I want, I discover a peace in prayer, a peace that doesn't happen if I ask for what I want. Praying my needs signals a trust in God's plan, even if I want something else in the moment.

Do you believe God is good? All the time? Do you believe God has your best interest at heart, no matter how your prayer is answered? With that kind of faith, it's easier to trust Him when He says, "No."

God's love isn't a mystery. Knowing I'm loved by an all good, totally loving, fully just, timeless God gives me what I need to keep on believing until I enter into eternity.

In the meantime, I'll quote Sonny from the movie *The Best Exotic Marigold Hotel*:

> "It will all work out in the end. If it hasn't worked out yet, it's not the end."

QUESTION

**Will you relax in faith, trusting God will
provide what you need when you need it?**

CONTENTMENT AND JOE MONTANA

Joe Montana had this freakish ability to forget the last play and focus on the next one. None of his energy was focused on what just happened, or what didn't just happen. He had no worries about the play after this one. He was all about current reality, about grasping the situation he was in and run-ning the next play.

Could this be the key to contentment? Contentment is realizing what's been given to you and being good with it.

Here's the Scripture that's informed my head and heart about contentment:

> "LORD, you alone are my portion and my cup; you make my lot secure. The boundary lines have fallen for me in pleasant places; surely I have a delightful inheritance." (Psalm 16:5-6)

A few things jump out to me . . .

1. **The Lord assigns "portions" and "cups."** He gives us something—that's our portion. *Cup* is translated as "suffering," meaning that we must trust the hand that gave us our portion to also measure out our suffering.

2. **My "lot" is secure and pleasant.** No matter what happens, my iden-tity, status, and eternal position are secure because of Jesus. This truth gives me unshakable stability when things get tough.

3. **Surely I have a delightful inheritance.** It's hard for us to let ourselves think about a divine inheritance, but it's something Jesus discussed repeatedly.

So can we become the Joe Montana of our circumstances? As the apostle Paul said, can we learn "to be content whatever the circumstances" (Philippians 4:11)?

QUESTION

Can we teach ourselves to be grateful, to "runthe next play"and trust our loving Heavenly Father for outcomes?

TESTING YOUR FAITH

Everything in your life is going to hell in a handbasket. House problems, marriage problems, business problems, kid problems, mother-in-law problems, money problems, boss problems.

"Maybe God is testing your faith," says your friend.

Really?

So your loving Heavenly Father puts you on a personal version of *Survivor* to see if you're really a Christian? To see how much you can take? God the "Faith Tester?"

All this started with James 1:2-3, which says,

> "Consider it pure joy, my brothers and sisters, whenever you face trials of many kinds, because you know that the testing of your faith produces perseverance."

James is talking about how to endure tough stuff and dangling the carrot of endurance (or perseverance) as the reward. He never blames God for setting up the tough stuff.

Read what Paul had to say about it.

> "Examine yourselves to see whether you are in the faith; test yourselves. Do you not realize that Christ Jesus is in you—unless, of course, you fail the test?" (2 Corinthians 13:5)

We can mouth the words and talk about trusting Him when everything is peachy, but when it really gets hard, we will know if our faith is real . . . or not. If we abandon our faith, we pretty well know it wasn't real to start with. We can doubt God, be angry at God, question His love for us—these are all very natural responses to disasters.

But the more you cling to Him versus question Him, the stronger your faith is.

QUESTION

Do you cling or question?

NO REGRETS

On a beautiful Saturday afternoon, my son's car flipped multiple times through the median of Interstate 20 near Madison, GA. It came to rest "wheels down" in the opposing lane.

A helicopter landed, loaded him, and headed off to Grady Hospital's Trauma Unit. Unable to keep the breathing tube in place, the crew was forced to land so the EMT could reintubate. Critical time was lost.

Brain bleed. Intracranial pressure. Damaged middle meningeal artery. His condition deteriorated steadily over those first hours. Into the night and through the next morning, worse and worse still.

All night, we knelt on the hospital floor and prayed. By daybreak, there were twenty of us. Pray. Wait. Pray some more. On Sunday morning, people prayed at churches all over.

On Sunday morning, his condition took a turn for the better. The next morning, he was moved from ICU to a regular room. A week later, he was released. A month later, he was back in school. Sixteen years later, he's helping people with skin cancer, loving and serving his wife and two little boys, and serving the God who gave him a second chance at life.

I've never heard anyone regret praying. I believe God gets glory when we humble ourselves and ask people to pray for us. And when we lay our heart's desires on God's altar and ask fervently and repeatedly for His help, that's all we can do. Outcomes are His business. Trusting Him is our only reasonable option. He may not get us out of our crisis, but I know He gets us through.

SCRIPTURE

"Therefore confess your sins to each other and pray for each other so that you may be healed. The prayer of a righteous person is powerful and effective." (James 5:16)

RAISING KIDS IN THE FAITH

These are the words we hear all the time:

"I want to raise good kids, kids who will believe in Jesus and follow Him."

There is no known formula, but here are three ideas.

1. **Talk about God . . . a lot.** If God makes no difference in your daily life and rarely comes up in conversation, how can you expect your kids to believe Him, trust Him, or follow Him?

2. **Pray out loud . . . a lot.** Invite your kids to *listen in* while you talk to God. Asking them to pray, especially at younger ages, may scare and frustrate them. But imagine how it feels for a child to hear his daddy and mommy pray for them.

3. **Let them see you in personal study, prayer, and worship . . . a lot.** Last year, one of my guys described waking up early and peeking downstairs to see his dad studying his Bible or on his knees in prayer. Sometimes he'd go down as soon as his dad left and put his face into the still-warm imprint of his dad's face on the sofa.

I'm not suggesting you do this for show; I'm suggesting you do it for real. You can't export what you don't have, so stepping into a deeper, more committed relationship with God is crucial. There may be nothing more vital to your kids' spiritual development than intentionally letting them in on what you're praying about and what God is doing in your life.

PRAYER

Lord, help me *go public* with my faith in front of my kids. Give me courage to start and the discipline to stay with it. Let my life leave a legacy that points my kids to You. In Jesus name, amen.

WINNING

We put a lot of effort into our work. We discover, develop and apply our skills, and, over time, we win. Winners earn the benefit of the doubt through past performance and a proven track record.

Don't get me wrong, there's nothing wrong with winning. For sure it's a lot more fun than losing. But we are called to think differently about winning and losing.

Jesus sends us to love and serve each other, win or lose. We can't "win" heaven; we don't need to. Jesus won it on the cross and gave it to us as a free gift. We can't win an award for being "super Christian" because accepting it would disqualify us. Pride destroys humility.

Winning as a Jesus follower means having more of Him in your heart every minute of every day.

Winning is walking with Him, praising Him, and listening to His voice. It is giving time, talent, and treasure to advance His Kingdom.

Winning is a life of gratitude. Humility. Selfless service to others.

Winning means allowing the Holy Spirit to constantly fill us, to bring peace, love, joy, patience, kindness, goodness, faithfulness, gentleness, and self-control.

Winning means loving the Lord your God with all your heart (your desires), all your soul (your personality and talents), and all your mind (your brain, thoughts, dreams, and aspirations), and loving your neighbor as yourself.

CHALLENGE

If you're a Jesus follower who's failed at something, made a huge mistake, or just doesn't feel much like a winner right now, know that your Heavenly Father loves you extravagantly. You are His adopted son (or daughter), and therefore you are a winner!

MAY 29

PRAYING ON THE SPOT

I thought back to the day I was walking into a restaurant and ran into an old friend named Lee. We shook hands, but instead of letting go, he pulled me closer, put his hand on my shoulder, and prayed for me. At first, I was embarrassed. But he made it short, specific, and real. "Amen," he said, releasing my hand, looking at me with a smile, and walking away.

My mind flashed to two conversations, both less than twenty-four hours old. I had listened, empathized, offered a little counsel, promised to pray for them, and hung up the phone. I never asked if I could pray right then and there.

Those two moments came to mind, but there are countless others. I can blame busyness, but more often it's my pride. I may feel God prompting me to pray on the spot, but I just don't do it.

Why should I push through my hesitation?

Here are five good reasons:

1. If it's an "in person" situation, I'm a *witness* to those who see us praying.

2. I'm an *encouragement* to the person I'm praying for.

3. Immediacy brings *clarity* to my prayers.

4. I demonstrate *obedience* to God's call to pray.

5. I'm not procrastinating; I'm demonstrating *urgency*.

I'm committed to praying more spontaneously with people who are hurting.

QUESTION

**Will you join me? Will you set aside your image
management, fear, ego, lack of faith, whatever it is that
holds you back, and just pray for your friend then and there?**

REASONS WE DON'T PRAY ON THE SPOT

God has challenged me to be more immediate and bolder in response to His unction to pray. But most of us would agree, it's not easy. I started thinking about what makes it hard and what we can do to push through the resistance and be bolder in praying with people on the spot.

Here's what makes it hard:

1. **"I don't want to be** *that guy"*—We all have a picture of an ultraspiritual, somewhat greasy, obnoxious, Bible-thumping zealot who's out of touch with reality.

2. **"I don't want to** *put God on the spot"*—If I pray one-on-one for a person, what happens if I ask God to do something and He doesn't come through?

3. **"I'm not** *hearing* **that unction to pray"**—When we get busy, distracted, and overwhelmed with our "stuff," we probably won't hear God's whisper calling us to pray.

4. **"I won't know what to say"**—Jesus told us to trust the Holy Spirit in those situations. When God gives us the unction to pray and we respond with a "yes," the Holy Spirit gives us the words to say to the Father.

5. **"I'm afraid I'll be rejected outright"**—People know it takes courage to offer to pray for someone on the spot. They'll know you care about them and their problems because you pushed through your fear and did it anyway.

QUESTION

**What if growth in your faith and your relationship
with Jesus hinges on your willingness to press
through this fear and pray for someone on the spot?
What kind of impact can you make on someone by
responding in obedience, even when it's uncomfortable?**

THREE KINDS OF PEOPLE

Dr. Henry Cloud wrote a powerful book called *Necessary Endings*, in which he gives insightful clarity on three kinds of people. The differences are important to know:

Wise people—Wise men and women evaluate their experience, learn lessons, and apply them. As learners, they regularly humble themselves, own their mistakes, and look for ways to do better next time.

Foolish people—A fool is someone who does almost the opposite of a wise person in every situation. Fools don't take feedback or learn from their mistakes. They are full of blame and excuses.

Evil people—Unfortunately, there are people in this world who are just plain evil.

The ultimate description of an evil person is one who "says in his heart, 'There is no God.' They are corrupt, their deeds are vile; there is no one who does good" (Psalm 14:1).

Evil people want to hurt you—to destroy you, your family, your business, your church. Your goal with evil people is *protection*. You're not going to talk them into or out of anything. God wants to redeem them, and He may invite you to participate at some point. But until He specifically directs, be very, very careful with people who have dark hearts and evil motives.

Cloud nets out his advice this way . . .

- Talk to *wise people*, give them resources, and you'll get a return.
- Stop talking to *foolish people* about problems, because they aren't listening anyway.

Evil people? Walk . . . no, *run* from those who would bring evil upon you.

QUESTION

Are you entangled with an evil person? Or walking in the company of a fool? Will you choose to devote your time and attention to wise people instead?

THE PARTIAL FOOL

Dr. Henry Cloud teaches a powerful principle on fools:

> "The definition of a foolish man is one who doesn't evaluate his experience and doesn't learn from his mistakes. They're defensive, play the 'blame game,' and make excuses. They don't listen . . . don't take responsibility . . . and constantly play the 'victim' card."

Most people I've met aren't 100 percent foolish. They're *partial fools*, dealing wisely with some things but foolishly with others.

Cloud's approach helps us deal with a specific area of foolishness without writing off the whole person. We learn from areas where they're wise, taking wisdom from their strengths and discovering how we can be like them. But in areas where they are weak, we stop talking. We might show them consequences and set boundaries, but we let them act as they wish. Oh, and we keep praying that they may humble themselves and grow in wisdom.

After all, the antidote to foolishness, whether full or partial, is humility. James 4:6 reminds us,

> "God opposes the proud but shows favor to the humble."

Dealing with foolish people as Cloud suggests will free you up. Boundaries and consequences put the responsibility for their decisions and growth on them, where it belongs. And if you choose to redeem the time and energy spent with fools and hang out with wise people instead, you'll almost surely go further, faster.

> "Walk with the wise and become wise, for a companion of fools suffers harm." (Proverbs 13:20)

PRAYER

**Lord, please let me perceive but not judge—
to be firm, fair, and forward-thinking as I set
boundaries and establish consequences for foolish
behavior. In the beautiful name of Jesus, amen.**

FIRST AND FINAL WORDS

Ask Christians what they want to hear thirty seconds after they die, and most will say, "Well done, good and faithful servant! You have been faithful with a few things; I will put you in charge of many things. Come and share your master's happiness!" (Matthew 25:23).

Why? Those words are from a parable. They're not a promise or a principle. Why do we take them out of context and so yearn to hear them upon our arrival in the great beyond?

Because we think what *we've* done will be on God's mind when we show up at the pearly gates. Not true. Isaiah 64:6 says, "our righteous acts are like filthy rags."

Our *righteous acts* don't cut it. No matter how well we behave, how pious we are, how generous, or evangelistic, or spiritual.

It's why the Cross is *everything* for us. Our hope of heaven is single-threaded through Jesus' death and resurrection, not through our righteous acts.

There is an alternative to, "Well done." What if God greets you with this:

> "Welcome (your name here), I'm so glad to see you. You're one of my favorites because there on earth, your heart broke for the same things my heart breaks for."

How do I do pursue what God's heart breaks for?

Ask Him. "Lord, You know what I have, where I live, who I know, and what I'm good at. What is it in my world that breaks Your heart?"

Then ask, "What would You have me do here, Lord?" Then, do the next thing He shows you.

QUESTION

Have you asked God in serious prayer to break your heart for a person, a people group, a need in your community, a specific cause He wants to connect you to? Will you?

A KISS ON THE FACE

I'm a huge David Crowder fan. One of his albums rocks me. Here's how it begins:

> "Well I didn't come here on my own accord. And I guarantee I can't leave like this.
>
> Where you are, I don't care, but whoever brought me here. Is gonna have to take me home.
>
> Yeah, you're gonna have to take me home."

I smile every time I hear this intro. It *so* captures how I felt when I'd wandered off in the weeds. I believed in God. I called myself a Christian, but I didn't know Jesus. Not personally. I felt empty, lost, alone, and helpless. Finally, I cried out to my Heavenly Father, and He responded. And thus my new life began.

Crowder ends his album looking back to that time of rebirth . . .

> "My heart was weary. My soul was heavy. My bones were aching, Lord.
>
> I needed waking. I needed breaking. I needed you, my Lord.
>
> And you took my hand. And led me to the river. And buried all I was.
>
> Then you kissed my face. And told me I was yours,
>
> And I knew I'd found my home."

Since I bought this record, I've carefully and prayerfully kissed each of my grandchildren on the face. Each time, I've teared up, thinking how much I love them and imagining my Heavenly Father loving me that much and more.

CHALLENGE

If you're still looking around for your *home*, stop. Get alone somewhere, get down on your knees, and give yourself to Him. Imagine Him kissing you on the forehead and saying, "You're mine. I love you. You're forgiven. You'll never be alone again. You've found your home!"

GOSPEL PATRONS

It seems that where God picks someone for powerful Kingdom impact, He often connects them with someone whose resources enable their impact to be bigger. The apostle Paul wrote about one of his supporters, a lady named Phoebe. Jesus and the disciples had Mary Magdalene, Joanna, Susanna, "and many others . . . helping to support them out of their means" (Luke 8:1-3).

In his book *Gospel Patrons*, John Rinehart tells the story of three historical giants. The most powerful of these was William Tyndale, who illegally translated the Scriptures from Latin to English—a work that launched the English Reformation and allowed the common man direct access to God's Word for the first time.

While many of us have heard of Tyndale, behind the scenes was someone we've never heard of. A mentor and champion, a businessman, a gospel patron named Humphrey Monmouth. Monmouth partnered with Tyndale and his work emotionally, spiritually, and financially. In fact, Monmouth served a year in prison for helping Tyndale, a penalty Tyndale never suffered.

There are three unique characteristics of a gospel patron according to Rinehart.

1. **Joyful giving**—It starts with a heart that seeks the things that are above (Colossians 3:1-2). They put their resources behind those doing eternal work.

2. **Gospel proclamation**—Billions of dollars are spent on humanitarian efforts each year, but we know the *best* work happens with the gospel at the forefront.

3. **Personal involvement**—These mentors—these gospel patrons—don't just write checks. They invest time. They give money but also *give themselves.*

QUESTION

Are you seeking His Kingdom personally? Are you backing someone who's been uniquely called to do the work of the gospel for greater impact? Is God calling you to do more?

IDENTITY THEFT

It's a travesty that over twelve million people in the US had their identities stolen last year. Somebody pretends they're somebody they're not, and over $24 billion gets confused in the process.

But there's a bigger identity theft happening. As of 2012, the number of adult Americans who identified themselves as Christians was 189 million. That's three out of every four. Do those numbers match up with your experience?

We've gotten careless with our identity, with who we are and what we stand for. The Christian "brand" is in trouble because these millions of people say they're connected to Jesus but aren't.

When someone connects personally with Jesus, they get a new identity. They don't have to go to the DMV for a two-hour wait and a bad photo. They get forgiveness, a clean slate, and a new identity. They become adopted sons and daughters of a perfect Heavenly Father.

Back here on earth, that new identity gets stolen. We screw up, and even though we're forgiven, we stop seeing ourselves as God sees us. We're defrauded of our legitimate identity and accept one that's ascribed to us, one that's not accurate.

On the other side of all this, King Jesus never forgets our identity. He's neither confused nor deterred by our wandering off or running away. You may not *feel* like a beloved son of the living God, but if you've ever humbled yourself and genuinely asked Jesus to be your Lord and Savior, then you've got an identity more permanent than a social security number. Your file says "one of mine."

QUESTION

Have you forgotten who you are in Christ? Will you reread 2 Corinthians 5:17 and Romans 8:1 and let God remind you of your identity?

SELF-FORGETTING ADORATION

I was bragging to my wife recently about how my "default setting" is gratitude. When I pray during the day, I'm usually saying, "Thank you, God," for something. Salvation. Forgiveness. Health. Family. Business. On and on.

That's a good thing. Scripture is filled with verses about being grateful.

But then I read this from Thomas Kelly:

> "When I give thanks, my thoughts still circle around me to some extent. But in praise, my soul ascends to self-forgetting adoration, seeing and praising only the majesty and power of God, his grace and his redemption."

There's a *me* and *mine* in my prayers that I hadn't noticed before. To some extent that is appropriate, but there *is* something else, something more. Something better.

How about prayers of pure praise, of adoration, prayer expressing our awe of God? The wonder of a Heavenly Father so big and powerful and creative that He made this world and everything in it, even life itself. Jesus rules over everything that happens, yet He cares enough to know each of us by name. What an amazing, amazing God!

The next time you turn to the Lord in prayer, before you get going with, "Thank you for this day," spend a few minutes in intentional praise. In personal worship. In self-forgetting adoration. If you're alone, pray, and praise Him. Don't just *think* the words, say them or sing them *out loud* so your own ears can hear them.

It's both/and, not either/or. He is worthy of both self-forgetting adoration *and* heartfelt gratitude.

QUESTION

Will you forget about yourself for a little while and express awe and adoration for our wonderful Jesus?

JUNE 7

GRACE IS THE CURE

How do I deal with stress and anxiety? What is God's role in my life? Do I exhaust myself trying to please Him or rest in the knowledge that He loves me just the way I am? When I sin, will He bust my chops? Or can I use my "get out of jail free" card, claim forgiveness, and party on with no fear?

I believe the answer is in understanding, receiving, and living in God's grace. That is the key to navigating this life without anxiety.

One of my favorite Bible stories is in Luke 17, where Jesus tells the story of the "returner," the one leper, out of the ten He healed who came back to say thank you. That guy got it.

That leper showed gratitude, and that is the place of deep gratitude we should enter into each day. Knowing we don't deserve anything, but God graciously gives us everything gives us a sense of humility deep in our hearts. As a result, God gets all the credit for everything good in our lives.

That's what I want you to *get* about grace. It's undeserved blessing. Deep, abiding trust in the Lord. Confidence you're loved. Faith that says, "Keep walking. What can man do to me?" Courage that can look circumstances (including death) in the eye, knowing we are not alone.

If God is with you, what else do you need to know?

Grace *is* the cure.

QUESTION

Will you receive it, embrace it, and humbly let others see it as you live your life? Because He's given grace to you, will you give grace to others?

SIX CHARACTERISTICS OF AN EFFECTIVE TEAM

Most of us have been on a sports team at some point in our lives. Your family is a team. You're part of a team at work. In *The Performance Factor*, Pat MacMillan says if you've ever been a part of a successful team, all six of these things were there:

Common purpose—The team purpose elevates the members and unites them around something great.

Accepted leadership—There's a clear leader, and everyone accepts his leadership.

Specialization of labor—Great teams happen when diverse people get placed into disparate jobs, but together create something special.

Good relationships—Team members don't have to be best friends, they just have to have healthy, respectful relationships.

Agreed-upon plan and process—Everyone knows what's to be done and who's to do it—the *when*, *where*, and *how*.

Good communication—On effective teams, communication is fast and efficient. There's high trust in the process and in each other.

Find a team where these factors are in place and you'll likely find one that's pretty effective. You'll certainly find one you'd enjoy being a part of. This *doesn't* guarantee a winning team. There are a ton of variables that drive winning and losing in the larger scheme of things.

But more often than not, in the real world, the here and now, looking at these characteristics can help a leader figure out what's wrong with a team and show him where he needs to start in making it better.

QUESTION

**Is your team working well? If not, which
of these factors is out of whack?**

LEVEL-3 CHRISTIANS

Men born into Western culture face three big decisions when it comes to Christianity.

1. **What will you do with Jesus Christ?** That's the foundational question. *Level 1: If you're reading this, the assumption is you believe in Jesus.*

2. **Will Jesus be Savior or Lord?** Is He your eternal Savior or is He Lord of all in your life? *Level 2: We surrender to Him.*

3. **Will we follow His call to serve other people?** His call always leads us to others. It's an outward turn, one that focuses our lives on helping those around us. *Level 3: We live to serve others.*

Jesus was serious when He said, "Go and make disciples." We believe He meant for us to take it personally, for every single one of us to have our own ministry doing some piece of Kingdom work.

Thousands of men have their own "ministries," and many happen in a local church. Thousands more find their ministries outside the church. Some lead support or recovery groups. Others lead Bible studies, serve as sports chaplains, coach kids, help the homeless, or feed the hungry.

I've found my ministry in mentoring younger men. But my real motive is for men to find the joy of Level-3 Christianity and the fulfillment of joining Christ in His Kingdom work.

CHALLENGE

If you're a Level-2 guy and you know where God wants you to have your ministry to others, say "yes." Obey. Act. Blessing waits on the other side of your obedience. Your life will never be full at Level 1 or 2. Jesus lived His whole life at Level 3, and He's calling us to follow Him there.

WHO IS "THEY" ANYWAY?

Most of us get defined by people we can't even name. Starting about middle school, *"they"* becomes the most powerful voice in our lives. *"They* expect me to do what they do, dress how they dress, say what they say. Otherwise, I'm ostracized and I don't exist anymore."

College? Same deal. *They* expect me to look like this, talk like that, pledge this or that fraternity.

Starting a career changes nothing. *They* expect you to work crazy hours. *They* favor people with MBAs.

It's not that different in church. What will *they* think if you raise your hands in worship? You'd go to church there, but *they* aren't real keen on people like you.

All this is a confession. I'm ashamed to say how much of this I succumbed to in my early years. I missed three years of my kids' lives working on an MBA because *they* would promote me faster. Even if they did, I look back now and ask, "So what?"

They usually exist in our heads. We put together a composite of our worst fears and ascribe the anticipated judgment to *they*. Few mentors or parents will ever push hard for us to think about who *they* are and why *their* voice is important to us.

Maturity starts with becoming comfortable with yourself. With being defined not by *they* but by Him. When I grasped God's personal love for me, everything changed. The Creator of the universe knows my name. I'm worth something.

We are defined by our Heavenly Father, not by *they*. We are chosen Sons, new creations in Christ. You are somebody because He made you, called you to be His, and loves you extravagantly in your humanity.

QUESTION

Who is your *they*?

STANDING IS WHAT'S REQUIRED

How's this for a big idea?

> We don't need to advance against Satan. We just need to stand and not give up any ground. It's up to us to *not* snatch defeat from the jaws of victory! The battle is already won.

When I read this concept in Watchman Nee's little book *Sit, Walk, Stand*, it was scary simple. Jesus defeated Satan at the Cross. The outcome of this war between spirits of the air has already been determined. Our side wins.

God makes Himself available to us through the Holy Spirit as we *sit* before His throne and let Him love on us while we praise and thank Him. Then we *walk* with Him as we live our lives, hopefully living examined lives where we do His will and apply His Word. We become His hands and feet as we love and serve others in His name.

Nowhere are we called to defeat Satan. We're simply challenged to *stand*. Ephesians 6:10-18 tells us to put on the full armor of God, but the elements are defensive in nature. Paul repeatedly tells us to *stand,* not fight.

What does this mean from a practical standpoint?

1. **Acknowledge he's there**—You can't stand against an enemy you don't believe exists.
2. **Draw lines, set boundaries**—Satan is trying to tug you into places Jesus doesn't want you to go. Draw lines far in front of those points of temptation.
3. **Call for help**—When Satan attacks, when you're contemplating doing something you know is going to open the door to evil, call on Jesus and phone a friend.

QUESTION

Doesn't it feel better knowing we aren't called to defeat evil, but simply to *stand* against it? That feels like a more doable deal to me. How about you?

THERE'S ALWAYS SOMETHING YOU DON'T KNOW

Many of us work somewhere other than "corporate" or "headquarters." That was me once. When orders where handed down to us in the field, they sometimes seemed dumb. Out of touch with the real-world situation on the ground. I'd say, "What are they thinking up there in the ivory tower?"

Then it happened.

I was promoted and transferred to corporate. One of my first tasks was complicated with all kinds of HR and union concerns, things I'd had no knowledge of a few weeks earlier. When the new instructions went out to the field, my phone lit up. "Regi, what are you thinking?" "It sure didn't take you long to forget what it's like out here in the field."

My boss picked up on it. He took me aside and taught me something I've never forgotten. He said, "There's always something you don't know." In a lower-level job or a remote position, there are things people "upstairs" know that you don't. You never have the whole picture.

This same principle applies in everyday relationships. When your wife comes home acting cross and impatient, *there's something you don't know*. When the guy races past then cuts you off in traffic, *there's something you don't know*. When your teammate turns critical and negative, *there's something you don't know*.

And when God doesn't cause or allow things to work out the way you want them to, *there's something you don't know*.

Lean into what you *do* know. God is good, and God loves you. That's really all you need to know.

SCRIPTURE

"Trust in the Lord with all your heart and lean not on your own understanding; in all your ways submit to him, and he will make your paths straight." (Proverbs 3:5-6)

THE COST OF COMMUNITY

I've never thought much about the *cost* of community until recently.

A close friend's wife has gone nuts and decided she wants a different life. We found out she's lived a lie for years. She says she's no longer interested in "the God stuff" and wants a divorce. My friend is decimated. Rocked to the core. And his two sons are confused.

But people in his community are stepping up big time. One guy buys dinner every Tuesday so my friend can keep his footing and remain sane. Another offered half his house as temporary housing. Others have disrupted their family lives to connect their kids with my friends' kids, trying to provide some normalcy.

The decision of this ex-wife is costing everyone in the community. A cost willingly paid, but still a cost.

Time is what we invest to be a part of a community, and *time* is the currency in which we pay the cost. And it's not always time that can be scheduled or planned in advance.

Some people have all kinds of time for hobbies and DIY projects. They don't make the investment in developing community, so they never pay the cost. But they live alone. They're rarely needed or called upon by others. Consequently, when they have needs, they'll likely go unnoticed and unmet.

That's the *secret sauce* of community. Love is expressed when we meet the need of another person. The only way to know about those needs is to be in community.

QUESTION

Will the six guys who will carry your casket know you?
Will you have paid the cost of being their friend in
such a way that they'll willingly do the same for you?

WHY HOLINESS MATTERS

There's not much talk about holiness these days. We make everything relative. Movies get rated G, PG, PG-13, R, NC-17 or NR, but none of these even touches on holiness. There aren't degrees of holy. It's yes or no. Black or white. Holy or unholy.

Here's why it's important:

1. **God is totally, completely, 100 percent holy.** "There is no one holy like the Lord; there is no one besides you; there is no Rock like our God" (1 Samuel 2:2).

   God cannot and will not be in the presence of evil. When Moses wanted to see God, he was told no because God is so holy and pure that if a regular, sinful human being were to be in His *physical presence*, they'd die.

2. **He wants us to be holy.** "Be holy, because I am holy" (1 Peter 1:16).

   God loves people. We're His highest and best creation. In the beginning, we were holy. Pure. Innocent. But we chose evil. It's hard to deny the natural pull toward evil and away from good, and holiness, and selflessness, and submission.

3. **Jesus makes us holy.** About 2,000 years ago, for some reason we aren't likely discover until heaven, God decided to change things. He gave us a way to regain holiness.

As Jesus followers, we are called to holiness. We see what that looks like in the example of Jesus. It's not relative, it's certain. The only question is whether we will choose to pursue holiness or not.

QUESTION

Will you get down on your knees before this day is over and praise God for His holiness? Will you thank Him for making you holy through Jesus' atonement for your sins on the cross?

GOD AND CARS

Imagine a teenager who wrecks the family car. His dad told him not to fiddle with the radio while driving, but he did. Then he drifted out of his lane and hit the median. Dad will be disappointed. There's going to be a price for that kid to come back into relationship with his dad.

When it's paid, Dad will receive his son back into full fellowship. Their relationship will be restored. If Dad refuses to forgive and provides no means for redemption, then the relationship will end with the wreck.

Messing with Almighty God is a lot more serious than bending the fender on a Chevy. The price to be paid is a heavy one. Scripture says that because of God's purity and holiness, it's the death penalty.

That's where Jesus comes in. He voluntarily stepped into history and took the death penalty we deserved. He died in our place and, as a result, made it possible for our relationship with God to be restored.

I lived this story when I was seventeen. I begged my dad to lend me the family car for my homecoming date. Less than an hour after I pulled out of the driveway, I was calling my dad to come to the accident site. Terrified, I waited for his rage, rant, and rebuke.

But instead, he gave me grace. On that day, I got a glimpse of my Heavenly Father. My wreck hurt him. It caused undeniable damage. But he chose to forgive, not because I deserved it, but because he loved me. Our Heavenly Father extends His forgiveness the same way—out of overwhelming love.

QUESTION

**Will you tell someone you know the
story about God's love?**

JUNE 16

TELLING ON YOURSELF

"Tattletale, tattletale, hang your britches on a nail." That's what we chanted at whoever told on us. No one liked being ratted out for things like throwing rocks or stealing M&M's. It took guts to go to the authorities (usually Mama) because the backlash from the other kids would be painful. We were supposed to stick together: it was the unwritten rule of the kingdom of kids.

Telling on your sister? Easy. Telling on your brother? Maybe a little harder. Telling on yourself? Never. Why would you invite criticism and immediate punishment, not to mention self-inflicted shame?

Five reasons we don't tell on ourselves:

1. Telling on yourself takes guts, so most men don't tell on themselves unless they get caught.

2. Telling on yourself takes faith in whomever you're confessing to.

3. Telling on yourself requires transparency and vulnerability.

4. Telling on yourself clears your conscience and is a step toward healing.

5. Telling on yourself attracts resources, which may mean you get help.

By far the best time to tell on yourself is *before* you do something you're going to regret. Confessing what you're thinking about doing gives your trusted friend a chance to *protect* you. The sooner you let him in on what you're thinking, the better chance he has to help you.

Men get paralyzed by the thought of telling on themselves because they think it's a sign of weakness. But in fact, true strength is demonstrated in vulnerability. And it's in that vulnerability that we bounce back, recover, and grow.

QUESTION

**Is there something you need to confess? Is there
a trusted friend or minister who might be able
to protect you if you tell on yourself right now?**

SHARING THE GOOD STUFF

Yesterday, you read about confession—the idea of "telling on yourself." Almost everyone agrees that coming out with your screwups is healthy.

But there's more good about telling on yourself than just purging your crap; there's the chance to share the better part of you. Here are three things to be vulnerable about:

Aspirations—When you share your aspirations, when you make yourself vulnerable by telling others of your inklings or dreams, you get resources you didn't have before.

Accountability—Bob Goff teaches, "Don't hold me accountable, hold me close." Behind that cool one-liner is the presumption that someone is there to do the holding. Do you have a trusted friend to open up to? By opening up, do you gain a trusted friend? That's natural accountability flowing from a love relationship between two friends who care about each other.

Acceptance—Something amazing happens when we open ourselves up to someone. They love us more, not less. We think they'll look down on us or run away, but instead, they pull closer. We feel accepted when we thought we'd feel judged.

I watched a young friend shed his mask as he opened up about his long bout with alcohol and drugs. He was shocked when I then took off mine and told him about thirteen years of drinking (almost) daily. He and I accept each other. We connected. We're closer than we could have ever been while wearing our masks. We are friends for life because he took the risk and told on himself.

QUESTION

Will you reach out to your best friend this week and share a secret you've been holding back? One aspiration? One daunting issue? One inkling?

JUNE 18

RATS IN THE DARK

When you screw up, how do you treat yourself?

What is your standard of comparison? When we compare ourselves to perfection, we inevitably fail and think of ourselves as failures. Those of us who grew up in critical homes where the shame that comes with criticism burned a false identity into our souls are prone to think this way. We forget we're adopted children of the King and start seeing ourselves as failures, as people who can never measure up and aren't worthy of being loved.

How we think of ourselves comes out quickly when we're startled. Our instinctive reactions reveal who we really are, or at least who we're convinced we are. Given time to think, we'll respond the way we're supposed to or how others would expect us to. But hit us cold and what's "down in the well comes up in the bucket."

C.S. Lewis talked about rats in the dark. Give them warning, and they'll be gone when the lights come on. But give them no time to respond, and you'll catch them cold.

This is why God continually reminds me He loves me. Whenever I take the time to ask Him, "Lord, what would you have me know?" I hear, "I love you, Regi." He must know how hard it is for me to believe that.

We may respond in some moments as if we forgot our true identity. We revert back to the false identity of failure.

But God graciously picks us up and reminds us who we really are.

CHALLENGE

Next time you're surprised, immediately remember your true identity.

JUNE 19

HOLY GROUND IN THE BACKYARD

What do Acts 7:33, Exodus 3:5, and Joshua 5:15 have in common? In each, the Lord says,

> "Take off your sandals, for the place where you are standing is holy ground!"

Taking off your shoes is important for three reasons:

1. **Stopping what you're doing**—It's a necessary inconvenience. You have to pause, sit down, and remove your shoes. It means you're staying for a while.

2. **Dropping your guard**—Taking off your shoes means you won't run off, at least not quickly. There's nothing hard left between the rocky ground of your circumstances and the tender soles of your feet.

3. **God is present**—When God chooses to speak to you, to bring you into His presence so He can let you know something important, you'll always remember the place it happened. It may mean nothing to anyone else, but for you it's *holy ground*.

The backyard of our first home in Roswell, Georgia, was holy ground for me. That's where I first met God. Oh, He'd been around me for a long time, protecting me, convicting me, calling me. I had just shut Him out. Until that night at age thirty-three when His love overtook me and I surrendered. "I believe in you, Jesus," I said. "I accept your forgiveness. I'm yours . . . no matter what. It's you and me, God."

Holy ground in the backyard. It's a place of remembrance, of worship, and of gratitude to God for His relentless grace.

Where is your holy ground? Can you remember when and where you received His love for the first time in an authentic, grown-up way? If you can't remember, your "now" moment may be ahead instead of behind you.

QUESTION

Will you take your shoes off?

FOCUSED ON YOURSELF

If you spend your life focused *on* yourself, at the end of your life, you'll be *by* yourself.

As far back as I can remember, until I came to Christ at age thirty-three, everything was all about me. I'd give my wife a milkshake-maker for her birthday, not because she wanted it or even liked milkshakes but because I did. Think how that selfishness lands with your family. With your friends. With your coworkers. Think about how people interact with you when all you are about is *your* life, *your* success, *your* wants, and *your* needs.

When I found and followed Jesus, my heart changed. I became *grateful* as I learned that my life, my forgiveness, my wife and kids, even my career success was *given* to me. It was from and through my Heavenly Father. He gave me a desire to love and serve others. I felt a compassion for people that wasn't there before. I wanted others to have the peace and purpose God was giving me through my relationship with Jesus. To have a friend you have to be one and since that night many years ago, I've tried hard to be one.

How about you? Are you getting a little fatigued of the focus on you and yours? Are you ready to love and serve the people God has placed in your life and pour into them?

Ask God to call your attention to someone in your life who has a need. Then meet it. The need for a visit, a ride, an extra pair of hands—whatever He shows you, just do it. He'll change your life.

SCRIPTURE

**"By this everyone will know that you are my
disciples, if you love one another." (John 13:35)**

BITTER OR BETTER? . . . LAW OR GRACE?

Here's a principle:

How you respond to the issues of life will make you bitter or better.

I'll go further. If you're a *law* person, you're headed toward bitterness. If you're a *grace* person, you've got a shot at a better life.

Law people use the word "should" a lot. "He *should* come back and fix that for free. After all, it's only been six years!" "She *shouldn't* have cut in front of me." Law people often banter fairness around. "It's just not fair. They should do their part." Law people decide what's fair, the way things should be and how people should act, then spend their life full of disappointment, anger, and resentment because what they thought should be, wasn't.

Grace people, on the other hand, use the words "thank you" a lot, especially when they're talking to their Heavenly Father. They know God loves them immeasurably and that He's trustworthy, so they can relax. Grace people take things as they come. Grace people give grace because they've been given grace. They don't presume what *should be*; they're grateful for what is. They find a way to be thankful for everything, no matter how hard.

We have the potential to add peace, love, and compassion to every person we meet. Granted, it's easier with grace people than with law people. But we're taking up God's job when we battle with bitter people. If we can't show them the love of Jesus, maybe we can at least do what He did . . . be quiet. Or walk away.

SCRIPTURE

"But the fruit of the Spirit is love, joy, peace, forbearance, kindness, goodness, faithfulness, gentleness, and self-control. Against such things there is no law." (Galatians 5:22-23)

PICK ONE (AND ONLY ONE): JESUS OR RELIGION?

God calls every Christian to pick a fight. To not sit and wait for evil to attack, but instead, to attack the effects of evil. To pick some wrong and go hit it in the mouth. In that fight, we discover who we are. Who God is. Our purpose. And we find meaning, because we are spending our lives for something that matters.

My fight is against religion. It almost killed me and my marriage. My kids barely escaped.

Jesus picked the same fight; He took on religion.

Religion is a distortion of Jesus. Religion tries to domesticate a God who is wilder, bigger, and better than that. Religion creates an *idea* of the thing instead of the thing itself. Religion veils love, truth, and beauty. Jesus amplifies it.

We gravitate to religion because it's easier. It allows us to stay at surface level, and we soon learn how to act in the system. Growing up in church, I learned how to navigate religion well. But we aren't called to serve a religion, we are called to serve Jesus.

Jesus changes everything. He changes how we think, live, act, serve, work, and lead. He changes how we approach our jobs, how we lead in our homes, and how we serve others in our community.

You can't serve Jesus and religion. Either you become slave to the rituals and routines of religious practice, or you become zealously devoted to Jesus.

SCRIPTURE

"What sorrow awaits you teachers of religious law and you Pharisees. Hypocrites! For you are like whitewashed tombs—beautiful on the outside but filled on the inside with dead people's bones and all sorts of impurity. Outwardly you look like righteous people, but inwardly your hearts are filled with hypocrisy and lawlessness." (Matthew 23:27-28, NLT)

JUNE 23

SUBMISSION TO ONENESS

Submit may be the most controversial word in the Bible, especially when it's used by a man talking about a woman. Submission doesn't come naturally. Start telling your wife how she's supposed to submit to you and you'll find yourself celibate—and not because you meant to be.

What God has for us in marriage isn't found in *making* anyone do anything. It's not about the *requirement* that the husband do "X" so the wife will do "Y" or vice versa. The jewel we're digging for is *oneness*. Voluntary, not obligatory. Filling, not draining.

As a husband, I feel oneness when I know I measure up. When she lets me know I have what it takes and when she listens to me.

She feels oneness when she feels cherished. When she feels loved, lovely, and lovable. Accepted and not criticized. When she feels my focused attention.

So, instead of battling over who goes first, whether love brings submis-sion or vice versa, why not make it mutual?

"Submit to one another out of reverence for Christ." (Ephesians 5:21)

Instead of doing things for the sake of our marriage, what would happen if we created an imaginary third party called *oneness*? What if we started thinking, *For the sake of oneness, I'm going to pass up the temptation to snap back to what she just said. For the sake of oneness, I'm going to let him off for forgetting that thing I asked him to do. For the sake of oneness . . .*

Recognize it's *oneness* you both want. Oneness "out of reverence for Christ," who put the two of you together in the first place.

QUESTION

"Out of reverence for Christ," will you do what it takes to pursue *oneness* with your wife?

KEYS TO ONENESS

Marital bliss, if there is such a thing, happens when we experience *oneness* with our mates. That oneness is elusive; it usually lasts a few seconds. We want it to last hours, days, weeks, months, and years.

But let's shoot for hours as a starter. Here are three simple things to preserve oneness with your wife.

1. **Hold it**—Don't say it. When that thought comes into your head, keep it there. It either won't be funny, or it may trigger negative feelings you forgot existed. It's just not worth it.

2. **Drop it**—Something you've seen or thought a hundred times keeps coming back when she says or does *that thing* that sets you off. Drop it. Let it go.

3. **Give it**—One choice that's always open is to give. We can give a point. We can give the benefit of the doubt. We can give forgiveness, even when it's not deserved and we don't feel like it.

In his book *Sit, Walk, Stand*, Chinese Bible teacher Watchman Nee says our response to *everything* must be through the Cross. Good or bad, right or wrong isn't the deal. When we *sit* long enough to consider what Jesus did and let gratitude fill us, we'll *walk* differently. Respond differently. Speak differently.

If there's one person to put ahead of yourself, it's the woman who gave herself to you.

QUESTION

Will you hold it, drop it, and give it? Will you sacrifice your pride and selfishness for a marriage of intimacy and oneness?

HOW ARE YOU DEFINED?

"You won't be defined by the mistake you made; you'll be defined by how you recover from it."

Profound.

Everyone makes mistakes. We even repeat the same mistakes. We've disconnected the word "mistake" from the word "sin," a word that's fallen out of our vocabulary.

In recent history, two examples stand out. One good, one not so good.

Chuck Colson was intimately involved in the Watergate break-in and the cover-up that followed. He went to federal prison for his mistake. But through Christ, Colson's life was redeemed. He owned his mistake. He founded the largest prison ministry in the world. Chuck is defined by his recovery more than his mistake.

On the other hand, there's Lance Armstrong, the famous cyclist who finished ahead of everyone else in the Tour de France seven times. After years of lying and denying, Armstrong was finally cornered on his use of performance-enhancing substances. His reputation was destroyed, his brand value reduced to almost nothing, and his legacy was stripped. Lance Armstrong will be defined by his mistake.

The beauty of the gospel is how it enables all of us to recover from mistakes. We can grab hold of the grace offered by Jesus, have our mistakes covered by His sacrificial blood, and then, by His Spirit, see them redeemed for the good of ourselves and others.

QUESTION

Is there a mistake you've allowed to define you? Will you instead choose to be defined by your recovery?

A CALL TO HUMILITY

If I could secretly reach into the heart of every man and turn the knobs, the first one I'd look for would be labeled, *Humility*. It would have an arrow pointing one way toward *Humble,* and one the other way toward *Proud*. Crank up the humility and you're turning down the pride. I'd crank humility all the way up.

The word *humility* comes from the same root word as *humus*, which means "fertile ground." When a man is humble, he becomes fertile ground for God to grow stuff in—stuff like love, peace, joy, patience, kindness, gentleness, faithfulness, goodness, and self-control.

Pride is the opposite. It says, "I've got this." "I don't need help." "I know what I need to know." Pride grows arrogance and isolation, rarely wisdom or relational intimacy.

Humility is also sometimes translated to the word "meek." In the Sermon on the Mount, Jesus said, "Blessed are the meek, for they will inherit the earth" (Matthew 5:5).

Humble people recognize it all belongs to God to start with, that we can *inherit* what He has for us. Humble people start with clear perspective that it's His. We have our life, our breath, our being, and our hope in Him. Humble people grasp that it all would end in death except for grace.

Turn your knob to humble and watch as people are drawn to you, want to help you, have empathy for you and your situation. Pride repels people. Humility attracts people *and* God's favor. Proverbs 3:34 says, "He mocks proud mockers, but shows favor to the humble and oppressed."

QUESTION

Will you turn your humility up and your pride down?

JUNE 27

THE BAIT AND SWITCH?

Everyone who gets married gets surprised. There are things you find out after the wedding that you didn't know beforehand. It's not intentional; it's nobody's fault. It just happens.

Infatuation is partly to blame. The *idea* of the person gets so jacked up by emotion and hormones that you can't see the actual person objectively.

Here's the thing: Love isn't a hole you fall into, it's a choice you make. Mature love is fueled by commitment, tenacity, and determination more than passion, romance, and flowers. It doesn't feel good a lot of the time. But it *is* good, and good *for us*.

Marriage isn't about falling in love once and staying in love with that same woman all your life. It's choosing to love her as she is in each stage of life, adapting your love to the woman she has become and is becoming.

A husband's love must mature as he and his wife mature. As Paul says in 1 Corinthians 13:11,

> "When I was a child, I talked like a child, I thought like a child, I reasoned like a child. When I became a man, I put the ways of childhood behind me."

I could paraphrase that to say, "When I was a newlywed, I talked like a newlywed, I thought like a newlywed, I reasoned like a newlywed. When I matured, I put the ways of a newlywed behind me."

Translated: I grew up, accepted her exactly as she is, and started to love her with a rock-solid, committed, selfless kind of love that never gives up or goes away–the same kind of love Jesus has for us.

QUESTION

Have you matured in your love for your wife?

FOUR KEYS TO DEALING WITH REGRET

I run into two kinds of Jesus followers. The *good guys* who grew up in church, mostly did the right thing, and ended up marrying the homecoming queen.

The other kind *wandered off the farm* and screwed up in royal fashion. These men (of which I am one) crashed and burned, then became humbled and broken. Jesus found them, forgave them, and turned their lives around.

This second kind of Christian deals with regret. A lot. Yet they don't know how to handle it. Over my years of being a member of this second group, I've discovered a few ways to deal with regret.

1. **Own the "new you."**–"I have been crucified with Christ and I no longer live, but Christ lives in me" (Galatians 2:20) isn't just a religious metaphor.

2. **Own the "dead you."**–The sins, failures, and decisions you made were *buried* with the "dead you."

3. **Put it away.**–Getting rid of physical reminders of things you regret can help you move on.

4. **Own what you did and learn from it.**–Experience isn't a great teacher, but examined experience is.

We all deal with regret. The apostle Paul had plenty. His words show that he struggled with the same stuff we do–owning his new identity in Christ, letting go of his past sins and mistakes, and owning the death of the "Saul" who did the horrible stuff.

CHALLENGE

Christ's death was payment for all your sin, and was intended to pay for them once and for all. When you bring those decisions back up and wallow in them again through regret, you're giving away the freedom He died to give you.

JUNE 29

PLAN OR PERSPECTIVE . . .
WHAT SHALL I PRAY FOR?

They say they are no foxhole atheists. When the chips are down—I mean *really* down—most people will cry out to God. "Get me out of here," or, "Please send help before it's too late," or, "I've *got* to make this huge decision! Please, God, if You're out there, tell me what to do!"

Jesus followers pray the same way in a crisis. But in calmer times, we're seeking God's guidance on all kinds of things—spending decisions, disciplining our kids (or not), and balancing the demands of work, home, church, friends, and family.

Some "pray-ers" come with high expectations of God. They expect God to act, to make things happen, to change the outcome. Or if it's a decision, they expect Him to tell them what to do. Other prayers come more to vent their issues with God but expect little of Him other than a loving, listening ear.

Perhaps God's most frequent way of helping is to give us perspective. I quote my friend John:

> "God might not always give us a plan, but He will give us perspective."

If we'll pause and ask, "Lord, what would You have me know about this situation?" we might get a clearer picture of what's actually going on, what people are thinking and feeling, and maybe even the wise thing to do.

When we see as God sees, we're more likely to respond as God would have us respond.

QUESTION

Will you pray for God's perspective on the issues you face?

JUNE 30

TRUE LOVE SHOWS UP

Nothing brings love into the conversation like pain and suffering. The other day, I called an old friend who lives in Texas and is confined to a wheelchair. He immediately burst into tears, telling me how he lost his five-year-old grandson to cancer four days after Christmas.

What was I to say? What can *anyone* say or do?

Often, we want to hide from tough situations like this one. If we can't fix it, we avoid it. We don't know what to say, there's nothing we can really do, so what's the point of just being there?

Love. That's the point. Love is being present with people. Love is just showing up.

Love is sacrificing your own comfort for the comfort of someone who is suffering. *Care* means "to grieve, to experience sorrow, to cry out with." We've morphed the word into another verb—an action word—because it's easier for us to do something *for* someone than to enter into the pain *of* someone.

I first got a glimpse into this when my friend Rick's wife died. I stood behind him as he manned the receiving line at the mortuary. I listened as person after person came through, saying things like, "She's better off," and, "She's in a better place now."

People have no idea how hurtful and inappropriate those phrases are when someone is hurting. I learned a major lesson that night: the power of presence, of just showing up in the middle of suffering—of simply *being present* with the person you care about.

CHALLENGE

Next time you find a friend in the middle of something awful, ask God for the courage to just go and, as uncomfortable as it might feel, be present.

SHIFTING GEARS

Some of the best practices from the business world can improve your marriage. Not all, but some. Here are three examples:

1. **Commit and Communicate**—People want to follow a leader who exhibits singular, all-in commitment to the company. Similarly, wives need to know we're committed. All-in for the long haul.

2. **Exclusive dedication**—The leader who spreads his time and talent to multiple endeavors won't garner much respect. At home, we will never have the wife of our dreams without *exclusive* commitment to her and her alone.

3. **Create an environment of acceptance**—A leader who creates a work environment of acceptance, positivity, and love will gain the heartfelt commitment of employees. Do the same thing at home.

On the other side, there are some work practices that never work out well at home. Here are three:

1. **Setting goals for your team**—*Don't try this at home!* Setting goals *together* is one thing. Assigning goals for your mate doesn't work.

2. **Specialization of roles**—At work, we divide duties and responsibilities based on skill and experience. Go home and start assigning your wife roles and responsibilities, and you might end up in the ER.

3. **Performance counseling**—Those higher in authority look at the work of those under them and measure their performance. I don't even need to say what might happen if you approach your wife this way.

A few things that work at work can help us at home, but in most cases, we diminish our marriages and homes when we forget where we are and act at home like we do at work.

Make a conscious effort to *switch gears* when you get home tonight.

QUESTION

What do I do at work that I do at home without thinking?

OUR TRIUNE GOD

Thinking about water helped me understand the Trinity.

H2O is water. It's the elemental construct—the core nature of the stuff. But water is embodied in three major ways: liquid, ice, and vapor. All are different, but at their essence, they're the same.

Water (the liquid) sustains life. We die without it. Water (the vapor) is the core element of our ecosystem. If there's no water vapor, there are no clouds, no rain, no crops, no life. Ice? Well, not only does it make our drinks pleasant, it makes the world's weather system work.

God is like H2O. He's the essential, the elemental, the core. Each of His embodiments has a specific purpose, which we won't fully understand until God connects the dots for us in heaven. But here's my take . . .

> **Jesus** is the *inward* connection. God the Son, our Savior who lives in and through us. We live *in* Him, and He lives *in* us.

> **God the Father** is the *upward* connection. We pray to our perfect "Father who is in heaven." He is the eternal lover of our souls.

> **The Holy Spirit** is the *outward* connection. He empowers, connects, and guides. When Jesus left, He sent the Holy Spirit to guide us through each day.

As H2O is to water, love is to God. Every atom of the Father, Son, and Holy Spirit is love. God *is* love. He loves us, and He created us to love as He loves. His Son died for us out of love. And the Holy Spirit is our helper as we love.

Any one of these dimensions would have been enough, but from His unfathomable love, God gave us not one, but *three* personas of Himself.

PRAYER

Thank You for adopting me into Your amazing family!

THE BELIEF METER

Belief in Jesus is essential, not optional, if one wants forgiveness and eternal life.

Folks who have grown up in church have a hard time remembering when they *didn't* believe. If your parents, Sunday school teacher, pastor, or priest told you about Jesus, why wouldn't you believe?

I once tried to convince my granddaughters that mermaids were make believe. They were loud and unanimous in reminding me that several key figures in their lives were invisible but *not* imaginary—unicorns, the Easter Bunny, Santa Claus, and Jesus. They got me.

But belief vacillates. It goes up and down. If we had a visible belief meter, I think there'd be wild swings in our belief level depending on our circumstances.

We're smart to recognize the up and down, the ebb and flow of belief. When we're in the Spirit, worshiping with all our hearts, surrounded by people who love Jesus like we do, our belief meter pegs 100 and stays north of 90.

Then Monday hits, with traffic, bosses, deadlines, conflicts, life, and our belief meter settles back between 60 and 65. Lose someone you love unexpectedly, and your belief meter sputters near 0. "Where were you, God?"

So how do we deal with doubt and unbelief?

Don't panic. Ask for help from the source of our faith. In Mark 9, the father of the demon-possessed boy asked Jesus, "If you can do anything . . ." Jesus replied, "If you can? Everything is possible for one who believes." Immediately the boy's father exclaimed, "I do believe; help me overcome my unbelief!" Jesus did, the demon was cast out, and the boy was healed.

PRAYER

Father, help me overcome my unbelief.

BIRDS OF A FEATHER

Birds of a feather . . . you don't need me to finish it for you. This saying has been around since the sixteenth century. Birds and animals of all sorts flock together with their kind.

It's part of our comfort, and, sometimes, our safety. There's power in numbers. The good guys defeat the bad guys when they stick together. It's natural.

But Jesus wasn't about doing what was natural. He was about doing what is divine instead of what is fallen. Things like turning the other cheek, giving away your coat, loving your enemies, and, yes, hanging out with birds of a *different* feather.

Is that true of us?

Confession time. I'm in a holy huddle that consists of my family, my well-off Jesus-following age sixty-plus friends, and my mentees. I don't mean to be, and mind you, I'm not complaining. I'm just challenging myself (and maybe you) to ask, "Where would Jesus have me be?"

Based on His life, it's not likely He'd spend His spare time hanging in the suburbs. Something tells me there would be more to Him than that. He would spend time with people who are different. Who are some of these people of a different feather?

Do you have a close friend from another race? How about a real, personal relationship with a Jewish or Muslim person? What about people of a different generation? Or prisoners?

Connecting with birds of a different feather demands intentionality. It demands we decide to step outside our comfort zone and build relationships with people radically different than us.

QUESTION

**Will you go beyond the "Jesus club" and
connect with birds of a different feather?**

JULY 5

THE THREE BIG DISTRACTIONS

Jesus was so smart. From a first-century world with no TV or technology, He spoke into our lives and put His finger on three things that take us away from the peace of His Presence.

From Mark 4:19:

> "But the worries of this life, the deceitfulness of wealth and the desires for other things come in and choke the word, making it unfruitful."

The worries of this life. Worry is when we visualize something in the future that we can't control and assume it's going to turn out badly. The things we worry about in this life include family, jobs, the weather, sports teams, terrorists, bad drivers, and much more.

The deceitfulness of wealth. Deceit happens when someone or something leads you to believe something that's not really true. Wealth says, "Get more of me and everything will be peachy." Liar.

The desires for other things. Humans can only think about one thing at a time. Multitasking is an illusion.

These things "choke the Word" in us. Jesus is the Word. The Word lives in and through us, but when stuff distracts us—when the thorns get our first attention—Jesus gets shoved to the back of our minds, and we're not fruitful.

The answer: Invite Him into everything, right up front. Catch yourself worrying about something? Pray. When your mind wanders over to money, ask Him for provision, wisdom, patience, and faith. Dreaming about things you want? Bring your mind back to Jesus and turn your dream into a prayer.

> "You will keep in perfect peace those whose minds are steadfast, because they trust in You." (Isaiah 26:3)

QUESTION

Jesus is the answer to peace and meaning in life. Will you use distractions as reminders to turn your thoughts back to Him?

JULY 6

EMPATHY FOR JESUS

Day in and day out, Christ followers ask Jesus to have empathy for them, to be with them. We thank Jesus for His love and forgiveness. We rest knowing that He *feels us*, that He understands, that He felt what we feel when He walked the earth.

What if we tried to get into Jesus' frame of reference? To *feel Him* for a change?

Paul talks about "entering into His suffering," and I guess that's what I'm suggesting.

Dwell on what happened as Jesus shared His last meal. As He went to the garden and asked God, with such fervor He sweat blood, to give Him a way out—a way to forgive our sins without having to experience what He was about to experience. Think about the rejection He must have felt as His Father offered no other way. Moments later, He was arrested. All night and all morning, beating after beating. No sleep. No food. Whipped and scourged. Pain.

Then visualize Him . . . beleaguered, exhausted, bleeding . . . carrying the cross He would die on. See Him nailed to it and then raised vertical. Hanging by nails in His hands and feet. Excruciating pain. He suffocates. Falls limp. Lifeless. Blood caked on what's left of His skin. His body is taken down and carried to a borrowed tomb, where it's locked away. Everybody leaves. It's dark, and it's over. Maybe the most brutal twenty-four hours ever lived.

Yes, Sunday comes. He is risen. But sometimes we rush to Sunday without considering what our forgiveness cost. Let the weight of the crucifixion settle on your heart this week.

PRAYER

**Thank You, Jesus. Thank You. Root
gratitude deep into my soul.**

GETTING OFF TRACK

How does it work that someone so close to God, so filled with the Spirit, so fired up and full of love, ends up distraught, angry, and alone in a matter of days? Puzzling, isn't it?

It's a fixation on the negative that gets us off track. We focus on the obstacle that robs us of joy and fall into "If only I could . . . if I just had . . . as soon as I . . . whenever she finally . . . then I'll be happy and everything will be OK." Without thinking, we create little gods that stand between us and the real God. Between us and joy. Worship means "to assign value and worth to." We accidentally worship little things that don't matter in the bigger picture.

But Jesus told us,

> "Ask, and it will be given to you; seek and you will find; knock and the door will be opened to you." (Matthew 7:7)

This verse can be twisted into, "Make Jesus your choice and get a Rolls-Royce." Or "Name it and claim it." You can come away questioning your faith, whether you have enough, or any at all.

But Jesus is talking about answers, not things. He is assuring us that if we seek answers *in Him*, we'll find them. They may not be what we want them to be, but we'll get answers. Jesus always points us to matters of the heart, rarely material things or easy circumstances.

CHALLENGE

Switch your focus from what you don't have to what you do. Since gratitude is the only sure cure for anxiety, thinking about things you're grateful for can lift your spirits and get you back on track.

WHY WOULD GOD WANT TO TALK TO ME?

Imagine having a child and raising him without ever speaking to him. He comes to you all the time, pouring out his needs. He worships the ground you walk on. But you never speak. With your wisdom, you could give him courage, insight, and comfort. But you stay quiet.

Carry it a step further. The son decides his father is mute, that he can't or won't speak. So he tries to handle everything on his own, never tapping into his father's strength, wisdom, or insight. The son could die without ever hearing from his father, just because he didn't believe he would speak.

So it is between God and us. Since God has been speaking all along, we may be the problem. Our fear of being weird, of looking stupid, of becoming *that guy* (e.g., our pride) have cut us off from our ultimate source of love, wisdom, encouragement, and confidence. My friend Larry mentions multiple ways God speaks to us:

- Scripture
- visions/dreams/visual pictures
- a felt sense (e.g., fruit of the Spirit)
- people
- music
- our thoughts
- nature
- miracles

Many people struggle with why the God of the universe would *speak* personally and individually.

Larry's answer is simple and profound. God loves us. He is our Heavenly Father, and we're His adopted children. He loves us personally and individually. And He wants to communicate with us. He wants us to hear His heart, know His nature, feel His love, and sense His guidance.

Don't take it from me, take it from Jesus:

> "My sheep listen to my voice; I know them, and they follow me." (John 10:27)

CHALLENGE

Open yourself up to hearing from God. Ask, "Father, what would you have me know?" Then, write down what you hear.

THE POWER OF SELF-PERMISSION

At his class reunion, a guy receives a directory with everyone's address and cell phone number, including that of Arlene, his high-school sweetheart. He doesn't think much of it.

A few years later, Arlene calls. "Hey, I've always felt we should've been together. My marriage is collapsing. Let's catch up!"

The guy loves his wife. He's deeply committed to Jesus. He says, "Arlene, I could only meet if your husband comes." She drops it.

One day, the guy's wife makes him feel deeply disrespected. Her words touch on his shame. In anger and hurt, he bikes away. He's riding, talking to himself, when he remembers Arlene and starts peddling toward her house. He is unsure what he will do when he gets there, but that's where he's headed.

This dude is about to sin. He hasn't inflicted damage on anyone . . . yet. But he's got himself a big-time fight.

When did his battle start? When he got mad? When he stormed out? When he remembered Arlene? Or when he peddled towards her?

I often quote, "Spiritual battles are won or lost at the threshold of the mind." John Lynch says the threshold is when we're hurt, wronged, bored, or ignored in such a way that we grant ourselves permission to do something wrong.

We turn sin into a reward, something we're entitled to. We think whatever we're about to do will make us feel better, but really, it'll make everything worse.

Lynch points to King David. David's sin didn't start when he saw Bathsheba bathing. It began when he didn't go to war. His sin and all that followed began when he gave himself permission to stay home.

QUESTION

Have you given yourself permission to do something you'll regret? Who has hurt you so badly that you feel entitled to sin in response?

THE POWER OF SELF-DISCLOSURE

We left our story with a guy peddling toward his high school girlfriend's house. Hurt by his wife, he's about to mess up. He's given himself permission to sin, deciding he's almost entitled to it.

Then he stops. He's in a battle. He's still mad, arguing internally about whether to turn around. He knows where he's heading is wrong, but as he revisits his wife's words, they sting him again.

He remembers his friend Randy. Randy knows *everything* about him. He calls and says, "Hey . . . I, uh . . . what's up?" Randy knows that something is wrong. The guy stammers, "Randy, I'm on my bike, heading to Arlene's." Randy knows about Arlene and the call a few years back. He says firmly, "Stay there, I'm coming." The guy interrupts. Exhales. "That's all right. I'm OK now. I'm heading home. Later." Disaster avoided with one call to the right friend.

Exposing his weakness and allowing light to shine into his life annihilated the power of darkness. The call to Randy didn't fix anything, but it took what was hidden and brought it out into the light. The power was gone. Instantly. Another John Lynch thought . . .

> "It's less important that anything ever gets fixed than that nothing ever gets hidden."

We need "Randys"–good men to stand with us. Men need spiritual safety and protective love. We need friends we can call who will think *more* of us for our weakness and vulnerability, not *less*.

Intimacy among guys correlates to what they'll confess. Confess to unpaid parking tickets, and you might as well just talk sports. Expose past sins, present temptations, and future fears, and you're headed to true intimate friendships.

CHALLENGE

Ask God to show you the men in your life with the highest potential for intimate friendship. Then reach out and begin the process of going deep.

JULY 11

WHY WE NEED GRACE

A young friend of mine made a major screwup, and now his marriage is devastated. He feels awful. He has a plan to never make the same mistake. He's begging for forgiveness. He is wearing God out on his knees, begging Him to protect him from the consequences of his stupid behavior.

Even though failure is a great teacher—we can "fail forward" and all that jazz—failure still stinks. It hurts. To both the people we let down and ourselves. It creates a scar that reminds us of the pain.

We can seek forgiveness, from God and others, and get it. But we still failed. We need grace. We've been forgiven; that's not the issue. It's grace we need.

Forgiveness is the quid pro quo. I ask for it, you give it. We're square.

But grace is this amazing thing that comes when the scales are put away, when we move beyond what's fair and volunteer to make it not matter. It's not a trade. It's restoration without a price, without penance.

QUESTION

**Who do you know who is in need of grace?
Is there someone on the downside of a screwup
who's beating himself to a bloody pulp right
now? Whether they wronged you or someone
else, is there a way to give them grace?**

THE QUESTION OF CALLING

When you don't understand something, find someone smarter than you and ask them for help. I've heard the word "calling" forever. I even read Os Guinness's classic book *The Call*. But I still didn't get it, at least not in a practical way.

Enter Andy Stanley. I heard him speak on the subject of calling, and what follows is my takeaway of what he said:

1. The value of a life is always measured in terms of how much of it was given away.

2. Whatever you accumulated is worthless the moment you die. We undermine the value of life by holding on to it.

3. I've never met a man who pursued a selfless second half of his life who would go back and trade it for golf.

4. We all think, "If I'm going to do something, I better do it now." We are aware that we're running out of time.

5. It's wise to start doing meaningful things while we still have enough time, energy, and health to do them.

6. A calling is more *meaningful* than *measurable*. What matters most is usually not measurable.

7. Our fear of not mattering *much* can drive us away from what matters *most*.

8. Calling is more about *burden* than *background*. It's less about what you know than seeing what needs to be done.

9. Burdens are emotional. What need bothers you? Sit in it. Let it bother you. God may be calling you to carry that burden and help those people.

10. Calling often begins as *partnering* rather than *pioneering*. Find some- one who's working on the problem and wade in with them. (But don't come in with guns blazing telling them how to do it better. Just help out and learn.)

11. Calling is always going to be more about *who* than *what*.

12. A way to test calling is this question: "If I don't do this, will it feel like I'm being disobedient?"

13. When you're in your calling, you measure success in a whole different way. At the end of the day, you say, "Today I did what You asked me to do." And that is enough.

14. John the Baptist, when he was pressed about who he was and what he was doing, said, "A person can receive only what is given them from heaven" (John 3:27). When God calls us into something, there's an abiding awareness of *who it's from* and *who it's for.*

15. My responsibility is to do what I'm called to do regardless of the outcomes.

We all want "the next thing." We seem to have a built-in restlessness that's looking for more. What if that's the fingerprint of God? He created a universe that continues to grow. Should it surprise us that He built into us a drive to reach up and out for meaning and purpose throughout our lives?

QUESTION

**What burden has your name on it? What
holds you back from moving toward it?**

CAN A SECULAR ENDEAVOR BE SPIRITUAL?

How can a secular job—dealing with inventory, code, contracts, deliveries, lawsuits, heart attacks, interns, HR—how can these jobs be spiritual? And how can the work of the senior pastor of a large church be anything other than spiritual? Here's how:

> A secular endeavor, approached from a spiritual perspective, is spiritual. A spiritual endeavor, approached from a secular perspective, is secular.

It's all about *motive*. It's about *why* you do what you do. If the business leader goes to work for spiritual purposes, his work is spiritual. If he works to bring glory to God by "doing his work heartily as to the Lord," it's spiritual. If he's passionately loving and serving people out of gratitude and obedience, then he's in the ministry, baby! And his work is spiritual.

If the senior pastor's motive is to keep up the growth, make the budget, raise the capital, expand the programs, and be famous for leading the great big church in town, then his work might be secular. And God may move far from it. And him.

God is about motive, about why. Science tries to explain how God created everything, but it has no answers to *why*.

Do you go to work to make money? To apply your gifts and abilities? To feel valuable?

Without a doubt.

But both you and your pastor get to choose every day: secular work or spiritual work? The challenge is in the true priorities of our heart.

QUESTION

If your workplace thoughts and actions could be put on an old-timey scale and weighed, which would weigh more: the spiritual or the secular?

LEARNING TO LOSE AND DROPPING THE ROPE

Both my wife and I have a hard time holding our tongues when something wrong is said. I speak, trying to explain the truth to her, and she does the same. It's on. And it's ugly.

Here's the stark reality: Your wife isn't going to change her mind. And you aren't going to change yours. So what do you do?

Drop the rope.

Imagine a tug-of-war. You're holding one end of the rope, and she's holding the other. As soon as you feel her tug, drop the rope. Let it go. Don't resist. The facts are still the same, but the emotional pressure never materializes. You simply refuse to tug back.

I'm not suggesting you turn this into the silent treatment. That's no good. And you can't be dishonest or disingenuous. Just drop the rope at the first tug and disarm the emotional grenade lying on the floor.

The people who win at tug-of-war go a step further. They pay attention to the other side and anticipate when the big tug is coming. If you pay attention to your wife, you can learn to see stuff coming and be ready to drop the rope before it's tugged. Better still, you can learn not to tug the rope yourself.

I'm not a psychologist. I'm just a business guy recovering from a serious case of defensiveness. Couple that with a critical spirit, and you've got a man who's very hard to be married to and get along with. I share this out of weakness.

As to the stuff you're in conflict over, the old saying, "Don't sweat the small stuff" is useful. What they forgot to say is, "It's all small stuff."

CHALLENGE

**Next time you feel tension building in
the conversation, try dropping the rope.**

JULY 15

IT'S NOT FAIR?

Sometimes you're going to feel the sting of unfairness; it happens to all of us.

Jesus knew we struggle with fairness, so in Matthew 20:1-16, He shared a cool story teaching us how to respond. Here's the setup.

Several groups were hired by a vineyard owner to help harvest grapes. The boss cut a separate deal with each group.

"I'll pay you a day's wage for a day's work," he said to the first group at 8:00 a.m. Fair enough. They went to work.

At 11:00 a.m., he hired another group, and he agreed to pay them a full day's wage, too, to work the balance of the day. Hmmm.

At 2:00 p.m., he hired yet another group to work the rest of the day, which was only a few hours. He agreed to pay them a full day's wage as well.

Believe it or not, he hired yet another group at 4:00 p.m., just an hour before quitting time, and he paid *them* a full day's wage to work just one hour!

When everyone saw the different amounts of work done for the same pay, they went postal.

"He's paying you *what*?"

"You got for half a day what I got for a *whole day*!"

"Those guys over there only worked an hour! They didn't even work through the noonday heat!"

You can imagine the outrage.

If you have the boss's perspective, it could make sense. He knew his labor requirements. Maybe the grapes would ruin if they stayed in the field another day, so he paid more as the day went on out of desperation. Maybe the workers who showed up later in the day were stronger, more experienced, and could pick more in the short time left in the day. Maybe the boss saw these workers in the town square and had pity on them because no one else hired them. Maybe he just wanted to give them a break. We don't know what was in his mind.

Jesus added another dimension to the boss's response. Maybe he's not to be questioned. It's his money. He owns the vineyard. He paid what he promised. So what's your beef?

My takeaway from this story?

1. God is the boss. We don't know everything He knows. If we believe that God is good and He loves us, we can relax, even when it doesn't look fair. The question is, "Will we trust Him?"

2. It makes us mad when He's more generous with someone else. Should it? Maybe it should make us proud to know Him, like we'd be proud if our earthly dad did something admirable. It's the opposite of jealousy.

3. When we get wrapped up in what someone else is getting, we forget about the generosity shown to us.

4. It's *all* His. He has all the votes. He is God; we're not. Learning to trust Him and accept what He puts in our hand—that's the ticket to contentment. Start questioning His fairness and we're judging God. Bad idea.

Don't get bogged down comparing yourself with everybody else. You don't know what God is up to in their lives, nor do you know what He's planning for yours.

Contentment is built on a foundation of gratitude and trust—gratitude for what we've been given and trust in Jehovah Jireh, "God, our provider."

CHALLENGE

Next time you get a hint that someone may be getting a little more than you, smile and relax knowing that the Boss loves you.

WHAT MAKES "FUN," FUN?

My daughter told me recently I'd become a little *intense*. (She's now out of the will!)

Part of it is age and maturity. When you're young, you think you're invincible. The older you get, the more you realize things *can* kill you. There is danger and risk. It's undeniable.

Another part is being *on purpose* all the time. Work demands intensity, and technology has scattered it into every corner of our existence.

But as a Jesus follower with eternal security, why should I let that happen? Isn't God in charge? Isn't He responsible for all the outcomes? What should I be afraid of? Why should any of us be intense or driven? We should be the happiest, most spontaneous laugh-until-you-cry people on the planet.

On a recent road trip with some dear friends, we decided to inspire ourselves to live a little lighter and have more fun. (You know there's a problem when you're developing evaluative criteria for fun!)

I can't find the word "fun" in the Bible, but the word "joy" is in there a lot. From what I've learned, joy is *in us* via the Holy Spirit; we just have to let it rise to the surface. We have to set aside our "stuff" long enough to let joy get loose in our hearts.

John Piper calls himself a Christian hedonist because he thinks God wants us to have more fun and enjoy our lives more than anything but Him.

Try to crank up the fun in your life. It won't happen without intentionality.

CHALLENGE

**Go have some fun! Set aside your to-do
list and to create a to-do-for-fun list.**

JULY 17

WILL YOU STOP FOR PEOPLE?

Recently, I met one of the coolest senior pastors, a Harley-riding mega-church pastor. With three services, nine church plants, and a growing staff, this man still makes time to be a radical mentor to two groups of younger men.

Within seconds of shaking hands, he asked me, "Who is the most important person in the world?"

I froze. Looked away. Mumbled. "The person you're with right now," he said.

He later explained to the Sunday crowd how Jesus stopped for people, and how we must, too.

Jesus stopped for the woman at the well, the centurion with the sick servant, the tax collector up in a tree, the lepers, the little children, and many more. Jesus stopped for people . . . faced them . . . loved them . . . no matter what.

I was tested on this twice recently. While driving home, I passed a lady with a flat tire. I drove back and offered to help. She nicely told me she'd rather wait for AAA.

A few days later, I was late for an appointment when I saw a lady stranded in an intersection. I'd have to U-turn twice to stop and help. Since I'd already held someone up for fifteen minutes, I drove on.

The difference in the two situations was how much time I perceived I had. Jesus *knew* how little time He had left. Yet He stopped.

I can talk all day about loving God, but if I don't focus on the person in front of me, I miss out on the chance to be Jesus to them. And to focus on them I have to stop.

I want to be a person who stops for people. Like Jesus.

QUESTION

Do you stop for people?

THERMOSTAT OR THERMOMETER?

Maturity happens when we learn to behave in an acceptable way. *Emotional maturity* is a little different. It's not directly connected to age or experience. I know a seventeen-year-old with incredible emotional maturity. And I know a fifty-seven-year-old who's an emotional child.

An emotionally mature person has self-control. They take responsibility for themselves. They consider not only what they're about to say, but how it's going to affect others.

I'm talking about controlling what you say and do rather than letting emotions control you. This means not taking things personally.

Most of the time, what "sets me off" wasn't meant *personally*, I just took it that way. I started a fight, all because I thought I was attacked.

This isn't about detaching. We were made to feel things. Buddhists say, "Not flattered by praise, not hurt by blame." That's detachment, not emotional maturity.

I'm talking about being a *thermostat* instead of a *thermometer*.

A thermometer *reacts* to the environment it's in. Hot temp instantly reads hot. Cold air drops the thermometer. But a thermostat *responds*. It sets the climate. It reads the thermometer and *manages its reaction*.

A husband who becomes a thermostat becomes comfortable with himself and his wife. And a dad who stops reacting and starts responding will raise kids who are more confident, less on edge, and more loving.

When we rest in the fact that God loves us, we can relax instead of getting worked up. Stop reacting. Start responding.

It's up to us, men, to establish and maintain a safe, comfortable climate in our homes. Step up and lead. Be a thermostat.

QUESTION

Are you a thermostat or a thermometer?

HOW LONG SHOULD YOU PRAY?

Prayer is a mystery. How does it work? Does God change His mind? I know He hears me, but can I hear Him?

There are lots of helpful resources that teach me *how* to pray. But how *long* should I pray? Am I hurting God's feelings if I only pray for five minutes? Am I more Christian if I pray for hours?

I believe a big part of prayer is about conforming our will to God's will. Since God knows what we need before we ask, He uses prayer to infuse peace and faith into our souls. As we pray, God slips little doses of faith, trust, and hope into our lifeblood. Sometimes it takes a while, especially when we really want a certain outcome.

But if we've emptied our ambition and are ready to trust Him with the outcome, we can be done praying. In Matthew 6:7, Jesus even cautioned about babbling on, saying, "When you pray, do not keep on babbling like pagans, for they think they will be heard because of their many words."

Prayer is God's idea. He gives us the urge to pray; it's not a natural human behavior. And just like He pings us to pray, He lets us know when it's OK to get up off our knees and go do something.

Don't get me wrong, there's time when we need to keep praying. When our son was clinging to life after his wreck, we wore God out for twenty-four hours.

But most days, praying until I've handed my burdens to my omnipotent Father is long enough.

QUESTION

How about you? How do you know when you've prayed long enough?

THE FOUR C'S OF PARENTING

It's not even funny how unprepared I was to be a dad. There should be a law against having a child when you are that clueless.

My son arrived, and I cried. My daughter was born, and I cried again. I cried at their baptisms, their graduations, their weddings, and at the birth of their children.

A few years ago, a friend shared something that put it all in perspective.

He told me about the four C's of parenting.

You start out doing nothing but *caring* for a child. He's fully reliant on you because he can't do anything on his own.

As soon as he learns to move, roll, crawl, and walk, you move into *control* mode. You have to *control* him to protect him.

When control becomes crucial, care decreases. Before you know it, he's pretty independent, feeding himself and changing his own diaper (just kidding!). Your care becomes more economic and logistic.

You soon find yourself coaching them on life, giving them *counsel* and pointing them to the best choices.

Eventually, you start to become friends–*companions*. You're not their buddy; buddies go along with bad ideas. Friends are companions; they hang out. They do life together. I love this definition of a companion: "One that is closely connected with something similar."

Ultimately, the day comes when, if you've done the four C's well, they'll come back and *care for you*. The cycle is complete.

QUESTION

Are you fully present with your kids? If you continue on the path you're on as a dad, will your kid come back and care for you?

THE GOOD, FAST, OR CHEAP TEST

One of my first mentors, Pat MacMillan, taught me this simple test almost 30 years ago: Good, fast, or cheap? You can have two, but you can't have all three.

If what you want is good and you can get it fast, then it won't be cheap. If it's good and cheap, you probably won't get it fast. And if it's cheap and fast, then it's probably not going to be good.

Most of the decisions we live to regret were made *fast*. One of the big seven sins comes with "feet that are quick to rush into evil" (Proverbs 6:18). When we don't have time to do things right, we usually have to find time to do them over.

Looking for *cheap* can also lead us to doing things over. "The bitter taste of poor quality lingers long after the sweetness of low price is gone." Vendors need to make a profit, but they can't just cut corners to do it.

But *good* is different. Good implies quality, excellence, and integrity. It means something will work as advertised.

Why does this simple test matter? We are stewards of the time and resources God gives us, whether it's our family finances, our daily schedule, or our team at work. We're responsible for making good decisions, and this little test can help us make wise decisions.

Maybe it helps to put the three in priority order

> **Good:** non-negotiable.
> **Fast:** as fast as possible, so long as it's still good.
> **Cheap:** best price I can get for the good thing I need when I have to have it.

Be wise.

SCRIPTURE

"Wisdom is a shelter as money is a shelter, but the advantage of knowledge is this: Wisdom preserves those who have it." (Ecclesiastes 7:12)

PARKINSON'S LAW AND OUR AVAILABLE TIME

In 1957, Northcote Parkinson coined the following phrase:

"Work expands to fill the available time."

Nobody wants to admit it, but I believe it's mostly true. If a thing must be done within a certain time frame, I usually find a way to get it done. If I have no deadline, it takes longer.

There are exceptions. Creative work can't be rushed; it's going to take as long as it takes. Relationship work, like building trust, can't be programmed or scheduled.

But generally, it'll take more time to do a task if we have two hours available instead of one. We work more slowly and carefully. We're easier to interrupt.

We deal with the other side of Parkinson's Law more often. How can we get ten hours of work into an eight-hour day?

Pick work you're good at and love to do, work that's important to you, the organization, and to others. Turn Parkinson's Law around. Tell yourself, "This task deserves my best. I'm going to be grandiose in allocating time to it."

Put less important projects on hold. If you finish early, go back over what you did to see where you can improve. Get input. Delegate things that don't add as much value.

On the "available time" question, deadlines are the deal. Most of our stress comes from self-induced time pressure. Negotiate longer lead times. If you're setting them, cut yourself some slack. If you work for someone, set realistic expectations.

Yes, there are jobs where none of this applies and times in every job where you have to hunker down. Parkinson's Law represents a tension existing wherever there's work to be done.

CHALLENGE

You now know Parkinson's Law. So decide to feed what matters and starve everything else.

YOU ONLY GET ONE CHANCE TO START

There are high consequences to our beginnings. We form habits quickly, some say in three weeks or less. The life habits formed early in marriage, the study habits formed as freshmen, the first impressions made in new jobs or neighborhoods, are huge.

First impressions are decided in the first twenty seconds of face-to-face contact, and a negative first impression requires nine hours of interaction to reframe.

Starting deserves our best efforts and our focused attention. You can't steer a parked car. There has to be movement. You have to start in order for anything to happen.

God shows up when you start.

I believe God's blessing waits on the other side of surrender. The quicker you cast off the lines and sail out of port, the sooner you'll see His hand. When you make your plans, do your best preparation, get the right people on the bus with you, and get started, God will show up, if you've surrendered the whole deal to Him. That doesn't guarantee success, but it guarantees you won't be alone.

To those who are waiting to start, here's the only poem I can quote by heart:

> "On the Plains of Hesitation bleach the bones of countless millions who, at the Door of victory, sat down to wait, and waiting—died!"

QUESTION

**What have you been thinking about starting
but haven't? Is now your one chance to start?**

DO YOU HAVE WHAT IT TAKES?

My psych professor said normal people have medium self-esteem. Everybody else is either too high or too low. Normal people say, "I'm gonna give it a shot. If I make it, great. If I don't, I'm okay."

Key words: *"I'm okay."*

Knowing you're okay is the target. Make a list of people you know who are truly okay–totally comfortable in their own skin. It's a short list.

Our self-esteem usually starts with the first person we admire. How they respond to us helps create the voice our souls listen to every day. The voice says, "You're okay." Or not.

For my generation, this person was Daddy. I so wanted him to like me. To think I was smart. Competent. Funny. To think I had what it takes.

He didn't. Or if he did, he didn't say it for fear he would "spoil me."

As a result, I spent years trying to prove I had what it takes.

But at age thirty-three, in a ten-minute conversation with my Heavenly Father, all that changed. It took minutes, not hours, or months, or years. It took surrender.

I relaxed for the first time I can remember. Instantly, I cared less about what everyone else thought and cared most about what God thought.

Did I have what it takes? No more than I did ten minutes before.

But I had peace for the first time in my life. I was loved. I measured up. And so do you. Why? We measure up because He stands in for us. And He's perfect.

QUESTION

Do you *truly believe* that you measure up?

CLEAN CONVICTION

Watching the news, I saw a criminal being convicted. The judge called him shameful, subhuman, and despicable, among other things.

He probably deserved it, but the impact of those words struck me. The crook was weeping, head hung as low as it could go.

I couldn't help but think how we're alike. Sure, my sins are different. To society, I'm fine. But to God, me and that guy are both sinners. We've both been convicted.

God's conviction is clean and specific. He never berates me when He convicts me, because I am a new creation in Christ. As a believer, I was forgiven at the Cross, so asking for forgiveness is asking for something I've already been given.

But there are steps beyond that, for our good and the good of the Kingdom. First, gratitude. Then, confession. Admitting our failure to God is important.

Guilt and conviction are different. Conviction helps us, calls us to account, and grows us. Guilt brings us down, makes us question who we are, and keeps us from receiving God's forgiveness and moving on.

Jesus died to remove our guilt and shame. His desire is that we gratefully accept His conviction. Then confess, repent, make restitution, and move on in love to do good deeds. Guilt paralyzes; conviction motivates and empowers.

Conviction is God's way of keeping us on track. It's for our good and His glory.

PRAYER

Lord I want to walk with You. You came and took all my guilt and shame so that I could live free. Speak conviction loudly into my spirit, and give me the courage to act . . . to believe when You assure me of Your 100 percent love and forgiveness . . . even for the things I've failed at today. Amen.

THE FOMO EPIDEMIC

FOMO is everywhere. The fear of missing out.

Men buying the next new thing, be it golf clubs or TVs. We've got to get the new one, the big one, the more feature-rich one because we're afraid of missing out.

Women are on Instagram, looking at pictures of their friends on expensive trips to exotic places. "We've gotta go next year! We just can't miss out on that next time!"

Where did it come from?

Adam was the first carrier of the FOMO virus. He stood there in paradise with everything a man could ask for. But then FOMO showed up.

Chomp! Infected. And it's been passed down in our genes ever since.

God has a different idea.

Maybe God would have us *want* differently because He knows what *satisfies*. He knows what fulfills, and His will is that we love and serve people, not things. After all, people are His most valued creation. We are made in His image and built for eternity. He even sent His only son to die for people.

What if hanging out with God, doing His work of loving and serving people is the only way FOMO is satiated?

QUESTION

Do you suffer from FOMO?

THE CURE FOR FOMO

So, how can I get rid of FOMO? How can I rid my kids of it and remove it from my family?

Here's a five-course treatment plan for FOMO:

1. **Simplify**—Make your life consist of fewer things. Fewer people, fewer possessions, fewer activities. Maximizing is human nature, but there will be fewer things to miss out on if you're focused on fewer things.

2. **Commit**—Make commitments to the things you keep in your life. When you commit to something, you're less likely to pick it apart and find everything wrong with it. Commit to your wife, your church, your house—all these commitments lead to reduced FOMO.

3. **Purpose**—When you discover your unique purpose for being here, it's easier to relax. You can maximize being who you are and spend less time dreaming about what you're missing out on by not being somebody else.

4. **Faith**—Trust God with the outcome of everything. Do what you can do —the next right thing— and then relax in your faith. God is in the outcomes business. We should be in the obedience business. We don't know what He's going to do in a specific situation, but we know He loves us, and that offers a quiet confidence that it'll turn out OK.

5. **Pace**—With fewer things to focus on, I live my days at a better pace. If I engage with just a few things I'm really committed to, things connecting with my purpose in being here, I'll have more peace, more time with God, and more margin in my life.

Do this and FOMO . . .

. . . will be no mo'.

QUESTION

Will you take on FOMO in your family?

TO HAVE A FRIEND . . .

I've heard the aphorism, "To have a friend you have to be one," all my life. Now I find it's not true.

It's right up there with, "God helps those who help themselves."

I learned the deeper truth from my friend John, who says, "To have a friend, you have to express your need."

That's a little deeper. It encourages me to humble myself by telling my friend I need something. I have to admit weakness.

We know God loves those who are humble and hates pride. Pride repels help. Pride says, "I can make it on my own." "Yeah, it's a problem but I'll handle it." "I'll get by." "It's *my* problem." Pride sounds downright American, doesn't it?

Someone recently challenged me to talk to Jesus like I talk to my best friend. When I talk to my friend, I tell him my needs. He listens to me. I trust his response. He takes on some of my needs and empathizes with me on others.

So that's the way I'm talking to God now— like my best friend. I'm telling Him my needs. I know He's listening. He'll hear them all, He'll take on some, but He'll empathize with them all.

And I'm listening intently for His Words of wisdom and guidance. I know He won't press His ideas on me, but I also know He cares and that He's there for me.

I love my friend Jesus. I'm thinking about Him even when I'm not talking to Him. I'm telling people about how great He is and what an important role He plays in my life. He's at the center of it all.

After all, He saved my life.

QUESTION

Do you talk to Jesus the way you talk to your best friend?

WILL YOU SING?

Years ago, I met Jan Smith, Justin Bieber's mentor and vocal coach. Jan said something that's riveted to my brain:

"Music gets access to your soul *without* your permission."

I think she spoke profound truth.

Think how a little ditty gets stuck in your noggin and plays over and over. That song is penetrating your soul without you knowing it.

Like most things, this can be bad or good. The tunes I latched onto as a kid, like "Double Shot (Of My Baby's Love)" and "(I Can't Get No) Satisfaction" didn't do a lot to build my character.

But good songs can be really good, even better than good.

Before C.S. Lewis came to faith, one of his obstacles was his perception that the God of the Psalms had a constant demand for praise, that He desired "our worship like a vain woman who wants compliments."

Later on, after God captured his heart, Lewis wrote:

"I think we delight to praise what we enjoy because the joy is not complete until it is expressed. It is not out of compliment that lovers keep on telling one another how beautiful they are. The delight is incomplete until it is expressed."

When you go to church on Sunday, *sing*.

As soon as you read this, *sing*.

All day today, *sing*.

Will you humble yourself and sing *out loud* to our amazing God?

SCRIPTURE

"Come, let us sing for joy to the Lord; let us shout aloud to the Rock of our salvation. Let us come before him with thanksgiving and extol him with music and song." (Psalm 95:1-2)

WHAT'S BEYOND SURRENDER?

Surrender.

The word comes from Old French and dates back to the 1400s. It first meant "to give (something) over" or "give back." A hundred years later, it started being used in a military sense, like a prisoner might "give himself up."

When we think about surrender, we picture tattered, bloodied, wornout soldiers in war movies. Surrender is never their idea. It's always after something bad happens. Maybe one of the reasons it's hard for us to "surrender our lives to Christ" is because of these pictures.

Maybe we should go back to the original use of the word—to "give yourself over."

When we surrender to God, we're not surrendering to the enemy. We're "giving ourselves back" to the One who created us in the first place.

But what happens after surrender? After we give over specific issues and situations?

When we surrender to an all-powerful, all-knowing, all-loving, all-good God, whatever comes our way is for our good. And when we see things from the long view, as God sees it, we can say, "Thank You," and keep going.

Years ago, I was diagnosed with interstitial lung disease. I surrendered it to God from the get-go. Last week, I finally thanked Him for it.

Don't get me wrong. I'm no martyr. I was sitting with a friend who has all kinds of family issues, and that still small voice said to me, "Thank Me for your lung disease." I thought about it until I got home, and then I just did it.

Thanking God for what we've surrendered before we know the outcome requires faith only He can provide—faith in a God we know is good no matter what happens.

QUESTION

**Is there something you've surrendered
that He wants you to thank Him for?**

JULY 31

YOU HAVE TO GIVE IT UP . . .

Maybe the most amazing thing about my life since I surrendered to Christ is how so many of the things I wanted have come my way unexpectedly. Let me explain.

After the first couple of years of marriage, I thought I'd married an unaffectionate woman. I didn't handle it well. But after I ran out of gas and surrendered myself to Christ, I started giving these desires up to Him.

A few years later, we were riding down the road and I noticed my wife's hand on my knee. I suddenly realized, she's become more affectionate! How could this be?

The same kind of thing happened with business.

I left AT&T to start a company and had no clients. Things were moving slowly when I felt led to make a big donation to our start-up church. I knew it was right, but it was scary. Within days of writing the check, someone visited my office and became my first client. A few days later, I got a call out of the blue that led to a big six-month contract.

I learned something about my Heavenly Father. Whatever I give up to Him, He seems to enjoy giving back to me, but more. Is it like a loving Father to take five from your hands and give you back three?

No!

Isn't it more like Him to take five and give you back seven? Or eight?

Visualize your clinched fist. How can God put anything into a hand that's clinched tight?

Open your hand. Turn your palms up. Give God the thing you want. The thing you're holding on to. Ask Him to give back not what you want, but what you need.

QUESTION

**What are you holding on to that's keeping
God from being able to give it back?**

ARE YOU GIVING 100 PERCENT?

I was in a conversation with someone about tithing, about how the concept is "so Old Testament" and not really found in the New. The guy I was talking to asked a question. I thought it was going to be one of those trick Bible questions like, "Can a donkey talk?" (See Numbers 22:28 if you're curious.)

He said, "The New Testament model for tithing is 100 percent. Wanna know how I know?"

"Of course," I said, a little skeptical.

"Look at Luke 21:4: 'All these people gave their gifts out of their wealth; but she out of her poverty put in all she had to live on.' Jesus affirmed 100 percent giving."

A little extreme? Yes. But just like His Kingdom had boundaries far beyond geographic lines on a map, His concept of giving did, too.

We're always talking about what happens when you go all-in for Jesus, when you move from believer, to follower, to disciple maker. You have a peace that surpasses understanding. You feel loved. Protected. Purposeful. Provided for no matter what.

The same pathway applies to giving. We go from, "It's all mine" to, "I'll give God a tithe," to, "I'll give God all of it." That's the 100 percent tithe my friend was talking about.

Only when we give it all to God, acknowledging His ownership of 100 percent of our money, can we experience the peace that comes from being under His protection. I'm the steward of what He gives me, but it's all His.

So, the question is, "Will you go 100 percent for Him?" He's already gone 100 percent for you and me.

QUESTION

**Will you trust Him with 10 percent
or 100 percent?**

THE WHY OF LIFE PURPOSE STATEMENTS

After reading *The Purpose Driven Life* by Rick Warren, I thought a lot about my life purpose. I created my own purpose statement.

> I, Regi Campbell, exist to glorify God as I love, serve, and challenge others to be all they can be and give all of themselves to Jesus Christ.

And that was it for a long, long time.

After a while, I realized I'd been emphasizing the wrong word. I'd become a self-appointed expert in *challenge* and neglected the *love and serve* part. I've been working on that ever since.

Like most good things, this whole idea of purpose started with Jesus. His purpose is stated in John 10:10: "I have come that they may have life, and have it to the full."

Jesus' life, death, and resurrection give us eternal life. What He taught, energized in us by the Holy Spirit, gives us meaningful lives *now* if we make our lives about serving others.

Easier to say than to do.

God cares about our motives, our hearts, *why* we do what we do. But when our *why* is about Him, He's in it with us. When our *why* is to make money or a name for ourselves, it's about us, and God isn't in it.

If you go to work to get what *you* want, you're living for you. But when you start with what *He wants,* your purpose bends toward glorifying Him instead of you. And you'll see over and over that what He wants is for you to love and serve people—His highest and best creation, made in His image. What He bled and died for.

CHALLENGE

Take a crack at writing a life purpose statement for yourself.

August 3

IS THE TASK YOUR BOSS . . . OR IS GOD?

I keep finding myself wrapped around the axle, bound up in the tension between getting stuff done and living a peaceful life. It doesn't matter what I'm working on—the task becomes the boss, and I'm consumed by it. The result is the same every time. I go and go and wind up tired and sad.

Then God . . .

Isn't that what it says a lot in Scripture? "Then God . . ."

Then God starts to show up. Starts to burden me. Starts to whisper. Starts to convict.

It's not that I've been doing bad stuff. Not at all.

It's that He wants me to have some company. He wants to be a part, not when it's finished or in trouble, but while it's going on. While I'm in it. Even before I start.

You see, the part I keep forgetting is inviting Him in at the beginning. I keep assuming I know what He wants me to do. It's not hard to figure out what He *doesn't* want me to do. But what *does* He want me to do?

A disciple of Jesus is a *learner* and *follower*. I learn when I obey. He knows where He's going, where He's working, who He's engaged with. If I go where He tells me, engage with who and what He points me too, He'll be working. But if I don't ask Him for direction, I can miss these divine appointments.

I can't be the hands and feet of Christ if my feet are always running and my hands are always full of things, to-do lists, and calendars He's not involved in. And neither can you.

Let's let God be our boss instead of our to-do list.

QUESTION

Are you setting your daily agenda or is God?

AUGUST 4

WHY IS LISTENING TO GOD SO HARD?

The other morning, I rushed into my time with God. I said a few words of praise, gave a blanket confession for anything I'd screwed up, and then prayed the trusty phase God often responds to. I used the words Eli gave Samuel when he figured out God was speaking:

"Speak, Your servant is listening."

Crickets. I glanced at the clock and prayed my other tried and true phrase:

"Jesus, what would You have me do today?"

Clear as a bell, here's what came into my mind:

"Regi, if you think you're going to rush in here, repeat your rote words, and expect Me to speak to you on cue, that's not happening. I love you more than that. I want a relationship. No magic words. I want a conversation."

I smiled. I was embarrassed, but I felt so, so loved. My perfect Father was giving me a clear rebuke. I so respect Him, the way He's my friend and my Father at the same time.

There are times when I hear nothing, no matter what I say or do. When that happens, I know it's me. Usually it's because I'm in a hurry. I'll say, "God, I love You. I'm depending on You today," and I'll move on.

Other times, if I wait and stay quiet long enough, He'll speak. "I love you, Regi," comes quietly into my mind. No matter what I wanted an answer to or how anxious I might have been over something, having the Creator of the universe say He loves me is enough.

QUESTION

Will you give God the time to speak?

INTENTIONALITY LEADS TO ISOLATION

People tell me I'm one of the most intentional people they know. I even own the domain *intentionality.org*. I'm not kidding about being on purpose and intentional.

But a couple of years ago, I found a downside to intentionality. I realized I had lots of acquaintances, but few real friends.

I discovered this on a retreat with some guys. They skewered me. They told me they felt I was too busy to be a real friend. When I flew by their lives, it felt more like I was trying to *fix* them than be *with* them. I was spending virtually all my time getting to know people, but I was unknown. At a deep, personal level, I was friendless.

The lesson?

Over time, intentionality leads to isolation.

It's the opposite of God's will for us to be isolated. One of the reasons He sacrificed His Son was so we'd never be isolated.

So I shifted gears.

I haven't stopped being intentional. Instead, I've begun to be as intentional about friendships as I am about everything else. God, in His awesome grace and provision, is teaching me how to love others *and* how to let them love me back.

Listen, guys *desperately* want authentic friendship. But someone has to initiate. And that someone has to be you. Granted, it's awkward. Maybe even a little weird at first. But when you put in enough "road miles" with a few guys, when you have enough hours of honest conversation, you'll realize you're in a safe place. A place where you're known and loved.

And you're no longer isolated.

QUESTION

Are there a few guys who *really* know you?
Who will call you out if they have to? Who
know your weaknesses but love you anyway?

THE AMAZING POWER OF APOLOGY

My daughter-in-law taught me something big.

She said, "If you find yourself rehearsing a conversation in your head, there's a conversation you need to have in real-time." Brilliant.

There was one particular guy who had a big hand in my leaving AT&T. He went off on me in an important meeting with our new boss. I left the company a few months later, but what happened in that meeting played over and over in my mind.

Almost two years later, I'd started my own company and was doing great. But I would find myself replaying the tape of that meeting and becoming angry.

I prayed. I said, "Lord, what would You have me do about this deal?"

Clear as a bell, these words came into my head: "Regi, you can be sure he's not sitting somewhere grinding over *you* right now." Bing! A light came on. The guy *had* me, but God wanted me free.

In that moment, I said out loud, "Boyd, I forgive you."

A few weeks later, I decided to call him and ask him to lunch. It was awkward. But after a quiet lunch and endless small talk, he offered up what was as close to an apology as you can get. Interestingly, I got a much bigger rush when I forgave him in the car than when he apologized to me face-to-face. Go figure.

But I learned something important.

When you're rehearsing a conversation with someone or rehashing one from a while back, *act!* Do something. Start by talking to God. Then do what He says.

QUESTION

**Are you rehearsing a conversation in your head?
Is there someone you're crossways with? Whom
do you need to forgive? Go see? Apologize to?**

AUGUST 7

WATCH ONE, DO ONE, TEACH ONE

My daughter did a photography workshop with some famous guy. He hired models, set up his shots, and took pictures. Then he had his mentees photograph the same subjects, critiquing what they did. They did it again. And then again.

A couple days later, she saw me taking a picture of my granddaughter. She stopped me and taught me a whole different way to take the picture. A better way.

Watch one, do one, teach one.

It's what Jesus did. In the beginning, He told His guys to follow Him: "Learn from me, for I am gentle and humble in heart" (Matthew 11:29). They learned by watching what He did and said.

Then Jesus moved to the *do one* stage. He started giving the apostles assignments. He gave direct feedback. Sometimes He encouraged. Sometimes He criticized. He loved them, and they knew it. He'd earned a voice into their lives because He lived a life they admired. A life they wanted to emulate.

Isn't this how we should operate?

Watch one means living a reflective life, objectively examining your life and learning as you go. Reading. Listening. Praying. Being a learner and follower of Jesus, getting to know God's ways and God's voice. You *do one* as you live your life, applying what you've learned, making new and different mistakes.

But the point here is the *teach one* piece—getting outside your comfort zone and sharing what you've learned with others. Having the courage to be vulnerable, available, and intentional with someone who can learn from you.

Jesus did it, and so should we.

QUESTION

If you're mature and you've been walking with the Lord for a while, you've got a lot to give. Are you *teaching one*? What holds you back?

HAPPINESS OR JOY?

One day I had a conversation with my wife about the future. She said she wanted more joy in her life. That sounded pretty good to me, so I started planning. What can we do that brings more joy? Where can we go? What projects can we take on? Yada. Yada.

I asked her, "What does joy look like to you?"

She said, "It looks like this very moment. This place. These sounds. The fresh air we're breathing. Think how God has blessed us. The joy of the Lord is right now!" She knew where I was going. She reeled me back in.

Joy isn't something you get, it's something you *receive*.

Joy isn't the same as happiness. The word *happy* comes from the root *hap*, the same root as "haphazard." Happiness is spurious. Situational. Circumstantial to a degree.

But joy . . . the joy of the Lord is there all the time. Joy isn't dependent on circumstances; it's intimately connected with God's love. We just have to step into it. Acknowledge it. Receive it.

Paul says this in 1 Thessalonians 1:6: "You became imitators of us and of the Lord, for you welcomed the message in the midst of severe suffering with the joy given by the Holy Spirit."

The Holy Spirit is the presence of God right here, right now. That's where joy comes from. When we recognize His presence, we find ourselves right in the middle of an outbreak of joy.

Just like my wife, I want more joy. But it's not happening with a check box on my to-do list. It takes putting the to-dos aside in favor of stillness, solitude, and being in the moment.

That's where joy hangs out.

QUESTION

When is the last time you experienced the joy of the Lord?

NAME IT TO EVADE IT

Here's a question: Why does AA work when counselors, pills, electric shock, and countless other things don't?

AA starts by calling it what it is. "I'm Joe, and I'm an alcoholic." "I'm Sam, and I'm addicted to sex." "I'm Larry, and I'm addicted to prescription drugs." Then comes calling on a higher power for help. It's like a huge one-two punch against addiction.

There is amazing power in naming the sin that owns you. Sometimes those sins are obvious, but sometimes they aren't. Many of us are owned by sins that we fail to name—things like fear, greed, anger, jealousy, adultery, selfishness, dishonesty, and dissention.

What I'm suggesting is that we call these beasts by their names. Just name them.

We know Jesus did this at least once. After He told of His upcoming murder and resurrection, in Matthew 16, Peter said, "Never, Lord! This shall never happen to you!" Instead of replying to Peter, Jesus spoke directly to *sin*, to the enemy who was trying to move Him off mission. He said, "Get behind me, Satan! You are a stumbling block to me; you do not have in mind the things of God, but merely human concerns."

What if we did the same thing? What if we said, "Get behind me (fill in your blank). You are a stumbling block to me."

Maybe by naming them, we can evade them.

And what about the things of God? Peace, love, joy, patience, kindness goodness, faithfulness, gentleness, self-control?

I bet if we call Jesus' name, we can be filled with them.

QUESTION

**Is there something the evil one is using to
bring you down? Will you name it to evade it?**

A DAILY PRAYER

I'm not a big fan of scripted prayers, but this one is powerful:

Heavenly Father,

I recognize that my primary struggle today will not be against flesh and blood. I know there is more to this life than meets the eye.

Give me the strength to stand my ground against this world. Enable me to recognize its twisted values and perspectives.

Today, I choose to stand firm with the belt of truth buckled around my waist. Bring to mind what is true when confronted with the lies that permeate this world. As I open Your Word, renew my mind to what is true.

I put on the breastplate of righteousness. Thank you for giving me a righteous standing with You. Give me the wisdom to know what's right and the courage to do what's right.

I put on the shoes of readiness. Lead me to those who have not yet accepted your offer of salvation. Give me boldness and sensitivity as I represent You to others.

I take up the shield of faith, which has the power to help me stand against temptation, rejection, doubt, and fear. On the cross, Christ overcame the power of sin on my behalf, and His resurrection took away the basis for all my doubt and fear.

I put on the helmet of salvation. My salvation is a reminder of all You have done and will do in me. It is a reminder of who I am and to Whom I belong.

Lastly, I take up the sword of the Spirit, which is Your Word. Through Your Word, bring my ways in line with Your ways and my thoughts in line with Your thoughts.

In the beautiful name of Jesus,

Amen

CHALLENGE

Pray this prayer every day for a week.

10 TAKEAWAYS ON INTEGRITY

I was put in front of some young men and asked questions about integrity. These guys were trying to learn how to make good decisions as husbands, fathers, and leaders.

I figured I'd empty my bucket. So here is my "Top 10" on integrity:

1. A lie accompanies every sin.

2. People usually know when you're lying.

3. Sooner or later, everybody knows everything.

4. "What you do speaks so loud that I cannot hear what you say." –Ralph Waldo Emerson

5. We feel good about ourselves when we do the right thing.

6. Telling the absolute truth simplifies our lives.

7. One of the most powerful things you can say is, "I don't know."

8. When there's an argument in your head, truth is often at stake.

9. Silent lies are some of the most dangerous.

10. Being truthful doesn't mean being boorish and mean.

Being a truth teller brings truth tellers into your world. And when you take the moral high ground and stand in truth, you'll find others are straight up with you. Even if they don't raise their game, they'll remember your honesty. And they'll respect you for it.

How can a man be consistently honest in a culture filled with dishonesty? By trusting God with outcomes. All of them. We do the right thing, but He's responsible for how it all turns out. He loves us, He'll take care of us, *and* we'll sleep well at night.

QUESTION

Are you around a lot of dishonesty?
What's it like to stand apart from it?

WHAT ARE YOU TEACHING ME, LORD?

"What are you teaching me, Lord?" is one of the best questions ever. It's more likely to jump into my head when something bad happens, especially if it's not my fault.

If a Christ follower who's grounded in the Bible has the presence of mind to ask this question, God will usually let him know what He needs to learn.

In the Christian world, there are two kinds of people. One has a little bit of Bible knowledge. They think they know enough, so they've stopped trying to understand more; it's just too hard and confusing.

The other reads and studies the Bible constantly. It's as much a part of their life as language or numbers. God's truth is ingrained in their values and thinking.

The Bible explains who God is, why we're here, where we're going, and what the future is going to be like. Its worldview creates a framework for our thinking, acting, and responding.

Reading and learning the Bible is the only way to get to the place where you kind of know what God would have you do without even asking. Only with an understanding of His Word will you be able to ask, "God, what are you teaching me here?" and get an answer that makes sense.

But God's way isn't usually the easy way. And His way of helping us walk in the Spirit is more like diet and exercise. It can't be faked, substituted for, or imagined in our minds.

It takes work. It takes Bible reading and study, memorization, listening to good Bible teachers, and reading "books about the Book," written by smart people who have spent years walking with God.

But it can start when you read your Bible and ask, "What are You teaching me, Lord?"

QUESTION

Will you start today?

ARE YOU CALM IN A STORM?

Jesus is the perfect role model when it comes to remaining calm in the storm.

In Gethsemane (Luke 22:47-53), Jesus is identified to His killers by one of His own *with a kiss*! Talk about irony. His followers rally to defend Him, and He calmly holds them back and performs a miracle, healing the severed ear of a soldier.

Then there's the time in the boat during a storm (Mark 4:36-40). Jesus is *sleeping* in the back while an intense storm is raging, a storm so intense His disciples—experienced sailors—fear for their lives. They wake Him up and He stills the storm with a word.

And the ultimate calm. Jesus is hanging on the cross (Matthew 27:34-44) in excruciating pain when one of His executioners dares Him to come down to save Himself, even mocks Him. Jesus had raised people from the dead. It would have been short work for Him to drop those soldiers dead and set Himself free. The holes in His hands and feet would have healed just like the soldier's ear the night before. Yet Jesus utters not a word.

So, what can we learn from Jesus?

Jesus knew that the *outcome*—the end result—would be all right.

And Jesus knew God was with Him and He was not alone.

Knowing He loves us so much, knowing the outcome is going to be all right and the situation is under His control, gives us the confidence we need to be calm in the midst of the storm.

QUESTION

What habits have you developed to help you keep calm in the storm? If you don't have any, take some time, talk to some people, and make sure you have a few strategies at the ready.

WHY INTENTIONALITY MATTERS

We're all intentional. It's in our nature. Intentionality drives our survival, our careers, our families, and our fun. It's not a question of whether we will be intentional, but what we'll be intentional about.

Many of us are intentional about our spiritual progress.

But will we be intentional for the spiritual progress of *others*? Think about the people in your life. Whom has God put on your heart? Given you a burden for?

Make a list of those people. It might be one or two. It could be ten or twelve. Just write down their names. No one is going to see your list. This is between you and God.

Now ask God to help you guess where they are spiritually. Then begin praying for each person. Be specific. Pray that God will move them one step closer to Him. Pray that He will use you or someone else to point them to Jesus.

The night I finally surrendered to Jesus, I thought it was just me and God, alone in the backyard under the stars. But much to my surprise, my friend's wife Delaine had been praying for me regularly for eight years. She was intentional about praying for my spiritual progress—for my salvation.

I had no idea, but I'm forever grateful she made the decision to intentionally invest in the spiritual progress of others.

We are all called to do the same thing. So look at your list and start praying. Change could take days or it could take years. Doesn't matter. Just pray.

QUESTION

**Will you be *intentional* about the
spiritual condition of others?**

"THE CHURCH IS FULL OF HYPOCRITES."

Almost every person I've met who is outside the faith has been turned off by the hypocrisy of a church person. They'd rather be authentically lost than inauthentically saved. This view shows they don't really understand grace or salvation through faith, but that doesn't matter. At least to them. Not right now.

Webster's says a hypocrite is "a person who puts on a false appearance of virtue or religion."

Jesus is the easiest to explain. He's perfect. "Full of grace and truth." There was "no error in Him."

The church hasn't been quite so pure because fallen men are involved. Men trying to do good things for God. Men with egos and a desire for power, comfort, and control. Men seeking the affirmation of God and other men.

But the hypocrites in the church, these are the hardest to explain to an outsider. Webster's second definition of a hypocrite is "a person who acts in contradiction to his or her stated beliefs or feelings." They believe in Jesus in the fabric of their being, but they still screw up.

So, what do we do with all this?

Don't blame God for the failures of church people. We're all hypocrites in some area of life. We all project ourselves different from the way we really are. Accept that fact, stop judging, and pursue consistency between word and deed.

The church is full of hypocrites, but there's room for one more.

PRAYER

Father, thank You that I and all the other hypocrites are Your forgiven sons and daughters. Help me to remember that, and to communicate to others that we're always welcome in Your house and family. Amen.

DEATH IS YOUR IPO

An IPO is the ultimate dream of many business people; it's the ultimate payoff for years of hard work and risk-taking. They call it public for a reason: Everything about your company comes out. Nothing is hidden.

The first hurdle for an IPO is the Securities and Exchange Commission. The SEC decides yes or no on a company's IPO. No company can bring its stock to market until the SEC weighs in.

Next, a large crowd of experts analyzes every facet of the past, present, and future of the company. They assign a value, then the first day of trading reveals what the market really thinks.

Someday you and I will have a personal IPO.

Our IPO happens when we die. God is like the SEC. He decides yes or no, based on our authentic faith in Jesus and His payment for our sins. The price paid was so high we can't fathom it—the cost of the Creator's only Son. All the good intentions in the world won't matter on our IPO day. You know Him, or you don't. Simple. Straightforward.

Once we've cleared "entry," we'll see how our work mattered. What created value. Our reward gets decided by what we've done with our lives. How much did we love and serve others? What did we do for "the least of these"?

And just like a company's performance, everything will be public, in clear view for God to see.

Our potential won't count for anything on our IPO day. There will be no pressure after that. No track record to worry about. It'll be life as originally designed with God in the middle of it all.

QUESTION

**Are you ready for your IPO? What
changes will you make to get ready?**

EVEN GOD CAN'T CHANGE THE PAST

These words are from Charlotte Church's song "Even God Can't Change the Past":

> "Even God can't change the past
> No matter how many tears I've cried
> Yes, I thought this dream would last
> Who am I to question why?
> Who am I?"

The opening line came from Agathon, an Athenian tragic poet who lived in the early fifth century. His complete thought was: "This only is denied even to God . . . the power to undo the past."

Maybe I'm weird, but I find great comfort knowing that even God can't change the past. Not that He's limited; I think it's just a choice He made.

God paid too high a price to cover our sins for us to continue to wallow in them. He gave us a do-over. A fresh start. He made us new creations in Christ. Being released from the body of death, the apostle Paul talks about truly accepting this free gift of starting over with a clean slate.

Is there still pain? Yes. Are we going to live with the consequences of our sins, maybe for the rest of our stay on this planet? Absolutely. Will there be other people hurt by our failures who won't forgive us and let go of our past? Unfortunately, yes.

But is it His will that we grovel around second-guessing what we did yesterday and let the evil one rob us of the chance to make a difference tomorrow?

Not a chance.

QUESTION

**Is there something from your past you're still chewing on?
Would you benefit from a personal conversation with God
about it? Maybe taking it off your hands and placing it in His
would free you up to receive whatever He has in store for you now.**

AUGUST 18

"THIS WAY OF LIFE . . ."

Reading Matthew the other morning, I knew I was about to read the great commission. I've quoted it forever, but this time, reading The Message paraphrase, I found words I didn't expect.

> "Jesus, undeterred, went right ahead and gave his charge: 'God authorized and commanded me to commission you: Go out and train everyone you meet, far and near, in this way of life, marking them by baptism in the threefold name: Father, Son, and Holy Spirit.'" (Matthew 28:19-20, MSG)

"Train everyone . . . in this way of life"—the way of life Jesus taught and modeled.

What does that mean in the real world, right now? Here's what *this way of life* means to me personally:

- God is at the center of everything. My constant thought is "Thank you."
- Don't worry. Whatever is in my future will come through God's hand.
- Be grateful for money, but never forget it all comes from Him.
- The first place I'm to train in *this way of life* is at home.
- Live your life *for others*. Jesus taught and modeled total selflessness.

Don't get me wrong. I don't live it out all the time. Far from it. But *this way of life* is what I want for me and everyone else.

We each have to figure out what *this way of life* means for us. Everyone has to seek God on their own, listen to His voice, and fulfill His unique vision for their lives.

CHALLENGE

Decide what *this way of life* means for you. Write it down. Think about it. Pray over it. Talk to your wife about it. Commit yourself to it. Then decide what you'll do to teach it to others, starting with your family and moving out from there.

PICK A FIGHT

I've read Bob Goff's book *Love Does* three times. I've never read *any* other book three times, other than the Bible.

Goff tells about a childhood bully, a good-sized seventh grader named Dale who bullied and beat up the little guys in his school. Goff was a big kid himself, and one day he was watching Dale beat up another classmate, a little kid. Goff called him out (junior high-speak for, "Let's have a fistfight").

They scheduled the fight for after school the next day, and by the time a teacher broke it up, "Dale was covered in blood. Nobody realized it was all mine . . ." Goff had taken up the cause of the helpless, laying it all on the line.

He doesn't say if Dale stopped bullying, but he does tell about how that fight helped him learn something about himself—how he's "driven by the need to stand up for the little guy." His work in Uganda is a shining example of how God uses him, his legal skills, and his love for Jesus to redeem the lives of hundreds of "little guys."

The point of the story is this:

> What fight have you picked?

It's one thing to defend ourselves when we're attacked. Most people will do that out of necessity. It's another to go pick a fight on behalf of someone or something.

When you think about it, Jesus picked a fight. A big one. Not with politicians. Not with poverty. Not with disease. He picked a fight with religion.

So that brings us back to me. And you.

QUESTION

**Have you picked a fight? Will you pray
and ask God to show you your fight?**

PICK YOUR FIGHT AND FIND YOUR PURPOSE

This idea of "picking a fight" has got me. I'm putting it in the category of a BGI (Blinding Guiding Insight). It's a clue as to why Christians are so passive—they haven't picked a fight. They're just sitting in church learning more stuff. They're useless . . . as Jesus said, "like salt that's lost its savor."

Purpose is about *why*, and we know that if God gives us our purpose, it's about other people. Jon Acuff says purpose is a simple formula:

> Your talent + Other people = Purpose

Until we "pick a fight," we won't know what we're made of. Or made for.

Bob Goff's story yesterday shows how intentionally taking on Dale the bully clarified his calling. Years later, he finds himself taking on bad guys in Uganda, Iraq, India, and Somalia, using his personality and platform to help others.

A fight musters resources. A fight pumps adrenaline. A fight creates urgency. A big fight forces you to look outside yourself and create alliances. In a fight, there are times you attack and times you protect. A fight keeps you focused on your adversary.

What kinds of fights could *you* pick?

- Pick a fight with fatherlessness.
- Pick a fight with homelessness.
- Pick a fight with loneliness.
- Pick a fight with divorce.
- Pick a fight with hunger.

Don't leave God out of this—He's given you talents and experiences like no one else. Ask Him to make it clear by giving you a *burden* for the fight He wants you to pick. Ask Him to wear you out until you act. You may have to pick several different fights until you find the one you were made for.

QUESTION

Is this your season? Is now *your time* to pick a fight?

DO YOU HAVE ANY FRIENDS?

"The tragedy at my father's funeral was not that I had to help carry the casket; it was that I had to grab the hearse driver to make four carriers. Two relatives, myself, and the hearse driver. No friends," says my friend Pete.

Imagine how sad your son would feel, knowing you lay dead and friendless.

Do you have friends? *Real* friends?

You have to decide that you *want* to have friends. Pick a few people you see God's love in and decide to pursue friendship with them.

How do you pick the people to pursue true friendship with?

Maybe you could ask these questions about each one:

- Will he be *for me*? Will he also be *for my family*?

- Will this potential friend tell me the truth? Help me think things through without judging?

- Will his reaction to my failings, pain, or suffering be "I am sorry. I'm here for you and with you"?

- Does he have curiosity about and willingness to challenge me toward the God-given and unique purpose for my life?

Of course, the backside of these questions is, "Am *I* ready to be that kind of friend in return?" If I'm not, the friendship will be one-sided and short-lived.

I know this sounds a little weird, but try it. Reach out. Schedule time with a few guys who could become true friends.

QUESTION

Will you live *a quiet life of desperation*, alone, like most men? Or will you push through the pride and the fear of rejection, take off your mask, and take a chance to *truly* connect with another guy or two or three?

MAKE A PEOPLE PLAN

The best way to predict future behavior is past behavior.

The definition of insanity is to repeat the same behavior and expect a different result.

You can't talk your way out of what you behave your way into. You have to *behave* your way out of what you behave yourself into.

I'm going somewhere with this. I promise.

If you and I want to develop close friendships, we're going to have to do something different. We have to be intentional. We have to act. Things get done when they get put on our calendar.

But how do you put "developing close friendships" on your calendar?

Here's what I do. I created these three spheres of friendship:

> **Intimate friends**—People you talk to every day. For me, it's God and my wife.
> **Close friends**—People you are close to and want to be closer to.
> **Friends**—Everyone else.

So, here's my people plan. I'm going deep daily with God and my wife, Miriam—ample time for conversation and companionship. I'm not going to let anyone or anything get in the way of these two intimate relationships.

I'm going to actively pursue close friendships with the people on my close friends list. I'm going to either call or visit two of them each week. I'm putting names on my calendar every Monday.

And for the "everyone else" list, I'm going to reach out to one of these guys each week. In the course of the year, I'll have a touch with each friend. When they call me or I call them for something, that doesn't count. Pure friendship calls don't have an agenda.

QUESTION

Are you intentional about developing *real* friendships?

DO YOU BELIEVE OR DO YOU KNOW?

I'm ten years old. All the other boys have "walked the aisle" and prayed with the pastor. I'm the only one left. Finally the Spirit moves on the third verse of "Just As I Am," and now I'm saved.

Or am I?

Oh, I believed, but I didn't *know*. And there's a difference.

When I uttered a desperate prayer one night twenty-three years later and God answered in dramatic fashion, my believing became knowing. I finally gave it all up that night. My doubts. My ambition. My guilt.

This just happened for a friend of mine. He's been a believer all his life, but he made some big mistakes years ago. He ended up divorced, remarried, and with two families. God has forgiven him, but he's struggled to forgive himself.

Driving down the expressway one Saturday, he did something he rarely does—he put in a CD. The song that played was "Grace Walked In." Seconds later, he was crying his eyes out. He exited the freeway, pulled into a grocery store parking lot, and bawled some more. God's love flowed over him. Grace walked in. He's free.

I can't make God show up like that. Neither can you.

What we can do is open our hands and let go. We can pray, "Lord, I'm letting go. I'm opening my clinched fists. I'm releasing my grip on my guilt. I'm letting it go. Please take it away and put Your peace in its place."

Then wait for His love to wash all over you. When it does, you'll no longer believe. You will *know*.

QUESTION

Do you believe . . . or do you *know*?

SCAPEGOAT

My friend Wikipedia says a *scapegoat* is "a person or animal which takes on the sins of others, or is unfairly blamed for problems." The concept comes from Leviticus, where the high priest put both his hands on the scapegoat's head and confessed the sins of the people, thus laying them on the goat and removing them from the people.

The goat was led away into the wilderness and intentionally lost so the sins of the people could never be found again. I'd never thought of Jesus as a scapegoat, but Charles Spurgeon did. In one of his devotionals, he quotes Isaiah 53:6, "We all, like sheep, have gone astray, each of us has turned to our own way; and the Lord has laid on him the iniquity of us all."

He also points to John 19:16 (KJV), "They took Jesus, and led him away." Just like the scapegoat in the Old Testament.

I've always felt sorry for the scapegoat, but that's not the right response to what Jesus did. He was not a victim; He was a *volunteer!*

He volunteered to be the scapegoat. He doesn't want us to feel sorry for Him, He wants us to appreciate Him. To live a life of gratitude for what He did. To respond to His willingness to take on our sins by forgiving ourselves and forgiving others. He wants us to love Him back and show our love for Him by loving others every minute of every day.

PRAYER

Thank You, Lord Jesus, for volunteering to be my scapegoat. I am so undeserving. I am humbled by the reality that You love me that much. I will live today in gratitude for what You've done, showing compassion, love, and forgiveness for every single person I encounter. In Your beautiful name, amen.

WHERE ARE YOU . . . REALLY?

Years ago, my company hired a consultant to help us improve. He gave us a lens to look through that has stuck with me for decades. He said companies are in one of these modes:

- Growth mode
- Even-keel mode
- Over-confident mode
- Trouble mode

I think these also describe marriage. Mine has been in all four at one time or another.

Growth mode, well that's obvious and wonderful. You're on the same page. You don't compete, or confront, or conflict; you collaborate. No one takes things personally. The bedroom is happening often and effortlessly. It's bliss.

Over-confident mode means you're taking things for granted. You're *assuming* things about your marriage, your wife, and yourself.

Even-keel mode is just that. "It's not great, but it's not broke," you might say. Sometimes what feels like even-keel to you may feel like boredom to her.

If you're already in trouble mode, it feels like your marriage is, in effect, over. Every marriage gets lost somewhere along the way. They asked Billy Graham's wife if she ever considered divorce. She said, "No, but I have considered murder."

These modes are just guesses about where marriages might be. Maybe none of these describe where you are. There are probably a thousand options for you to "one-word" your marriage.

The important thing is to *pick a word*. Then go sit down with your wife and ask her to pick a word. You'll learn something, maybe a lot. Hopefully you will learn where you really are, and that's the first step if you're going to work *on* your marriage versus just living *with* your marriage.

QUESTION

Do really know where your marriage stands? Have the "what's your word" conversation with your wife.

TAKING RESPONSIBILITY

Regardless of which mode your marriage is in, the question is the same: What are you going to do? Moving forward, how will you look at your marriage? How will you lead?

The starting point is *taking responsibility*. Not for *her* marriage, not for *the* marriage, but for *your* marriage. Three out of those four letters spell y-o-u.

That takes us back to Jesus, the greatest leader of all time. And what kind of leader was He? A *servant* leader. "Husbands, love your wives, just as Christ loved the church and gave himself up for her" (Ephesians 5:25).

To really love someone, you have to get into that person's frame of reference. How does she feel when you say or do certain things?

I figured out (after forty-four years . . . duh) that my wife loves to be cooked for. So I get to decide: Do I delight by serving her? Or do I take the selfish route and let her cook all the time?

Genius me also finally figured out that the quickest way to shut my wife down is to cut her down in front of others. Usually it's a good-natured joke. But no matter how silly or immaterial I may think it is, I'm tearing down my wife and tearing down my marriage. Taking responsibility says I stop.

How we respond to what our wife says may be more important than what we initiate. Mark Batterson says, "It's easy to act like a Christian. It's much harder to respond like one." Taking responsibility means we throttle our emotions. We don't take things personally. We let things go without returning fire.

CHALLENGE

Step up, take ownership, lead selflessly, and give your highest and best effort. Take responsibility for your marriage. That's what real men do.

AUGUST 27

SATAN IS FOR REAL

You can't read the New Testament without learning there's a mighty dark power behind death, disease, pain, and sin.

Satan is old school, and for Christians, he provides an example of a true paradox. We say we believe in an invisible spirit-God who created everything, sent His Son into the world to die for our sins, and whose promise of unconditional love and eternal life fuels our hope every day.

Yet we struggle to believe in an invisible spirit of evil whose handiwork is plain as day. God's Word, which we totally depend on for truth about everything, speaks of Satan more than fifty times. Jesus, the reason for all our hope, encountered Satan personally and suffered "all the temptations known to man." Yet only 57 percent of us believe Satan is real. Older surveys put the number closer to 35 percent.

A close friend was going through one of the toughest situations I've ever seen. His wife turned on God and turned on him. As our group prayed and listened for God's guidance, I heard, "She is not the enemy."

The next morning, my Bible reading happened to include 2 Timothy 2:25-26, "Opponents must be gently instructed, in the hope that God will grant them repentance leading them to a knowledge of the truth, and that they will come to their senses and escape from the trap of the devil, who has taken them captive to do his will."

Forewarned is forearmed. Satan is real, and he's working against you and the God you love and serve.

QUESTIONS

Do you believe Satan is real? Will you spend some time in the Scriptures and learn how to deal with him?

CAUTION: CHRISTIANS WORK HERE!

When I became a follower of Jesus, they hadn't even started making fish symbols to stick on the back of your car. But in the workplace, people who were living for Jesus were pretty obvious.

Maybe they had a giant Bible on the desk, shared gospel tracts, invited everyone to church events, or wore Christian jewelry. Their faith was quite external and on display for all to see.

Yet all too often their faith never made an impact on their work. Their Bible reading and prayer time didn't lead them to think differently about how they approached work. I've heard leaders say, "I'm not hiring Christians anymore. They're disruptive. They're focused on everything but their jobs!"

Today, though, a lot of people see their work as an opportunity to demonstrate their faith. They work with integrity, pursue excellence, and serve others. Their humility is on display when people ask some of life's toughest questions, or when a critic offers a difficult criticism to Christianity.

As we mature in faith, we better understand how our faith changes every nook and cranny of life, even down to how we treat the people we work with.

Stop and think for a minute. Who has the most positive influence for Christ in your workplace?

If you can't call up a name, *it might be you!*

QUESTION

**Will you commit to leading and living this way?
Your workplace *needs* a leader like this.**

AUGUST 29

GOD'S WORD, SO WHAT?

Since Jesus says God's Word is one of the two things that will last beyond this life, maybe we should think a little more about it. In heaven, we'll recognize the words, wisdom, and authors, and we'll never tire of learning what it means.

What's the big deal about this old book? First, consider its source.

> "All Scripture is inspired by God and is useful to teach us what is true and to make us realize what is wrong in our lives. It corrects us when we are wrong and teaches us to do what is right." (2 Timothy 3:16, NLT)

Second, God's Word has been around, unchanged, for thousands of years. It is unchanging truth, yesterday, today, and tomorrow. Isn't it smarter to build your life on truth that's been time-tested for thousands of years, versus a few weeks?

Every day we have reasons to be scared out of our skin. But read 2 Timothy 1:7. It says that God "has not given us a spirit of fear, but of power and of love and of a sound mind" (NKJV).

Suddenly, we realize, "Hey, I can do this! I don't have to be afraid. God loves me! This fear I'm feeling isn't coming from Him. I have His power within me. I can discipline myself. I have a sound mind! Let's get on with it."

The Bible doesn't spoon-feed. God requires us to dig on our own, to initiate, to pick up the Book, pray, and search it for ourselves.

QUESTION

Will you pick up the Book, pray, and search the Bible for yourself?

DINNER TOGETHER

I can count the things my wife has been *insistent* on with one hand. Dinner together was one.

"When will you be home?" she'd ask.

"I'm tied up. It'll be a little while," I'd say.

Undaunted, she'd retort, "*Untie yourself* and get on the road. We have dinner together in this family. It'll be ready, and we'll be at the table at 6:30!"

I'm exaggerating a little, but not much. My wife consistently insisted we have dinner together every night as a family. At first, I didn't quite see why it was important.

But over time, especially as my kids moved into adolescence, I saw the value. It was the one time every day when we were eyeball-to-eyeball. We talked about things. We could hear their hearts and they could hear ours. They could see how their parents talked, worked together, and loved each other. Brother and sister sat there for a little dose of family.

If not at home, where will your kids learn about committed love, family dynamics, loyalty, empathy, relational problem-solving, and forgiveness? Who will prepare them for marriage and family life? I'm not aware of a "husband school" or "wife school" where our kids learn this stuff.

> "Love the LORD your God with all your heart and with all your soul and with all your strength. These commandments that I give you today are to be on your hearts. Impress them on your children. Talk about them when you sit at home and when you walk along the road, when you lie down and when you get up." (Deuteronomy 6:5-7)

QUESTION

Does your family sit together at home with any regularity? Ask yourself, "Twenty years from now, will what they got from outside activities be more important than Family 101?"

THE HAPPY WIFE PLEDGE

I used to think marriage hinged on picking the right woman.

Now I believe it's almost entirely up to the man. And I can prove it. This is *The Happy Wife Pledge*.

Get your Bible out. Put your left hand on it, raise your right hand, and repeat the following pledge . . .

"My wife is more important than the house being messy. I will shut up and start helping out."

"I will no longer criticize my wife about how she uses her time. It's her life to live."

"I am grateful for a wife who cares about our kids. I will thank her, encourage her, and never allow myself to think I'm unimportant to her."

"I recognize my wife was her mom's daughter before she was my wife. She has a right and a responsibility to be a good adult daughter and to honor her mother."

"I will never again complain about the food in our house. Instead, I will offer to stop by the store and bring whatever she needs without complaint."

"I will never criticize my wife for her desire to be with just me versus going out with friends. I will thank her and pour myself into loving her when we're together."

"I recognize that my wife gets tired. I will drop all my demands and make space for her to rest, and I will not take it personally."

"I acknowledge it's difficult to identify, screen, and coordinate schedules with babysitters. I will not criticize her nor take her efforts for granted."

"I will look for the good in my wife's appearance. If I can't say something nice, I will keep my mouth shut."

"I will never again comment on my wife's weight. That is off-limits to me forever. I will love and accept her regardless. It is none of my business."

"I will never say anything negative about my wife, even in a joking way, in front of any other person, male or female, friend or foe."

"I will never again bring up my wife's performance in earlier parts of her life. For example, I will never talk about how she 'used to like to dance' or anything of that nature."

"I will stop talking about sex. I will make no other comments, jokes, side comments, or criticisms about the frequency, quality, or any other dimension of our sex life. I will love her, and we will enjoy sex only when she is clearly in favor of it. I will put her first, be grateful for what comes my way, and be content."

"I recognize that my family of origin is just that—*my* family. I will drop my expectations for my wife to engage with my family. I hope she does, but I will not require it of her."

"I will go through a complete review of our finances. I will make sure she fully understands our income, our budgeted expenses, and our saving and giving commitments. And I will never again criticize her regarding money."

Live this pledge consistently and you will have a happy wife and a better marriage.

Guaranteed.

QUESTION

Which part of the pledge will be hardest for you?

A FAITH OF YOUR OWN

As I watched videos of middle schoolers share their stories before being baptized, I was stopped in my tracks by these words:

> "I have a faith of my own."

That's it! These young people have moved beyond the faith of their parents and decided to believe independently.

Everyone has faith in something—in a job, a savings account, a boss, a spouse, a doctor, a pension plan, a best friend. The question is who or what we have faith in. Everything I just listed falls short at some point. Then what?

Faith in a God who loves me, who never leaves, never dies, never moves away, never implodes, never turns his back on me—that's what we all want.

Three things are necessary to have faith in someone or something:

1. **You have to believe it exists**—You won't put your faith in Jesus unless you believe He's real.

2. **You have to have access to it**—You might believe that God exists, but if you can't get to Him, then you won't have faith.

3. **You have to trust it to do what it's supposed to do**—Many people lose faith in God because He didn't do what they thought He was supposed to do.

Are you struggling in your faith? Can you trace it back to one of these three issues? Pray *right now* and ask God to give you more faith.

SCRIPTURE

"The apostles said to the Lord, 'Increase our faith!'" (Luke 17:5)

THE CHALLENGE OF SEX

Here's one part of The Happy Wife Pledge that's hard to take:

> "I will stop talking about sex. I will make no other comments, jokes, side comments, or criticisms about the frequency, quality, or any other dimension of our sex life. **I will love her and we will enjoy sex only when she is clearly in favor of it. I will put her first, be grateful for what comes my way, and be content.**"

Yes, husbands *need* sex. And yes, a wife should meet her husband's need for sex. But when she doesn't, what's he to do? What's the answer?

Trust God.

With my sex life?

Yes. Totally.

Men are the initiators because we have the highest drive and need for sex. When we focus on our wives and woo them with attentiveness, selflessness, and patience, our needs usually get met. Maybe not a lot more than met. Maybe just barely and just in time.

But when we do everything right and our wife's heart is just not there for lovemaking, that's when it's up to us to look to the Lord for the grace to accept our wife's heart, not take it personally, and not dole out retribution.

What if God gave men more and women less sex drive for the purpose of leading men to love and women to submit? What if He wanted frustrated men to have no other legitimate place to turn other than his wife and to Him? So crank up your kindness, patience, understanding, and attentiveness. If she's still not motivated, your next stop is your Heavenly Father.

QUESTION

Will you drop your demands for sex, gently pursue your wife's heart, and let God meet your need for sex in His timing?

MEN AND EMPATHY

Empathy is feeling *with* people. It drives connection. There are four qualities of empathy:

1. Taking the perspective of another person.
2. Not judging that person.
3. Recognizing the emotion in the other person.
4. Communicating true understanding of their emotion.

Empathy is getting into the other person's frame of reference, taking them exactly as they are and where they are, sensing what they're feeling, and letting them know you understand. Nothing more.

Because men are doers and fixers, empathy is hard for us. When we see someone hurting, we say, "I know how you feel. What you need to do is (fill in the blank)" or, "Let me help you. I'll (fill in the blank)." We want to make things better. That approach is well intended, but not empathetic.

The best place to see the power and wisdom of empathy is watching people comfort a grieving parent or spouse. Friends and family who show empathy –who *feel with them*, who cry with them and don't judge their despair, who feel their pain and let them know they feel it–they bring healing. Everyone else–the folks who are rushing them to move on–are working *against* healing, not for it.

Back this down to day-to-day situations. People don't need us to fix them, they need us to *feel* them. They can choose to look at things differently. They can choose to believe different things if they want to behave different ways. We can't do it for them.

We men can become more empathetic if we want to help people badly enough to keep our mouths shut.

What would Jesus have us do?

Feel or fix?

SCRIPTURE

"Rejoice with those who rejoice; mourn with those who mourn." (Romans 12:15)

EMPATHY AND SELF-ESTEEM

If empathy is simply connecting with people's feelings, why is it so hard? All Jesus followers want empathy, right? "They will know we are Christians by our love," falls apart if we can't meet people where they are and connect with their emotions. It's hard to love someone well without knowing their heart.

I believe the problem is self-esteem. If I have healthy self-esteem, if I know who I am and I'm OK being me, I don't worry as much about who *you* think I am. If I'm at peace with myself, I can set aside my issues and focus on yours.

But if I'm using all my energy to take care of myself—if I'm trying hard to make you like me—I've got no capacity left for you.

It seems like Christ followers should have the perfect amount of self-esteem. There's absolutely no reason for us to have low self-esteem, right?

When we have self-esteem from our identity in Christ, empathy gets easier. We *choose* to love people and truly value them. We *choose* to consider others more important than ourselves.

Remember, empathy is feeling people, nothing more. I mess this up because I want to help. When I go beyond listening, I replace the feeling of being *connected* with the *content* of my thoughts. What they need is love, understanding, and *connection*.

Try being empathetic in every conversation today. In each moment of personal interaction, set aside *all* your stuff and totally focus on the emotion being felt by the person you're talking to. Resist the temptation to offer advice, to self-reference, or to cut them off.

Let them know that you feel what they feel.

QUESTION

Will you pause your thoughts and feelings long enough to engage the thoughts and feelings of others?

"I JUST WANT TO BE HAPPY"

How many times have you heard, "But I just want to be happy!"—or said it yourself?

Happiness is something we trade for. "I'll give up (fill in the blank) in return for being happy." But it never seems to work out, does it?

Three things make us *un*happy:

1. Not getting something we want.
2. Not getting to do what we want to do.
3. Not having people think what we want them to think.

Anxiety comes from unmet expectations, and all three of these start with expectations—for ourselves, other people, or God.

Even when we get what we think we want, we're not happy for long. Soon enough, we want something else.

Happy is defined as "a state of well-being, a pleasurable or satisfying experience." It comes from the same root as "haphazard." It connotes something random. Spurious. Unpredictable.

But "joy," which comes from the word "rejoice," means "to feel great delight, to welcome or to be glad." The Bible uses the words "happy" and "happiness" about thirty times, while "joy" and "rejoice" appear three hundred-plus times.

For me, joy rides on two things: love and hope. I first experienced it when I grasped that I was loved by my Heavenly Father. Knowing that I'm loved gives me an irrevocable hope that I will always be loved. Personally. By the God of the universe.

The only sure cure for anxiety is a grateful heart. And for the Jesus follower who gets it, gratitude is the default setting of the heart.

SCRIPTURE

**"May the God of hope fill you with all joy and peace
as you trust in him, so that you may overflow with
hope by the power of the Holy Spirit." (Romans 15:13)**

MATURITY: NOT SAYING EVERYTHING YOU KNOW

In a casual, friendly conversation with a banker one day, I made an off-the-wall wisecrack about something going on inside the company that had bought ours. It wasn't confidential information, it was criticism of what I thought was an obviously bad decision.

Three years later, I was sitting with my mentor who is now on the board of that company, and we were talking about people being critical.

My mentor looked at me and said something that let me know he had heard about the criticism I'd shared with that banker three years back. Ouch. It was embarrassing. It was humbling. It hurt like crazy, but I got it. *I mean, I really got it.*

I admire that quality in a mentor–the ability to observe, perceive, hypothesize, and crystalize an insight for someone, but not act on it.

Isn't that the way God works with us?

He doesn't miss a thing. He has the truth we need, but He'll often hold it while we struggle, flail around, and wear ourselves out.

As a mid-level field manager in a large company, it was easy to be critical of corporate staff decisions. When I moved into the head office, I got a different perspective.

Imagine the complexity of the relationships and motives our Heavenly Father sees every day. In every single one, He's working to grow His kids in their faith and influence, and to draw everyone else to become His kids.

If you're wearing yourself out trying to teach your employees, kids, team, or mentees important things, maybe you'd do better by holding back some of the truth until they're ready to learn.

QUESTION

**Do you have the maturity to not
say everything you know?**

"YOU HURT MY FEELINGS EGO!"

"You hurt my feelings," is really hard for a man to say.

The truth is, it's usually our *ego* that's been hurt, not our feelings. Feelings are emotions. They come upon us unannounced, unfiltered, and real. We feel what we feel.

My definition of ego is, "the combination of the person I think I am, the person I want to be, and the person I want others to think I am." The borders between these three are fuzzy. I don't know which one is running the show until I run into someone and get hurt.

When that happens, it means I've set myself up as a god, deciding what other people should think, do, and say. When they let me down, I'm upset.

It's pride. Plain and simple.

There's a lot of things God seems to be neutral about, but pride isn't one of them. James 4:6 says, "God opposes the proud but shows favor to the humble." Of everyone I don't want opposing me, God is at the top of the list! And I sure do want His favor! Another translation says He *"gives grace to the humble."* Grace. Undeserved blessing. To the humble.

Next time you get your feelings hurt, recognize that it was your ego, not your feelings. Humble yourself. Instead of rehearsing the conversation you're going to have where you express your hurt feelings, turn to your Heavenly Father and tell Him how much you love Him and how grateful you are for all He's done for you.

See, it wasn't your feelings at all. It can be healed in a moment of humility and gratitude.

QUESTION

Will you confess that your ego is lording expectations over people in your life? Will you humble yourself, let go of the hurts, and let the amazing love of God wash over you?

WALKING AND TALKING WITH GOD

Over these years of following Christ, I've learned that God speaks to us. Not always audibly, but in our thoughts. It's that "still small voice" described in 1 Kings 19:12.

I read this the other day, (and you can substitute *I* for *man*):

> When man listens, God speaks
> When man obeys, God acts
> When God acts, men change

But how can I know when it's God who is speaking?

Prayer. Ask Him to shut out the other voices that may be speaking at the same time.

Here's a sample listening prayer:

> *Father, I come to You in the name of Jesus Christ, Your Son, and according to James 1:5, I am seeking wisdom for (fill in the blank).*
>
> *In the name of Jesus, according to Matthew 28:18 and Luke 10:19-20, I take authority over Satan and his fallen angels and command that they be rendered deaf, dumb, and blind to my prayers and removed from my presence. I place my own voice under subjection to the shed blood of Christ, according to 2 Corinthians 10:5. I ask, Father, that only Your Holy Spirit will speak to me as I wait on Your wisdom, insight, and direction for (fill in the blank). What You show me and direct me to do I will quickly obey.*

Then be quiet. As thoughts come, write them down. Thank God and put what He told you to do on your calendar. That's the first step to obedience.

Where God guides, God provides. If we'll act on His instruction, step out in faith and do what He leads us to do, He'll provide the outcome.

QUESTION

Do you have enough faith and humility to ask God specific questions and then obey what He tells you?

NO ONE DIES

We existed before we started wearing these "earth suits." God says, "Before I formed you in the womb I knew you . . ." (Jeremiah 1:5).

And we have to decide where we go next.

For a time, I got caught up in life and let myself act like this is all there is. I slipped into short-term thinking. I lost sight of the fact that this *isn't* all there is, and where I end up is awfully important.

How do I know there's life after death?

Easter.

It was a brutal execution, watched by hundreds of people, followed by the public removal of His dead body. Then He came back to life in recognizable human form and lived again. No other religious figure ever did that. Mohammad, Buddha, they died and they were dead and have been dead ever since.

Jesus coming back to life is an extremely important and personal point. He was human and He died and then He lived again. That means I, as a well-documented human being, am going to die and live again. Somewhere.

If I *know* I'm going to exit this life and I have pretty good evidence this man Jesus exited and then came back to life, it makes sense that doing what He said might be the key to ending up in the right place when this life is over.

What He said to do is so simple: *"Whoever believes in him shall not perish but have eternal life"* (John 3:16).

If He lived, you will too. But where?

QUESTION

Is there someone you know who has never said what they *really* believe about Jesus? Do you care enough about them to have a conversation about it?

SEPTEMBER 10

DON'T HOLD ME ACCOUNTABLE ... HOLD ME CLOSE

That title comes from Bob Goff's book *Love Does*, and I think it's true. Who is close enough to you to know when you're off the rails? Whom can you call for advice with the stickiest of questions? Which of your friends will challenge you on the hours you're working?

For most of the guys I know, the answer is *nobody!*

You can't hire someone to be this kind of friend. You can't will it. You can't manufacture it. You have to work for it.

A few years ago, I was challenged to find some friends. Not guys to *save*, and certainly not guys to mentor or fix. Guys to do life with—to draw close to and allow to draw close to me.

The answer came in one word: group.

I wormed my way into a group of guys who were meeting once a month. They knew each other, went to the same church (not mine), and had a lot of "road miles" together, having met for a few years before I came along. Now, years later, they know my junk, I know theirs, and we're still friends. Actually, we're now *real* friends.

Of course, nothing can replace the intimate friendship of our Heavenly Father. And no earthly friendship should rival the one we're developing with our wives. But every single one of us needs at least one friend who will hold us close. The light of that friendship, shining into the deepest recesses of our desires, temptations, strengths, and broken places beats any other kind of accountability.

Do you have that friend of inestimable value?

If you don't, start talking to some of the guys you know.

QUESTION

**Will you make developing close friends a priority?
Will you give this group thing a try?**

SEPTEMBER 11

"ARE YOU JESUS?"

A friend sent this anecdote to me:

A group of salesmen were late for their flights. Rushing through the crowded concourse, one of the men inadvertently kicked a display of apples. Apples rolled everywhere. Without looking back, the men reached their nearly-missed boarding . . . all but one.

He took a deep breath and experienced a twinge of compassion for the girl and her overturned apple stand. He waved goodbye to his colleagues and returned to the apple-strewn terminal.

He was glad he did. The sixteen-year-old girl was blind! Crying softly, tears running down her cheeks in frustration, she helplessly groped for her spilled produce as the crowd swirled about, no one stopping or caring. The salesman knelt down with her, gathered up apples, and helped her reorganize. As he did, he set aside those that were now battered and bruised.

When they finished, he pulled out his wallet and said, "Are you OK? Take this $40 for the damage." She nodded through tears. He continued, "I hope we didn't spoil your day too badly."

As the salesman started to walk away, the bewildered girl called to him. He turned to look back. She asked, "Are you Jesus?"

He stopped mid-stride and said gently, "No, I am nothing like Jesus. He is kind, caring, loving, and wouldn't have bumped into your display."

She nodded. "I ask because I prayed for Jesus to help me gather the apples. He sent you to help, so you *are* like Him. Only He knows who will do His will. Thank you for hearing His call."

Slowly he went to catch the later flight with that question bouncing around in his soul:

Are you Jesus?

QUESTION

Are you Jesus? Do you stop for people?

THE LAWS OF APPLAUSE

Years ago, somebody taught me, "You won't have peace until you figure out who your audience is, and God is the only audience that matters." While this is true, living it out risks two misunderstandings: 1) Believing God is an audience we perform for, which ignores grace, and 2) Thinking that what people think doesn't matter, which ignores reality.

Everyone likes positive feedback. Andy Stanley said, "There's a Lady Gaga in all of us." He went on to share the laws of applause.

1. What's applauded as exceptional the first time will be expected next time.
2. Those most applauded *for* feel most entitled *to*.
3. Applause is intoxicating, and applause-intoxicated people don't make good decisions.
4. Applause is addictive. We start looking for it. We'll even manufacture it.

Once you get a little applause, there's an appetite for more. I know because I've sought it forever. The first half of my life, I wanted my dad's applause. Without consciously deciding, I set out to make him proud in the only arena I had a chance in: work. Intoxicated by the accolades, success became my audience and my path to applause.

But my "then God . . ." moment happened. When I grasped God's love for the very first time, I felt acceptance, approval, and peace. The love I felt wasn't tied to performance. I no longer craved the applause of people, including my dad.

I still like applause. That's human. But I'm not addicted to it nor intoxicated by it. I try to graciously and gratefully deflect applause to my Lord. He deserves all of it and more.

QUESTION

**Are you clear about whose applause
you're working for and why?**

EMOTIONAL INTELLIGENCE

Years ago, John D. Mayer, now a professor at the University of New Hampshire, and Peter Salovey, now president of Yale University, developed a conversation into articles that introduced the concept of *emotional intelligence.*

But it wasn't until 1995, when Daniel Goleman's book, *Emotional Intelligence: Why It Can Matter More Than IQ,* became an international best seller, that the field appeared on the map and the term entered our vocabulary.

Before I rattle on too much further, let me explain. There are five key elements of EQ:

1. **Self-awareness**—The ability to recognize and understand your moods, emotions, and drives, as well as their effect on others.
2. **Self-regulation**—The ability to control or redirect disruptive impulses and moods along with the ability to suspend judgment.
3. **Motivation**—A passion to work for reasons that go beyond money or status.
4. **Empathy**—The ability to understand the emotional makeup of other people.
5. **Social skill**—A proficiency in managing relationships and building networks.

People who have these attributes are better husbands, fathers, mentors, and leaders. And unlike IQ, emotional intelligence can be improved with effort. Jesus followers have a leg up in raising their EQ because we know we are loved by our Heavenly Father. We have the Holy Spirit to help us selfregulate. We're motivated to *"do our work heartily as to the Lord."* And we're directed to be about loving and connecting people to God and to each other.

I can never have an IQ of 140. But I *can* challenge myself to grow in these five areas. And I'll become more like Jesus and more effective for Him as I do.

QUESTION

Which of these five areas do you struggle with most?

SEPTEMBER 14

DON'T TAKE IT PERSONALLY

I'm an expert on arguments. I've got a lot of experience. My brother-in-law casts me as "often wrong, but never in doubt," and "my way or the highway." I confess, I can be pretty committed to my ideas.

What leads us to argue? What sets us off and makes things emotional?

Arguments start the moment someone takes something personally. And most of the time it wasn't meant to be personal.

Nowhere is this more true than in marriage. We need to train ourselves to listen better, to live and let live and assume what's said *isn't* personal until it undeniably is. You know when it's really personal, don't you?

Here's some examples of things not to take personally:

> Your wife gets wrapped around the axle because of a disagreement with her sister. As a result, she's not in the mood for sex. Don't take it personally. *It's not about you.*

> Your wife asks for help in the kitchen or with putting the kids to bed. She's not calling you a slug. She's not saying you're less tired than she is. She just needs help. Don't take it personally. *It's not about you.*

> Your wife enjoys meeting a friend for lunch or going shopping with her mom. She spends a little more money than she should have. Don't take it personally. *It's not about you.*

Do you want better a relationship with your wife?

Train yourself to hear what's being said and consider *the motive* of the person who's speaking. Instead of listening with your ears perked up and your finger on the trigger, listen with patience, love, and compassion.

CHALLENGE

**Decide not to take anything personally.
More than likely, it's not about you.**

THE MARRIAGE CAGE

Marriage is easy when you're feeling the love. When you aren't, marriage feels like a cage. But think about this: *What if the cage is there to protect you?*

If you were alone, and it was dark, and you were deep in the jungles of Africa with lions, tigers, leopards, jackals, all kinds of hungry animals looking for fresh meat, you'd give anything for a cage. You'd gladly lock yourself inside.

Maybe that's why God created the institution of marriage. Maybe it's there to protect us from the dangers and the temptations we're drawn to, things that might kill us if we were set free.

Why should we value or protect institutions? Because institutions are ways to sustain important activities over time.

Let's say there's a good-hearted doctor who takes care of everyone in his community. What happens when the doctor dies?

We created an *institution* to *sustain* the healthcare we all need. The good-hearted doctor is still at the heart of it, but now he's connected to an institution, the hospital, which is a system that will carry on.

Marriage is sort of like that. It's a system that carries two people through when they don't feel love for each other. Consider this:

Love *initiates* marriage. But marriage *sustains* love.

Remember that God created marriage, and He put you in yours for your benefit. Probably for your protection, as well. Marriage will only be sustained if people think long-term, stay committed even when they don't feel like it, and trust God for the love and protection He provides through marriage.

QUESTION

Are you actively working to protect your marriage?

MAD, SAD, OR GLAD

A lot of really smart people have written about the four access points to a kid's world. These are the four times in day-to-day life when a dad has physical and emotional access to his kids. They're outlined in Deuteronomy 11:19:

> "Teach them to your children, talking about them when you sit at home and when you walk along the road, when you lie down and when you get up."

"When you lie down" is what I want to talk about here.

My wife and I constantly maneuvered around who was going to put the kids to bed. It was a daily adventure and a grind. We prayed for them and, after I committed to Christ, we prayed *with* them.

But here's what I wish I had known. I wish I had known how important it was to bend down over their beds, put my hand on their heart, and ask these three simple questions:

1. Has anyone made you mad today? Is anyone mad at you?
2. Has anything made you sad today? Can you tell me about it?
3. Did anything make you glad today? What can we thank God for tonight?

Imagine the love relationship that would come out of those three questions, coupled with the physical touch of a father to his kid's heart, patiently asked every possible night of a kid's life, and followed by a simple prayer to a loving Heavenly Father.

Dad, how you respond to what your kids share will determine the depth, quality, and trust level of your relationship. If you *feel* them rather than *fix* them, you'll get invited back into their world again and again.

Inside their world, you have influence. Outside, you have none.

QUESTION

Will you take the time to check mad, sad, or glad with your kids tonight? Every night?

ACTIVITY, PROXIMITY, OR INTENTIONALITY

Men are lonely. We put on masks for our friends, and they put on their masks for us. We look at each other's masks, never really seeing or knowing each other.

To overcome this, we connect through *activity and proximity*. Passion for activities like golf or tennis draws us into relationships. Or we connect with the guy down the street, or at work, or at church because we're in the same place at the same time. Generally, because of some activity.

But is this the best way to decide who your lifelong friends are? Who's going to be in your inner circle? Who'll have significant influence on you?

Maybe it's time for a friend inventory. Who has the Lord put in your life? Why might He have put them there? If He's put outsiders in your life—people who don't know Christ—maybe He wants you to invest in them.

There may be other friends in your life you need to fire. They may be pulling you down instead of lifting you up. Leave them behind. Stop being available.

Instead, pick a guy whose life you admire, who can add value to your life and walk. Reach out to him. Ask him to breakfast or lunch. Meet. Eat. Talk. Share your story and ask him to share his.

It will feel awkward. Get over it. A real friendship, intentionally initiated, prayerfully pursued, and patiently developed over time, is worth the risk of being rejected.

In fact, it's worth far more. It's priceless.

QUESTION

Is God's unconditional acceptance real to you? To the point that you would cold call a potential friend and risk being turned down for a breakfast or lunch?

ARE YOU WAITING? OR PROCRASTINATING?

If the seed of making disciples and disciple makers was planted in you, a process started. You may be waiting to lead a group, but you're procrastinating if you're just sittin' and soakin' and not engaging anyone in conversation about Jesus.

It's so tempting to play it safe and do nothing for anyone else's soul. After all, "I have *my* church, *my* Sunday School class or small group, *my* Bible, *my* salvation, *my* Heavenly Father to walk through life with." It's all about *me* and *mine*.

The problem is, Jesus didn't point us toward me and mine. In fact, He said we should abandon ourselves, even our mothers, fathers, brothers, and sisters for the sake of others. For the sake of their souls.

Start with prayer. Ask God who He wants you to engage with. Pray for them intentionally. It's amazing how God can change the heart of someone we consistently pray for. And you will find that as you pray for someone, it's easier to love them. You can't really minister to someone you don't love. Praying leads to loving.

Finally, look for opportunities to serve them. Unconditionally. Don't make them a project, just make them the focus of your attention and acceptance. Little by little, God may warm your heart and theirs, both for each other and for Him. They won't "care to know" about anything until they "know you care" about them, as a person, as a friend.

Let God lead wherever He wants.

Something changes in *us* when we invest in others for Kingdom purposes. That's not why we do it, but it's a sweet benefit of following Jesus and not procrastinating.

QUESTION

If you're not intentionally engaged in helping someone else from a spiritual perspective, ask yourself, "Am I waiting, or procrastinating?"

SPIRITUAL BIRTHDAYS

Today is the anniversary of when I cried out to God for the first time. Oh, I'd been a "Christian" since fifth grade. I'd been to church a thousand times. Baptized. Taught Sunday School. But God didn't influence my life. I didn't *know* God personally.

There's a big difference between believing things *about* someone and believing *in* someone. The first requires enough intelligence to say, "I believe Jesus was God's Son, that He died on a cross and came back to life." I started to believe that when I was twelve. But it was *intellectual*, not *relational*.

Believing *in* someone requires a relationship. You can't have a relationship with an idea or a set of rules. You can't have a relationship with a church, no matter how great. Relationships are only possible between *individual living things*.

The game changer was grasping that the Creator of the universe *loves me*. He wants more for me than just salvation. He wants me to embrace Him as Father! I cried out that night, "God, I'm yours. I want what You want for my life. I accept Your forgiveness, and from now on, it's You and me." Something changed in me. God was suddenly real.

I wonder how many Christians have a relational, emotional connection with God. Do you tear up thinking of times He has shown up in your life? Do you have a deep-seated peace in your heart when things get tough?

I didn't before that night. But I have ever since.

SCRIPTURE

"See what great love the Father has lavished on us, that we should be called children of God! And that is what we are! The reason the world does not know us is that it did not know him." (1 John 3:1)

THE "GOD LIFE" AND EXCLUSIVITY

In my first business after leaving AT&T, there was a significant Christian culture. One day on a flight from Chicago, I started talking to the lady next to me. She told me her boyfriend loved his new job. "The only downside is it seems a little like a 'Jesus club,' and he's not sure he's gonna fit in."

I said, "Really? What's the name of the company?" Yep, you guessed right, it was *my* company. I nodded my head politely as I used my foot to flip over the tag on my briefcase broadcasting our company logo.

In that moment, I was ashamed of the very club I had been so proudly building. I never let on, but I never forgot.

If you've been to a party where everyone seems to know everyone except you, you know how this feels. They're talking, sharing stories, and catching up. Your stories aren't connected. You have nothing to catch up on. You feel alone, excluded.

Is this what we're doing at work every day? In our neighborhoods? Even in our churches? Are we talking to the people who share our faith and unconsciously excluding those who don't? Are we spending our relational bandwidth with our Christian friends and unconsciously excluding those who don't know Him?

Including outsiders gives purpose to our lives. "Let your light shine before others, that they may see your good deeds and glorify your Father in heaven," says Jesus (Matthew 5:16). That means let it shine around those who live in darkness.

Of those who become Christ followers as adults, 84 percent do so through the influence of a trusted friend. I'm betting the percentage among those treated like outsiders is close to zero.

QUESTION

**Are you unconsciously *exclusive*
to people outside the faith?**

DADDY'S MONEY

My dad might have failed in a lot of ways, but managing money wasn't one of them. He knew exactly how much he had and what it was going to be used for. I followed in his footsteps, using the envelope system to teach my kids to manage their money.

When they went off to college, I noticed a strange phenomenon. When we visited and offered to take them out to eat, they would start inviting people. Come one, come all! You'd think even a college kid might feel guilty ordering up a feast on someone's tab. But no, they ordered food like protesters coming off hunger strikes. Appetizers. Desserts. You name it.

I finally figured out that there are two kinds of money in the economy of college students: their money and Daddy's money. When it's *their* money, they're tight. They hold back, stretch it out. But when it's *Daddy's* money, they're wide open. Enjoy! No restraint. Eat, drink, and be merry (for tomorrow we'll be back on *our* money)!

Do we do the same thing?

After we set aside Daddy's money (e.g., a tithe), do we spend like crazy? Has it dawned on us that it's *all* Daddy's money?

All our money comes from and belongs to God. Every spending decision we make has a spiritual component. Just because we have tithed and met our giving goal doesn't mean we should carelessly throw the rest away.

There are not two currencies, just one. And Christ followers believe in stewardship, not ownership. Jesus' parable of the talents says there will be a day when the Master returns and requires an accounting for what we did with our time, talent, and treasure.

Be thoughtful with *all* of Daddy's money.

QUESTION

Do you believe it's all Daddy's money?
Does that influence your spending decisions?

TOO BUSY

I'm not going to go off on how busy we are. I'm not going to mention the study showing that young people almost *never* unhook from smartphones and technology. I'm pretty sure I'm not the only one who gets mindnumbingly busy and forgets who he is and what he's about, who becomes a "human doing" instead of a human being.

Instead, I'll share the five questions I ask myself when I sense things are going off the rails (and what Scripture says to each question):

1. Have I become less kind and patient?

"Love is patient, love is kind. It does not envy, it does not boast, it is not proud. It does not dishonor others, it is not self-seeking, it is not easily angered, it keeps no record of wrongs. Love does not delight in evil but rejoices with the truth. It always protects, always trusts, always hopes, always perseveres." (1 Corinthians 13:4-7)

2. Have I become less forgiving?

"Repent, then, and turn to God, so that your sins may be wiped out, that times of refreshing may come from the Lord." (Acts 3:19)

3. Am I a good friend right now?

"A friend loves at all times, and a brother is born for a time of adversity." (Proverbs 17:17)

4. Am I praying? And how?

"Rejoice always, pray continually, give thanks in all circumstances; for this is God's will for you in Christ Jesus." (1 Thessalonians 5:16-18)

5. Am I *present*?

"For though I am absent from you in body, I am present with you in spirit and delight to see how disciplined you are and how firm your faith in Christ is." (Colossians 2:5)

QUESTION

Have you gotten too busy?

IF YOUR LIFE IS A DOLLAR . . .

I was just past my thirty-fourth birthday and was a four-month-old Christ follower. Friends had come in from out of town, and we decided to visit First Baptist Church of Atlanta. I opened up the bulletin, and Charles Stanley's name wasn't there. The guest speaker was Ronald Blue, CPA. I thought, *I didn't come to hear a bean counter drone through some boring talk about money. I came to hear Dr. Stanley. The motivator. I came to be inspired, not guilted about giving.* But there was no way out. Ron Blue walked to the podium and asked a question that changed my life:

"If your life is a dollar, what are you spending it for?"

I was stunned. Embarrassed. Knocked off balance. He continued:

"My purpose in life is to glorify God by using my financial knowledge, skills, and experience to help people become better stewards of the resources God has given them."

Wow!

I had never before heard someone state his purpose in life. If I'd written down my answer to his question, it would have said:

"My purpose in life is to glorify Regi Campbell by going as far as I can, as fast as I can, within AT&T."

Pretty lame, huh?

Since we know God doesn't screw up and "there is a time for everything, and a season for every activity under the heavens" (Ecclesiastes 3:1), let me ask you: What's *your* purpose? Have you thought about it? Not something generic, but something specific to you.

QUESTION

Is there some unique thing about you that, if given over to God, could make a huge difference in people's lives? Is there something designed into you that, if unleashed, could bring tremendous meaning to your life and glory to your Heavenly Father?

SEEING AS GOD SEES

God loves you. Completely, totally, unconditionally. Just as you are.

Warts and all.

But what does that really mean, and how does it change your life?

In the safety and security of knowing God loves me, I can be honest with myself about myself. I can unpack things I'd otherwise be ashamed of and ask God to take them away.

The night I surrendered to Christ in my backyard, I grasped God's love for the first time. I saw that my life had been all about me, driven by my need *to matter*. When I realized I already mattered to God, everything changed. I began to see myself as God sees me, not as I see myself.

As I gave God unfettered access to every part of me, He showed me things about myself that He'd built in. Good things. Things He didn't want to change, just redirect. Other things in there, from my sin nature or from stuff I'd added along the way, well, they had to go. Back then, I'd write when I was angry. God kept and grew the writing, but He replaced the anger with gratitude.

Receive God's love for yourself. Then you'll be free to examine yourself, build on the unique gifts and talents God placed in you, and, with God's help, remove the parts He wants out—parts that have no place in the life of a Christ follower.

QUESTION

Have you grasped the fact that God loves you? That He sees you as His son?

THE MAIN THING

If we grow up and live in a "Christian country," how do we get so screwed up?

I think it's because we've forgotten the *main thing*. We've let church take the place of God. And we've neglected, or maybe never understood, the Holy of Holies.

The Holy of Holies was the place in the center of the Temple where man connected with God. In Old Testament parlance, only the high priest could go in and hang out with God, and even for them it was only once a year.

Outside this space was the Temple, where God's people could worship, make sacrifices, give offerings, and hear the Scriptures read and taught. Outside the Temple was the courtyard where anyone could go.

The *main thing* for us is that central place where we meet with, talk to, and are personally loved by our Heavenly Father. At the moment Jesus died, the veil enclosing the Holy of Holies opened up. It was ripped from above, from top to bottom, by God Himself, inviting *all of us* in!

Jesus' death gave each of us access to the Holy of Holies. We have the same access as the most holy man anywhere. No one can take away that unfettered 24/7/365 availability, that unconditional, unwavering love of and access to the King of kings.

The *main thing* is to enjoy continuous fellowship with the Father. That's what He created us for. The church we attend, the denomination we were raised in, even the faith we want our children to have—all that is secondary to connecting with God in a personal way through Jesus.

That's the *main thing*.

QUESTION

**Have you let church become the main thing?
Do you have the guts to move church to
second place and make the Father first?**

THE MYTH OF MULTITASKING

I consider myself a pretty good multitasker. I always have fifteen or twenty things going, am reading multiple books, and am thinking about not just the next thing to do but the next several.

But I have learned that there's no such thing as multitasking. Our brains are wired so we can only focus on one thing at a time. And that's true for all of us.

The difference is how we switch from one thing to another. Some people switch quickly; others more slowly.

Sometimes people use one thing as a "reason to be" but also as a "reason not to be" doing anything else! Emotional/relational things require more switching time than transactional/task-type things, in part because the logical left side and emotional right side of the brain are both required.

So, if our brains can only work on one thing at a time, what do we do?

First, we need a place to *park* stuff that we're not ready to think about when it flashes into our minds. The common wisdom is to write it down.

The second thing we need to do is *schedule* ourselves and the stuff that's on our minds. Writing it down is step one. Deciding if it's worth spending time on and then scheduling it, well, that's the biggie.

Just as God made some of us right-handed and some left, He made some with the ability to switch between tasks more quickly than others. Work with your divine wiring, not against it.

CHALLENGE

**Find work that matches your switching speed.
Adapt your plans and schedule yourself in
harmony with the way He made you.**

CLOUD VS. SERVER DEPENDENCE

In technology circles, cloud computing is all the rage. Keep your music, contacts, apps, projects—everything—in the cloud. When it's on your computer or server, it can be lost, stolen, corrupted, or lose relevance quickly. But when it's in the cloud, it's safe, portable, backed up, and current.

For years, I've focused on becoming all I can be. I've been about learning and growing, as a person and as a Christ follower. I've been developing my *server*.

Don't get me wrong, that's a good thing. But the risk is becoming more about self-improvement than self-surrender and dependence on the *cloud*, on God.

Many people see Christianity as a set of principles and beliefs, mostly centered around deciding what to do or not do. That's a *server* mentality, building our in-house capabilities.

But if a disciple is a learner and follower of Jesus, what about the follow part? The connectivity? The dependence? We can focus so much on the learning part—so much on ourselves and our performance —that we cut God out of the equation. We can get smarter but miss His wisdom and the fellowship He wants with us decision-by-decision, minute-by-minute, day-by-day.

So, in the analogy, God's wisdom is in the cloud. If we turn to Him when we make decisions, before long we'll be totally dependent on Him. On the other hand, the more we depend on our *server*, on our brain and experience, the less dependent we are on Him, and the more vulnerable.

> "For the LORD gives wisdom; from his mouth come knowledge and understanding." (Proverbs 2:6)

Q UESTION

**Are you moving toward dependence
on God or independence from God?**

A FATHER WITH FEW REGRETS

There was an era in business when the "rational method" of decision-making ruled. We created formulas and shot for the highest probability of success and the lowest of failure. We played the odds that if we did certain things, we'd win most of the time.

As fathers, we don't want to "play the odds" with our kids. No matter what we do, we can't guarantee they'll turn out to be wonderful, Jesus-following adults. But we can make decisions that lead to the lowest coefficient of regret for ourselves! We can choose not to do things we'll regret later on.

So many men live with scars from dads who didn't control their tongues and tempers. "Fathers, do not exasperate your children; instead, bring them up in the training and instruction of the Lord" (Ephesians 6:4). At a minimum, we *must* shut up. Control our criticism and anger. We don't usually recognize we're doing it until it's done.

We longed to hear words of praise and affirmation from our dads, but many of us never did. It's amazing how pride paralyzes us. We'll ride mechanical bulls, motorcycles, and wakeboards, but we won't push through our fears of sounding weird or soft by telling our sons and daughters how special they are and how much we love them.

Are you all-in for your kids? Are you fathering so you'll have the least coefficient of regret down the road?

CHALLENGE

Ask God to show you the biggest thing you'll regret as a father years from now. Then ask Him to give you the courage to tackle it.

APPLE OR ONION?

Too many of us try to be apples instead of onions. We put a shiny, red skin on the outside for our kids and others to see. But inside, we might be sweet, sour, crisp, mealy, bruised, or just plain rotten.

An onion is the same all the way through. When a man decides to be all-in with Jesus, life gets simpler. No more posing. No more posturing.

Our kids are always watching what we do more than what we say. And they can tell apples from onions.

One of the unforgettable pictures from my "BC" (Before Christ) days was heading out to the driveway to wash the car one Saturday afternoon. I had my jam box in one hand and a six-pack of Miller Lite in the other. I looked back and noticed my son was following me, toting his kiddie jam box and a six-pack of Coke he'd taken from the pantry.

It was a moment of clarity I've never forgotten. He was doing his version of what he saw me doing. That's what kids do.

Matthew 6:33 says, "Seek first his kingdom and his righteousness, and all these things will be given to you as well." *Seek* is an action word. You can't seek passively; you have to initiate to seek.

The first place for leadership is self-leadership, and "seeking His righteousness" means *becoming an onion*—asking Him for the courage to remove everything that's not onion from our lives. And then mustering the will to lead consistently—to be God's man—inside and out.

QUESTION

**What do your kids see as they
watch your life: apple or onion?**

EGO: EDGING GOD OUT

Our egos fuel us to contend with God. We get a little success, and we start feeling pretty good about ourselves.

But just like there's only one steering wheel in a car, there's only one CEO in our lives. When we're going for what we want, irrespective of what God wants, our ego is in charge, and we start *edging God out*.

I've been reading a Psalm every day. Sometimes the words of David bother me. When things are going badly, he calls for the Lord's wrath on those who deceive, covet, and kill. But then when he's blessed with success, his ego takes over and what does he go and do? Deceive, covet, and kill.

Handling success may be harder than handling failure. One of the things I've tried to do since I surrendered to Jesus years ago is to not take credit for stuff. When awards, recognition, or praise come my way, I try to *deflect*, to *never* take credit personally.

I'm all for healthy self-esteem. And of course we can't quash our egos and live in selfless, sinless perfection. But it's important for Jesus followers to stay grounded. We miss out big-time when our egos *edge God out,* and we forget that every single victory comes through His hand, no matter how smart we are, how hard we work, or how much we sacrifice to get there.

QUESTION

How's your ego lately? Are you getting pretty big on yourself? How are you stacking up on self-centeredness versus God-centeredness?

THE SILENCE OF THE LIE

Telling the truth is one of the linchpins of character. There are fifty-four verses in the Bible about lying. Proverbs 12:22 is one of the best:

"The LORD detests lying lips, but he delights in people who are trustworthy."

Lying lips. That's straight-up speaking something that isn't true.

But there's another side to truth telling. Staying silent in the presence of a lie is a lie, especially when the lie provides an advantage to us.

Mike Moye is a big-time sports agent who made news because he found a mistake in what a player was paid—a $500,000 mistake. He was under no legal requirement to admit the mistake, nor to do anything about it.

But Mike is a trustworthy man, a man of integrity. He and his client chose not to live with a silent lie. The price of that choice was a half a million dollars. Mike sleeps well at night.

People feel good about themselves when they do the right thing. When we step into the silent lie and speak the truth, when we correct the mistake or clear up the confusion, there's a release. A burden is lifted, or avoided altogether.

It's easy to see *why* we should deal with silent lies. The *how* is harder. Being a man of character is going to cost you. But the beauty of being a Christ follower is that our Father is the God of all outcomes who delivers us from evil. He delights in people who are trustworthy.

He's got your back.

QUESTION

**Is there a silent lie you've allowed to
go unaddressed? Will you trust God with
the consequences of cleaning it up?**

LIVING WHOLEHEARTEDLY

Brené Brown's work on vulnerability points us toward wholehearted living. Simply put, her message is, 1) Deal with your shame, 2) Decide you are worthy, 3) Get up enough guts to make yourself vulnerable, and 4) Go take risks—be creative, start your own business, and be all you were meant to be.

The root of all these concepts is our relationship with Christ.

Shame—The truth sets us free from all our guilt and shame, if we will just accept it.

Worthiness—God wants this for us so much that He sent Christ to die in our place. If that doesn't show we're worthy, nothing's going to.

Vulnerability—Since we're worthy of being loved, we can take risks. We have nothing to fear. We have assurance of God's love. I don't have to be enough because He is. I just have to be me.

Courage—Yes, we can drum up the courage to be vulnerable all by ourselves. But how much better it is to remember we're not alone that God is in it with us and for us.

> "The LORD is with me; I will not be afraid. What can mere mortals do to me?" (Psalm 118:6)

To live *wholeheartedly*, I have to be able to engage 100 percent of my heart's capacity. Harboring anything other than pure desire takes away from my 100 percent and my ability to live a wholehearted life.

Wholehearted living is living strong, energetically, and confidently. It's engaging, living on purpose, and living 100 percent in obedience to and for the glory of Jesus Christ.

QUESTION

Will you commit today to living wholeheartedly?

THE PROBLEM WITH EVANGELISM

Why can't we get it through our thick heads that unchurched, non-Christian people aren't "buying" Christianity because they don't think they have any problems (at least none they think our faith can solve). Here's a principle:

People don't buy solutions to problems they don't have!

Here's my short list of problems people have or will have, whether they acknowledge them or not:

Death—I will die at some point.

Fear—I don't want anyone I care about to be sick, hurt, or dead.

Guilt—I want to feel good about myself, but my past is a train wreck.

Meaninglessness—I want to matter and make a difference, but I have no idea how.

Belonging—I want to *belong* somewhere, to be known and accepted.

Acceptance—I want to be loved for who I am, not what I can do for people.

Jesus Christ has answers to every single one of these problems. But if a person isn't disrupted— if they don't feel any of these "problems," we just need to wait. To be there. To love them where they are. Will they buy into our faith? Will they embrace our Jesus at some point? There is no way to know, but that's not our job. If we obey what God calls us to—if we love, and serve, and pray consistently, and we don't let fear keep us from offering the gospel when the time comes, we've done our job.

SCRIPTURE

"Jesus answered, 'I am the way and the truth and the life. No one comes to the Father except through me.'" (John 14:6)

NOT DECIDING IS DECIDING

There are some things we don't ever really decide. We think one way, then we swing back the other way. We don't commit.

Are you *not* deciding any of these things?

- to consistently give to the Lord
- to spend time with God every day
- to regularly pray with my wife
- to send an encouraging note to someone each day
- to spend more quality time with my wife and kids
- to turn off technology at night and be *fully present*
- to volunteer and help the "least of these"

God is decisive. He says, "yes," or "no," or "wait."

Think about it. There's no anguish when we say "yes," mean it, and do it. There's little angst when we say "no" and clearly mean it. It's when we're tentative, when we don't want to commit, when we "need time to think about it," that's when we get in trouble. We decide by not deciding.

A popular way of not deciding is saying, "Let me pray about it." Yes, there are big decisions that we need to pray about. But isn't it true we often *know* the best option right then? We're just putting off the commitment.

Try this. When God speaks, act immediately. Get out the card, make the call, put a reminder on your calendar. When a decision stands in front of you, make it. If you need more data, advice from others, or time with the Father to decide, schedule those actions on your calendar.

If you don't decide, you're deciding anyway.

QUESTION

What decisions are you deciding by *not* deciding?

COMMERCE OVER CHARITY

Over the last twenty years, the number of children dying each day from malnutrition and preventable disease has dropped from 33,000 to about 19,000. Before you relax, remember, that's an NBA arena full of kids under five years old dying *every single day*.

As a Jesus follower, I want to do something. These are helpless kids. The poorest of the poor. The *least of these*. So I do what most of us do. I write checks. Those checks, written by people like us in the developed world, have totaled over one trillion dollars over the last fifty years.

But by all accounts, our charitable generosity has had the *opposite* of the intended effect. Instead of solving issues like hunger and poverty, we've inadvertently perpetuated these crises.

The problem is that we've confused *compassion* with *charity*. Charity is sending clean water to drink after an earthquake. Compassion is helping create commerce so people have jobs, produce income, and build sustainable water and sewer systems.

So what can we do to make a difference?

Do some of both. Give for compassion *and* charity. Don't just write checks; look for a ministry partner with boots on the ground—someone who is deeply connected to and engaged in the work at a local level.

And look for organizations built around sustainability. Too often our charitable efforts fail because they hit like a tidal wave, creating more chaos than charity. Long-term solutions happen from sustainable models built around commerce and business.

It *is* possible to make a difference in the midst of a crisis, it's just a matter of doing the work to find partners in our Father's business.

QUESTION

Will you plug in somewhere? Will you be about our Father's business of helping brothers and sisters in need?

OCTOBER 6

SHAME *IN* ME

I asked my counselor friend why she was so good at getting men to open up and make progress. "I avoid shame," she said. Men have this huge hole in their souls called shame. It's an abject fear that they don't measure up or have what it takes. I used to think it was defensiveness, but it's more than that. It's deeper. More innate.

The root meaning of the word *shame* is "to cover or conceal." When we men feel like we've been attacked, or exposed, or criticized, or rejected, or questioned, we react with either *fight* or *flight*.

I'm amazed by this truth. As I've listened to myself and tried to track what's going on with my emotions as I interact with my wife and others, it's amazing how easy it is to let my desire to avoid shame drive my responses and behavior.

Why would God wire us this way?

He didn't.

There was no shame—no fight or flight—until the fall. Until we lost our innocence and found ourselves struggling with right and wrong, life and death, pride and humility.

Recognizing what's happening in our bodies when this shame *in* us is triggered gives us a split second to turn to Jesus and ask for help. We can say, "Jesus, I know you love me. I know you accept me. What would you have me know about myself right now? About this situation? How would you have me respond?"

Then we can respond as He would have us rather than react to protect ourselves from shame.

SCRIPTURE

**"Therefore, there is now no condemnation
for those who are in Christ Jesus." (Romans 8:1)**

OCTOBER 7

SHAME *ON* ME

Guilt says, "I *did* something bad." Shame says, "I *am* something bad." This kind of message is devastating to a boy, and it makes for a messed-up man later on.

I'll bet you could go back and find some defining moments in your childhood. We all have them—moments where we were made to feel shame.

The key to all this is not that we *feel* shame but how we *respond* to shame, whether we respond to the facts or the feelings. We behave out of what we believe, so we must get *truth* in our noggins and keep on believing it instead of being shaken when we're attacked, questioned, or criticized.

We can't go it alone in this stuff. We need a way out.

There are three components to shedding shame:

> **Facts**—Romans 8:1 says, "Therefore, there is now *no condemnation* for those who are in Christ Jesus." God loves us enough to redefine us. We are *His kids*. We are loved. We are special. We have no shame.

> **Feelings**—Take a deep breath. Process who's talking and why they're talking. Recognize their motivation. Believe it or not, it's usually coming from a misguided desire to help. Patiently respond and don't take it personally.

> **Friends**—Every man needs a buddy. Someone he can safely talk through these very personal things with. An equally transparent, equally vulnerable friend who's on the journey, trying to figure it out along with him.

This shame thing is huge. I think it's foundational. If we can get our minds around this, we move further and faster toward being the man God made us to be.

QUESTION

Will you get this shame thing off of you?

DON'T PROMISE WHEN YOU'RE HAPPY

Our emotions amplify what we're thinking. When we're on a roll, endorphins lubricate our happiness. They make it go higher and faster. We're optimistic. We see abundance. And we can easily get carried away.

It works the other way, too. When we suffer a loss, get turned down or rejected, our lack of happiness accelerates our fall. We lose confidence, see scarcity, and think, *I'm an idiot. Why didn't I see this coming? Bad stuff always comes in threes, right? What's next?*

Anger is the most intense. When someone sets us off, we're ready for fight or *flight*. Responding intelligently in this "red zone" of hormones is about as likely as a pilot giving Boeing feedback on their new airplane while he's trying to pull it out of a death dive.

God gave us emotions for our good. He wants us to experience a full life. I think that's why we have music, and worship, and sex, and sunsets, and grandchildren.

The key to finding wisdom is to slow down the process and extend the time horizon. Big decisions need to be made slowly, and with long-term consequences clearly in focus. That means waiting until the hype wears off. Until the sadness clears away. Until the anger subsides and clear thinking returns.

To protect myself from myself, I have a personal guardrail that says I don't make any big decision the same day I'm confronted with it. I sleep on it, give it twenty-four hours. I've been amazed at how different a decision can look the next day, after a little rest and reflection.

QUESTION

Can you remember a decision you wish you could do over? What effect did the emotions of the moment have on the choice you made?

PRIDE: GOD'S ULTIMATE ENEMY

Look behind almost anything *ungodly* and you'll find pride. Pride is the opposite of humility. It's the enemy of vulnerability. Pride says, "I've got this." And pride is what sent Satan to hell.

Think about it. Here's a spiritual being who's right there with God. In His innermost circle. Maybe like His COO, His Executive Pastor, or His Vice President. He's the number two guy.

But pride, by definition, doesn't want to be number two. Pride wants to be in charge. Pride always wants more. So Lucifer launches a campaign to unseat his boss. He convinces Adam and Eve to join his cast. He says, "Your eyes will be opened, and you will be like God, knowing good and evil" (Genesis 3:5). They bite, and instantly pride infects humanity and the struggle begins.

Pride is like a voice. Pride's voice says, "Keep going. You're right, she's wrong. Stand your ground. Your boss doesn't need to know. You've got this. You don't need help. You don't need anyone!"

Does that sound like God's voice? Like what Jesus would say? Like the Holy Spirit? Like humility?

No.

Check out 2 Chronicles 7:14.

> "If my people, who are called by my name, will humble themselves and pray and seek my face and turn from their wicked ways, then I will hear from heaven, and I will forgive their sin and will heal their land."

God's voice takes us to humility. It reminds us that we're His. That we're called by His name. That He hears us from heaven. And that He forgives and heals.

CHALLENGE

When you feel pride swelling up inside, when pride's voice starts pumping you up, stop and call on Jesus. Then choose humility.

BAD NEWS EARLY, BAD NEWS OFTEN

Somewhere along the line, you're going to have the responsibility to break some bad news to your superiors. No one likes to deliver bad news up the line.

But you have to.

Early in my career, my boss fell while jogging and suffered a head injury. He started talking like he was off his rocker, giving erratic instructions and weird responses when we'd ask him questions.

After a little while, I took what could have been a career-limiting risk. I called his boss (who was in another city) and said, "You might better get up here. I think Mr. Simpson needs your help." His boss came quickly, talked with him long enough to see that something wasn't right, and then drove him to the hospital, where he stayed for a week.

My boss was scared to death of his boss, and he would have fired me before he'd have let me report his temporary insanity. But I delivered the bad news for the good of Mr. Simpson and for the company, and it all worked out.

When you go to your superiors with the truth of a situation, when you present the facts clearly, without prejudice and without placing blame, you actually *gain* credibility and respect. (Notice I said *facts*, not opinions!)

Sure, there are stories of the messenger being shot for the message. But those are overstated. Usually when the messenger gets shot, his fingerprints are on a few things connected to the bad news. And even if they weren't, getting fired for telling the truth is way better than getting whacked for covering it up.

CHALLENGE

Have you been sitting on top of some bad news your bosses *really* need to know? Will you man up, trust God, and tell them?

OCTOBER 11

ARE YOU DONE WITH RELIGION?

I'm done with religion.

Every day, I run into someone whose story has the same plot: born into a churchgoing family, baptized as a kid, hammered with rules and rituals, walked away, and wound up with a messed-up marriage, family, head, or heart.

Religion kind of vaccinated me from a relationship with God. Without meaning to, it taught me that saying a few magic words would somehow make everything perfect. At twelve years old, I wasn't very aware of my *sin,* but I knew I was supposed to feel really happy for being forgiven.

What I missed was the *love* part. It just didn't get through. The part about Him being personal. About Him knowing my name. About Him caring about what I was facing and how I was feeling about it.

Grasping God's love changes everything. Realizing God loves us personally unconditionally and personally and regardless of our performance allows us to relax. When I thank Him for loving me and ask Him what He'd have me know about the situations I'm in and the people I'm with, He gives me thoughts and spurs me to action. He reminds me of Scriptures, or things He's taught me in the past.

See the difference?

If you have children, which do you want them to have? If all you have is religion, that's the best you have to give them. But a relationship is something you can tell them about. Let them watch. Invite them into. Over time, Jesus might just become their best friend and father them too.

I've lived twenty-one years with religion and thirty-five years in relationship. Relationship beats the snot out of religion.

CHALLENGE

**Are you ready to drop religion and
enter into a relationship with God?**

YOUR COHERENT NARRATIVE

Your *coherent narrative* is the story of your life. It's usually chronological, starting with where and how you grew up and the big things happening *to you* leading to big changes *in you*.

It starts with remembering. Mark Buchanan says, "To remember is, literally, 'to put broken pieces back together' . . . to re-member. It is to create an original wholeness out of what has become scattered fragments." To *dis-member* something is to take it apart, to *re-member* is the opposite.

And the most important piece you can decide to put in or leave out is God. Was He in your story? Where was He involved? Is He in it now?

I'm one of those nutcases who believe God is in my story *big time!* His omnipotence, omniscience, and omnipresence mean He's there throughout, every day of my life. By definition, everything came through His hands.

If God is not in my story, life is out of control. If He is, it all makes sense. God uses everything for my good. He wastes nothing. It comes down to Romans 8:28:

> "And we know that in all things God works for the good of those who love him, who have been called according to his purpose."

Everyone's coherent narrative has a version that includes God and one that doesn't. The version you believe affects everything—your outlook, attitude, relationships, confidence, peace, and hope (or lack thereof). It shapes how you see God and everything else.

Isn't it more glory-giving to *figure God in* than to spend the rest of your life futilely trying to *figure Him out*?

CHALLENGE

Think about how you tell your story, to others and to yourself. Is it the truth? Is it God's story in your life or a version you pieced together to stay safe?

OCTOBER 13

LUCKY OR BLESSED

When things go your way, are you *lucky* or *blessed*?

And the other side, when things fall apart, are you *unlucky* or *cursed*?

Two thoughts:

You don't cause God to bless you by being righteous. Jesus said, "He causes his sun to rise on the evil and the good, and sends rain on the righteous and the unrighteous" (Matthew 5:45). It's not cause and effect.

- You don't cause God to curse you by being wicked. You can bring earth-ly consequences on yourself, but God's punishment comes after you die.

- No doubt a just God levels severe punishment for wickedness. But in an amazing, mysterious, and merciful act, God placed all our punishment on Jesus at the cross. The punishment doled out 2,000 years ago cover-ed all wickedness, then and now.

Someday in heaven maybe we'll understand why God decided to discon-nect our performance from His earthly reward and punishment. There are times when I know He's blessed me in some personal way. I know He loves to give good gifts to His children, but I believe that's because we're His children, not because we've done something good. Remember, our right-eousness is like filthy rags compared to His.

We'll never bring God down to the level where we understand, control, or predict Him. And don't ask me about the part prayer plays in all this; that's beyond my pay grade. But I do know this:

> "The LORD does whatever pleases him, in the heavens and on the earth, in the seas and all their depths." (Psalms 135:6)

And it's my job to respond in gratitude.

QUESTION

Are you lucky or blessed? Unlucky or cursed?

GOD AND GOOGLE

I'm on a lifelong guilt trip for not reading my Bible. I can't understand why it's so hard. Where do I start? What do I read? Do I read all the way through? Take a single book and study it deeply? Do I take a topic and read every verse about it? Or follow a guide of some sort?

Then there's the question of circumstance. Some folks swear by reading early in the morning. Others say reading the Bible at night helps press meaning into the events of the day.

Let me offer a different approach: Google.

Instead of cramming God into a time slot, try turning to Him throughout the day. Google what you're thinking or feeling. Type in a fragment of Scripture and Google usually takes you to a Bible website where you can find the full verse. With one click, you can read it in any translation. And God speaks from His Word specifically to what you're facing or feeling.

Sometimes I'll type in, "What does the Bible say about (fill in the blank)?" That'll take me to an article, or book, or sermon which includes a Scripture reference. I go there, and I'm in His Word.

God is not going to force Himself onto your radar, onto your calendar, or into your mind. You choose where you turn for guidance and what you do when God comes to mind.

The Internet is like money—it's amoral. It can be used for God, for good, or for evil. We get to choose.

When there's a pause in your day, pray. If God brings something to your mind, Google it. Find the Scripture He has for you and thank Him for staying so close.

CHALLENGE

**Will you use Google and other web
tools to move toward God?**

OCTOBER 15

THE CHOICE NOT TO CHASE

At a good friend's sixtieth birthday party, his son raised a toast. He said something that piqued my interest.

"My dad is the most content person I know."

I started processing those words and realized his dad is the most content person *I know* too! So I asked him for his *secret sauce*. Here it is:

1. **A heart of gratitude**—His default setting is gratitude. No matter what may be lacking or missing, his focus goes back to, "Thank you, God," for all he's been given.

2. **A historical perspective**—The past reminds him how far he's come and how blessed he is.

3. **A choice not to chase**—He doesn't chase riches, or titles, or relationships, or fame, or power. He waits for God to send whatever He wants, and he's decided to be satisfied with whatever happens.

When I think about the people I know, those who are the most content are the most grateful. They have a good grasp of where they've come from, and they aren't chasing anything. They're pursuing God and His righteousness in their lives and families.

Solomon, the wisest man in history, may have summed it up best:

"What do people get for all the toil and anxious striving with which they labor under the sun? All their days their work is grief and pain; even at night their minds do not rest. This too is meaningless.

"A person can do nothing better than to eat and drink and find satisfaction in their own toil. This too, I see, is from the hand of God, for without him, who can eat or find enjoyment?" (Ecclesiastes 2:22-25)

QUESTION

Are you content? What are you chasing? Is it worth it?

DADDY AND THE CHECKERED FLAG

It's crazy how much our dads shape us. No one escapes the power and influence of their earthly father.

Mine was more absent than involved. When I grew up and realized it, I was hurt. And mad. After I came to faith in Christ and realized the "Father-son" relationship God wanted with me, I replaced my earthly father with my Heavenly Father.

It freed me from my dad's expectations. I forgave him. We became friends. I loved and served him as a choice, not an obligation. Those were sweet years. Then he died.

Paul wrote in Ephesians 6:2-3,

> "'Honor your father and mother'—which is the first commandment with a promise—'so that it may go well with <u>you</u> and that you may enjoy long life on the earth.'"

I underlined *you* because it may not be obvious that honoring your father and mother benefits *you*.

I chose to invest time with my dad during his last years. It was hard. It was a one-way street because he didn't know how to love me back. But choosing to love on him, hang out with him, and take care of him was one of the best decisions I ever made.

My dad passed away twenty years ago. As we drove home from the funeral, I told my wife, "I feel like sticking a checkered flag out the window, like the winner of a NASCAR race." I did good by him. Even if he didn't do good by me, I did good by him.

Do well by your dad while you can, so "it may go well with <u>you</u> and that you may enjoy long life on the earth."

QUESTION

Are you holding your dad's performance against him? Will you choose to forgive and start to honor him from here on out

IS JESUS SATISFIED WITH ME?

I grew up Baptist, and my mind sometimes goes to the B.B. McKinney hymn, "I Am Satisfied." Written in 1926, it had a good tune but bad theology in the chorus.

> But the question comes to me,
> As I think of Calvary,
> Is my Master satisfied with me?

This question can create so much confusion. If you're a follower of Jesus, then God is satisfied with you. When He looks at you, He sees the holiness of His Son, who swapped His purity for your sin. What performance could you possibly add to that?

The question is, "Are *you* satisfied with you?" Knowing the incredible price God paid to give you this holy status, don't you want to at least turn away from the stuff His Son died to free you from?

Our obedience gives God glory, just as we get a little glory when our kids do what we want. Because the Holy Spirit lives in us, we *know* right from wrong. We usually *know* what He'd have us do in a given situation or relationship.

Mustering the courage to do the right thing and trusting Him with the outcome—that is the challenge.

Jesus' birth put all this in motion. Imagine the Father's angst as the day approached when Jesus disappeared from heaven and showed up in a stable. Imagine the knot in God's stomach knowing Herod would kill thousands of innocent babies hoping Jesus would be among them. And that was *before* He started threatening the political and religious establishment with His message of redemption. God suffered all of that to create an opportunity to be satisfied with us.

QUESTION

Do you really believe that God is satisfied with you regardless of your performance? It's the gospel. Believe it.

ARE YOU SATISFIED WITH JESUS?

As Christ followers, we know where we've come from. We know our story, what we've been forgiven for and maybe some of what we've been protected from. And we know where we're going: to heaven to be with God, and Jesus, and the Holy Spirit, and with Christian friends and family.

But what about now? Today?

John Piper says, "God is most glorified in me when I am most satisfied in Him. He's on a crusade to bring our satisfaction to 100 percent. If I'm satisfied in Him, then I know I'm loved and not just used."

"There is a God-shaped vacuum in the heart of every man which cannot be filled by any created thing, but only by God, the Creator, made known through Jesus," wrote Blaise Pascal. When God's presence fills the entirety of that vacuum, there's nothing else to want. Nothing else needs to be satisfied.

Jesus is ultimate. The ultimate Savior of our souls when we die, the only chance we have of forgiveness for our past here on earth, and the complete answer for every issue in our current circumstance.

And there's not a single question Jesus doesn't answer. Not a single need He doesn't meet. Not a single outcome that can't be understood when we see as God sees. Only He can completely fill that God-shaped vacuum in our hearts. He loves you and me, and He wants what's best for us long-term.

SCRIPTURE

"God, who is rich in mercy, made us alive with Christ even when we were dead in transgressions—it is by grace you have been saved." (Ephesians 2:4-5)

October 19

SINGING THE SAME SONG

Angie worked with me at Radical Mentoring early on. She passed away from breast cancer. As I drove to her funeral, I sang praise songs, as I often do. But then I realized, when we started singing at the celebration service, *Angie would be singing with us*. Simultaneously praising our Father.

It's comforting to know we're together in doing what we were made for, even though she is gone from the flesh and we're not. It's so cool to know her soul is alive and well, singing really loudly to Jesus!

Dallas Willard, the brilliant theologian, philosopher, and teacher, taught that a person is "a collection of conscious experiences" that will go right on, un-interrupted by death. Jesus said that those who trust in Him will not taste death (Matthew 16:28).

I translate that to mean we go to sleep in this world and wake up in the next. We're still conscious of who we were, but with transformed bodies, sinless hearts, and unfettered exuberance for what comes next.

I've heard widows ask, "I wonder what my husband is doing up in heaven right now. I so wish I could be with him, to do stuff together like we used to."

Well, the closest you're going to get to that is to sing a song of authentic praise and know he's singing the same song at the same time to the same awesome God.

And that's pretty good.

PRAYER

Lord, thank You for wanting to be with us. From the beginning, that's why You made us and all You ever wanted. Thank You for giving us a way to get back to where we started—walking with You and experiencing Your presence in our praise and in the smallest of moments.

A WRAPPED PACKAGE

If you found a wrapped gift in the park or on the subway, would you open it?

You'd think twice, wouldn't you? I would. Not knowing where or who it came from would scare me off.

How many of God's gifts have we chosen not to open because of the packagin? Race, culture, denomination, economic level, educational background, gender? We turn away or choose not to engage, missing blessings and divine appointments left and right.

Life is defined by relationships. That's why we exist. God's whole deal with Jesus was about relationships, offering a way to be forgiven for the sin in our past *and* a way to live forward, facing toward God and others. Forgiveness allows us to deal with people in our past. Acceptance lets us connect with people in our future.

Writer and poet Carl Sandburg once said he hated the word, "exclusive." I think about that a lot. Who am I *excluding*? Who scares me? Whom do I turn away from? Whom do I avoid? Whom do I dread spending time with?

Church people talk about "open" and "closed" doors all the time. What if strangers are open doors into lives God wants to touch through you? And maybe even gifts He has for you that can't be opened until you disregard the wrapping and connect?

Yes, it takes time. But if we are the light of the world, how can we shine into the lives of others unless we open some packages from strangers and engage with people outside our holy huddle and comfort zone?

CHALLENGE

Will you ask God to give you *just one* divine appointment with a stranger today?

WHEN GOD BREAKS YOUR HEART

I've been challenged with the question: "What does your heart break *for*?"

It's not, "What breaks your heart?" Those things are momentary.

When your heart breaks *for* something, it says you have more than momentary sympathy. You feel a conviction to do something. And it's really about *someone*. Maybe the question is, "*Whom* does your heart break for?"

How do you know when your heart breaks *for* someone? Two clues:

1. When you see or think of this person/these people, you get emotional.
2. Your mind keeps coming back to them. They just won't go away.

If your heart doesn't break for *anyone*, you may need a wake-up call. You may have let selfishness grow to the point that it has pushed empathy for others out of your heart.

We talked a few days ago about Blaise Pascal's idea of the God-shaped hole in every man's heart. No one can be satisfied or have peace without filling that hole, and Jesus is the only thing that fits and fills it.

But filling that hole with Jesus doesn't mean wholeness on its own. There's more. When He said, "I have come that they may have life . . ." (John 10:10), that's about filling the hole.

But when Jesus went on to say, ". . . and have it to the full," I think He was talking about the abundant life we can only experience when we move beyond "me and mine" to loving and serving others. If you want more (and if you'll let Him), He'll punch a hole in your heart that only "doing for others" will fill.

And when you do something, when you start to move, He'll fill it to overflowing.

QUESTION

Whom does your heart break for?

HISTORY GIVES PERMISSION

Years ago, I had a debate with a good friend about how much of your past to share with your kids. He'd used drugs in school and thought full transparency was best.

I don't need to tell you what happened. Oldest son ended up in rehab. Police record. Drugs changed the trajectory of his life.

Would the boy have avoided drugs had his dad not revealed his history?

I don't know.

What I do know is that certain parts of our story should be reserved until our kids grow up and mature.

Parents can tell their kids, "Do as I say, not as I did," but kids are deaf until they grow up. Kids listen to what you say, but they watch what you do, and they remember your stories. If you did it, they interpret that as permission to do it. No matter how wrong, how selfish, or how devastating.

John Maxwell teaches "the law of the lid"—how we never exceed parameters we set for ourselves. But some lids are put there by our parents. If my mom and dad worked out their marriage problems and stuck together, that's a lid—a parameter that guides you. Their tenacity gives you permission to be tenacious. If they give up and get divorced, their behavior gives you permission to do the same thing.

Living out good habits and good deeds invites your kids into Christlikeness. Modeling bad stuff and bragging about your childhood adventures gives your kids permission to do everything you did.

QUESTION

**What are you giving your kids permission
to do? Will you think and pray about what
God would have you do about it? And will
you then ask Him to give you the courage
to act on what He shows you?**

WHAT DOES LOVE REQUIRE OF ME, RIGHT NOW?

I needed a way to remember to respond to my wife better. Something catchy that might fit on a bracelet or a coffee cup.

I remembered this great question: "In light of my past experience, my present circumstances, and my future hopes and dreams, what is the wise thing to do?"

Awesome. But too long for a wristband.

Listening to the sermon one Sunday, there it was:

"What does love require of me, right now?"

This may be the most useful question ever for Jesus followers. Since the second commandment is about loving one another, and since all of life is experienced *right now*, tell me a better way of managing yourself. Of responding to your wife, your kids, the people at work, whomever.

We could ask, "What does God require of me," but somehow using the word "love" in the question makes it more actionable. It's quicker to know what to do than opening up all the theology attached to "God."

And I like the word "require," too. It says, "Hey, this ain't optional." If I'm to be loving, *right now*, what's required of me? Love may require something totally different long-term. I may have to change something in the relationship. I may have to exert tough love. I may have to stand up to an issue or stand up for myself. Relational stuff requires thought, and prayer, and wise counsel, and time. "What is the wise thing to do?" is a great question when you have time to think about things in the bigger picture.

But *in the moment*, I haven't found a better way of seeking and finding the Lord's will than to ask, "What does love require of me, right now?"

QUESTION

So, what does love require of you, right now?

ELEVATOR BUTTONS

My pastor friend Brian said this in a sermon: "Friends are like elevator buttons. They'll take you up, or they'll take you down. Show me your friends, and I'll show you your future."

This is certainly true about teenagers. If you want to raise them well, help them choose great friends.

Dads want to hold their kids accountable, but Bob Goff says to *hold them close* instead. You gotta be close to know what they're dealing with or whom they're listening to. The further we are from our kids, the less we'll know and the more misreads we will make.

I went all-in with Jesus when my kids were small. My son was ten, my daughter was seven. Up until then, I'd been present at everything they did, but my mind was always elsewhere.

Here's the switch that happened: I went from emotionally unavailable to emotionally available. Not perfectly, not all the time, but a lot more than before I met Jesus.

Instead of just being there physically, I started listening to their words *and* their hearts. I started paying attention to my kids' interactions with other kids. Slowly my wife and I began to curate those friends, encouraging some into our circle and gracefully leaving others behind.

I've always said love is spelled t-i-m-e. That's not true anymore. "Love is spelled a-t-t-e-n-t-i-o-n," says Pastor Brian.

Focused attention. They'll feel your love. You'll earn influence. And you'll become a friend who can help with the elevator buttons.

PRAYER

**Father, when we think back to how little we knew
when we were younger, we're in awe of your grace
and mercy toward us. Please help us choose our
friends wisely, and help us as we help our kids choose
friends who will walk wisely with their God. Amen.**

HONOR YOUR FATHER AND MOTHER

Blake is a new friend. When his mom began to experience dementia and was diagnosed with early-onset Alzheimer's, he spent the next ten years caring for her. His company's IPO gave him the resources to do it. He became known as "the guy who cared for his mom." That's honoring your mother big-time.

But what about the rest of us? Facing the normal circumstances of parents growing older, how can we honor our parents? What can an adult child do or say that will bestow *honor* to their parents?

Here are six ways to honor your father and mother:

1. **Praise them behind their backs**—The highest compliment you'll ever receive is the one not intended for your ears.

2. **Track your parents' loved ones and express interest and concern**—While they might not have been an important part of your life, they're important *to your parents*. Ask about them and show you care.

3. **Always say thank you**—Unexpressed gratitude feels like ingratitude.

4. **When they're sick, check on them**—Not just once, but consistently until they're well. They want your concern out of love, not duty.

5. **Offer to pay whenever they take you out**—Our offer to pay validates the value of what's being given.

6. **Remember *their* important dates**—Birthdays, anniversaries, and special dates from their life are especially important at this age.

SCRIPTURE

"'Honor your father and mother'—which is the first commandment with a promise—'so that it may go well with you and that you may enjoy long life on the earth.'" (Ephesians 6:2-3)

ARE YOU CONTENTIOUS?

Contentious: given to arguing or provoking argument.

A contentious person likes to be right. They're pursuing the truth while protecting themselves. They won't stop until they've gotten their point across. Their arguing is a habitual response to their spouse, the stimulus of conversation, or both.

Why do we attribute contentiousness to women? Maybe it's because it's something we see multiple times in the book of Proverbs. But men are just as prone to that trait.

Whether it's her or you, contentiousness is a deadly, debilitating habit that can be stopped with focused effort. It doesn't matter who it starts with; it's who stops it that matters.

Jesus was never contentious. One of the best examples of His lack of contentiousness was when He met Mary and Martha after Lazarus died. Verbally assaulted by Martha, Jesus replied patiently, then went about raising Lazarus from the dead.

He didn't push back or contend; He kindly went on with His business.

When you're tempted to be contentious, don't. Stop with the facts and leave off that extra phrase that causes all the problems. If your spouse tends toward being contentious, talk about it. Ultimately, someone has to go first, either to stop the contention or to process it differently.

Leaders go first.

PRAYER

Lord, it's clear from Proverbs that You don't want Your children to live in an environment of contention. Give us patience as we attempt to live with each other in an understanding way. Help us to forgive when we feel challenged, criticized, and contended with by our spouses. Help us to relax in Your complete, unconditional love and acceptance. In Your Son's precious name, Amen.

JESUS-FOLLOWING DADS

Jesus-following dads start by helping their kids understand *who they are in Christ.* Does your kid know he's an adopted child of the King of kings—completely forgiven, totally adequate, and perfectly worthy?

When teens understand who they are in Christ, they discover a meaningful identity. This identity makes it much easier to know what to do in those moments when right and wrong seem fuzzy, or when parents push back on a decision.

Their thought process becomes based on, "What would Jesus have me do?" because their identity in Christ is the foundation of who they are.

My friends Craig and Kerry have three wonderful daughters. When decisions come up about short skirts and low-cut blouses, Kerry asks, "Do you think that's appropriate?" A lot of kids would push back, thinking mom is putting her idea of appropriate on them.

But these girls have developed their own identities, their own standards of what's appropriate and what's not. They've avoided most of the fights about what can be worn and what can't because they have thought it through for themselves. "I know who I am. People like me don't wear stuff like that. People like me don't do those things."

CHALLENGE

If you want to reduce the teenager tension in your house, focus on identity. Lead your kids to know who they are in Christ.

OCTOBER 28

LEARNERS AND THE LAZY SUSAN

There's a restaurant I know that serves food on a Lazy Susan in the middle of the table. The server puts on the food, and you spin it around to fill and refill your plate.

I think God grows us in a similar way. He keeps life interesting by serving it up on a Lazy Susan. Sometimes it's meat, sometimes it's cake. Sometimes it's a party, sometimes it's an issue we're forced to deal with.

One way or another, with or without God, you respond. If you're wise, you learn from your "serving." You learn more about God and about yourself. If you're foolish, you don't.

Learning is rarely pushed onto your plate—you get to choose. You're listening to a sermon, reading a book, listening to a song or talking with someone, when "BAM!" There it is.

Like a dad fathering his son, or a mentor leading a younger one, God brings something to our attention and invites us to class. Check this out:

> "Take my yoke upon you and learn from me, for I am gentle and humble in heart, and you will find rest for your souls." (Matthew 11:29)

A yoke in Jesus' day was the specific teaching of an individual rabbi. So when Jesus challenged His followers to "take my yoke upon you and learn from me," He might have been saying, "Watch me as events occur in my life. Listen to my teaching. Model what I do, how I respond, and who I am. Life with me is the only life where you'll find rest for your souls."

When the Lazy Susan of life spins trouble your way, will you stop and ask, "Lord, what are You teaching me here?"

PRAYER

Father, please create in me a gentle, humble, teachable heart.

WHO'S SPEAKING?

Sometimes I catch myself saying stuff that shocks me. I hear words come out of my mouth and think, *That was awful. Where did that come from? I thought I was a new creation!*

But then I'll be in another situation, and I'm amazed at how God seems to speak through me. I come up with just the right question or the perfect comment. How can this be?

It seems there are three *voices* with which we speak.

1. **My voice**—Not much spiritual about that one.

2. **God's voice**—Christ living in me is loving, kind, generous, understanding, merciful. He is love. When we *choose* to respond in His power, we speak His words. Knowing Scripture gives our brains the words to express what God would have us say.

3. **The non-God voice**—The voice of evil. Sadly, we sometimes listen to the evil one, giving him a foothold in our hearts. And before we know it, he's speaking through us.

So what should we do?

1. Stay close to the Father. God's presence in your life is your first defense against evil intruders and saying bad stuff.

2. Pause and consider which voice is about to speak. *Is this going to sound like me? Or Jesus?* If it's not Voice #2, call on Jesus and zip it.

3. Set this filter for yourself:

   "Do not let any unwholesome talk come out of your mouths, but only what is helpful for building others up according to their needs, that it may benefit those who listen." (Ephesians 4:29)

QUESTION

Will you choose today to stop using unkind, judgmental, accusatory, critical, harsh, or insensitive words?

DON'T STAY IN THE HALL

In his classic work, *Mere Christianity,* C.S. Lewis shares timeless words about Christianity and the church.

> "Christianity . . . is more like a hall out of which doors open into several rooms. If I can bring anyone into that hall I shall have done what I attempted. But it is in the rooms, not in the hall, that there are fires and chairs and meals. The hall is a place to wait in, a place from which to try the various doors, not a place to live in."

One recent study uncovered the rising trend of Americans who mark their religious affiliation as "none." A lot of them are people who "waited in the hall" but never connected with a church.

Check out this line from the survey. It's even more disturbing!

> "For every person who has joined a religion after having been raised unaffiliated, there are more than four people who have become religious none's after having been raised in some religion."

We've got to change some stuff, and fast. The local church has to get real and connect. Fathers, we've got to disciple our kids personally and passionately. And publicly, we've got to replace our *two-faced hypocrisy* with *true-faced authenticity*, love, and grace.

If you're "in the hall" and not in a local church, find one and get involved. Our churches need men to stand up and lead.

CHALLENGE

Are you still "in the hall"? Are you a consumer who keeps shopping for the perfect church? Pray for God's guidance and courage to get out of your lethargy and into a local church.

TAKE COURAGE

Where does courage come from? Why does it matter? If I want to be brave, what do I lean on, especially when the outcome of my bravery can't be known?

Sometimes courage comes *from within* (courage of our convictions), meaning we believe in something so much we'll stand up or even put ourselves in danger because we *have to*.

Then there's courage *from others* (courage from our identity). "You're a Campbell." "Airborne!" "Semper Fi." "Eagle Scout." We lean on our identity, our heritage, the bravery of our forebearers, or the expectations of our colleagues past and present.

But then there's courage *from God* (courage to obey). This one's all about who the order comes from and the *why* behind it. It's obeying God no matter the consequences or outcome. For His glory. Out of love, respect, and honor for God.

Some think letting go of fear equals courage, but I don't. The absence of fear is not courage. It may bring peace, but not progress. Courage is *moving through fear*, doing something in spite of it. John Wayne said, "Courage is being scared to death . . . and saddling up anyway."

Try this.

The next time you hear someone misrepresent something and you get that nervous lump in your throat, ask the "next tough question" and expose the lie. The next time you think about talking to one of your kids about what God is doing in your life, act on it. Right then.

They say we learn more about God in one moment of obedience than in a lifetime of sacrifice.

QUESTION

**Will you take courage, obey, and watch
what happens in your heart as a result?**

KIDS LOVED JESUS. DO THEY LOVE YOU?

"Then people brought little children to Jesus for him to place his hands on them and pray for them. But the disciples rebuked them. Jesus said, 'Let the little children come to me, and do not hinder them, for the kingdom of heaven belongs to such as these.' When he had placed his hands on them, he went on from there."
(Matthew 19:13-15)

Some well-meaning parents cut their kids loose, and they swarmed Him. They wanted to get close to Jesus. They read Jesus' face, they looked at His eyes and His body language, and they sensed acceptance.

When Jesus saw the disciples' reaction to these kids, He paused. He said, "Let the children come to me and do not hinder them."

Paraphrase: "I love them just as they are." Innocent, raw, and real-time. There was no processing, calculating, qualifying, or parsing, no hesitance at all. That's what flows from a pure, unhurried heart.

Then Jesus reached out in love and touched them. "He laid hands on them." In that culture, children were often blessed by important people in their families and communities.

Imagine the impact this kind of courageous prayer and vision-casting can have on kids. God works through us to shape future generations.

I think our reaction to little kids reveals the status of our hearts. When you catch yourself hurried, impatient, or irritated, see that as a poke from the Holy Spirit to check up, to slow down and figure out how to bless that child in some way. Like Jesus did.

PRAYER

Please give me the sensitivity to hear Your prompting and the courage to act wisely in response. In Your beautiful name, amen.

JESUS KILLED THE CURVE

Do you remember when a teacher or professor would grade on the curve? They'd give the test, take the scores, and scale them out on a bell-shaped curve, declaring the top 10 percent A's, the bottom 10 percent F's, and the rest of us B, C, or D by default.

Some teachers would curve the scores by taking the highest grade on the test and adding enough points to make it 100. If the best score was 92, then everyone got 8 points added to their score. Occasionally, someone would blow the curve by making 100. I hated that guy; I needed those 8 points.

Jesus killed the curve. Through His perfection, He brought justice. He made 100. No curve. No points added. He set the standard of perfection because God is perfect, and He only connects with perfection.

We *pass* through perfection. Anything less, and we *fail*. With pass/fail, you make it or you don't. And we don't. We are doomed to failure on our own because we can't make 100.

But Jesus went to the cross to pay the price *for us*. He made 100 *for us*. Everything He did was *for us*, not for Himself. He voluntarily took the test, performed with perfection, and turned in His test score for us. We get full credit for His work. It's totally not fair, but grace is the opposite of fairness; it's a gift. Undeserved blessing.

Why would Jesus do this?

So you and I would be forever grateful. We were created to worship. For God's glory.

QUESTION

What kind of worship tops gratitude? Say, "Thank You, Jesus," and acknowledge both who He is *and* what He's done for you.

DEEP FAITH

How does one develop deep faith?

Through evaluated experience. To have faith in someone, I have to trust them. That means I take a chance on them and then watch what they do. When I take another chance, trust them, and they come through again, I trust them a little more. Over time, I see they're dependable, and I trust them.

Eventually my faith grows beyond their *performance for me.* Now I have faith in their *love for me.* It's personal.

This happens through surrender. The proverbial "leap of faith" is usually only taken when there's no other option. It's an all-in, all-at-once experiment in faith. You jump off the building and hope for the best. If your friend catches you and saves your life, you'll have faith in him big-time! He came through for you; you can trust him.

Faith, by definition, is "confidence in things not seen." If it was made of concrete and steel, it wouldn't be faith, and it wouldn't require the heart.

Jesus Christ, the Divine Presence of God in a human body, came to personalize and energize our faith. He came miraculously, performed all kinds of miraculous things, then died and came back to life miraculously, all so we can have a real faith.

Grow your faith a little at a time. Pray, listen, ask, receive, express gratitude, walk, and talk with Him every day. Watch how He never leaves or forsakes you.

CHALLENGE

**He's calling you to grow your faith
through a bold leap. Go for it. Jump.**

EUCATASTROPHE

It seems like every day there's another catastrophe, another shooting, massacre, tornado, or capsized boat. With instant news and constant repetition, we're hit in the heart with shocking events and bad news.

But the God of the universe is good . . . all the time! He hasn't lost His way. He hasn't gone bad. He isn't dead or asleep. He loves us. His love, truth, and beauty are all around.

J.R.R. Tolkien coined the word *eucatastrophe* when he added the Greek prefix *eu* (meaning "good") to the surprise implied in *catastrophe*. It's the unexpected appearance of goodness. In *The Letters of J.R.R. Tolkien*, he defined it as "the sudden happy turn in a story which pierces you with a joy that brings you to tears." It has this effect on us "because it is a sudden glimpse of Truth" in which we "feel a sudden relief as if a major limb out of joint had suddenly snapped back."

Take a few minutes to recall eucatastrophe moments in your life. When did something incredibly joyful overtake you? In a moment you least expected, something good happened, and you were in tears before you knew it. Yeah, it'll take a few minutes to pull them up because that garden of good stuff is paved over with disasters, close calls, bad news, and worries. But I'll bet you can remember a few moments so joyful and good you were overwhelmed.

Jot them down. Then tell Him thanks!

SCRIPTURE

"I will remember the deeds of the Lord; yes, I will remember your miracles of long ago." (Psalm 77:11)

CARE QUADRUPLES COMPLEXITY

Guys just want to get stuff done. We don't want to think about it; we know what we're doing. We don't have the time or patience to consider how it's going to make her feel, how it sounds to the children, or what the repercussions might be down the road. Ready-fire-aim. Just do it.

Jumping in and doing and saying what you feel is quick and easy. *Being careful* with people, with money, with decisions, with what we say—well, it makes life more complex.

Why?

Four reasons:

1. **Careful slows us down**—Thinking about the consequences of what you're about to do takes time.

2. **Careful involves others**—Once someone tells you what they think, there's an obligation to do what they say or at least tell them why you didn't follow their advice.

3. **Careful thinks longer-term**—Slowing down to be careful takes you beyond *right now* and asks you to think about *down the road,* about longer-term consequences. It takes extra effort.

4. **Careful requires humility**—Ego says, "I've got this." Careful says, "Whoa, maybe I ask around. Gather input." It says, "I don't know everything about everything."

Think about the arguments you and your wife wouldn't have had if you'd been more *careful* with your promises.

Think about the money you could still have if you'd been more *careful* about investing, spending, saving, and giving.

Think about the people in your life you'd still be close to if you'd been more *careful* to forgive, reach out, express gratitude, and show you care.

QUESTION

Will you take the time to live a little more carefully?

DOUBLE-MINDED

As I'm reading Matthew's account of Jesus' last hours, I see Peter and imagine what it was like to be him.

He'd healed people, seen the dead raised, and walked side-by-side with the Messiah for three-and-a-half years. From all that experience and with total confidence, Peter swears to Jesus, "I'll be there with you, even if it means dying."

Then reality bites. A switch gets flipped. Jesus is carried off and put before the authorities, flanked by soldiers brandishing weapons of torture and death. All the disciples except Peter scatter like rats into the dark.

Peter sticks around. He wants to stand up, but he's torn. Double-minded. All-in for Jesus one moment, faithless the next.

There are two *processors* constantly running in the mind and heart of the Jesus follower: the flesh and the Spirit. The flesh is looking out for physical needs, making everything about me right now. The Holy Spirit is Jesus living in us, living in light of eternity. His still small voice guides, corrects, comforts, and affirms.

We get to *choose* to respond in the Spirit or respond in the flesh. Our flesh will speak lightning-fast. The Spirit will cause us to pause and respond from the truth, the wisdom, and the love of Jesus in our hearts.

When the pressure comes, which way will you flip your switch? Will it be the flesh? Or will you decide to be Holy Spirit-led?

PRAYER

It's so easy for me to flip the switch and respond wrongly in everyday conversations at work, at home, and in my neighborhood. I back down from opportunities to reference my Savior Jesus and His beautiful name. Help me, Lord. Give me steeled courage to stand tall in my faith today, even if it's just in a small way. Amen.

SPIRIT LED, SINGLE-MINDED

The idea of being double-minded bothers me . . . a lot. The thought that we have these two parallel *processors* inside—one of God and one of the flesh—vying for control, is sobering and troubling.

There's an old saying: "When two people are in charge, no one is." At the end of the day, one voice will rule. When anything competes with God, aren't we forced to choose? Aren't we constantly deciding between *me and mine* and *He and His*? Between *my way* and *His way* of responding to life, to people, and to circumstances?

Here's one simple approach I learned from Skye Jethani's *With:*

> Walk through your day in constant contact with the Father, saying to Him, "I thank You, Father. I trust You, Father."

That's praying without ceasing in the best kind of way. It's being *with God* and being reminded that *God is with me*. It reinforces the "default setting" of gratitude in my heart, and it reminds me that God is who I'm trusting with everything.

I've been doing this for a while, and it's been amazing. My awareness of God's presence and care for me has spiked. I feel less double-minded because "my mind is stayed on *Thee*" instead of *me*.

PRAYER

**I thank You, Father. For Jesus. For the Holy Spirit.
For the life You've given me as an adopted son in
Your family. I trust You, Lord. Give me the wisdom
to know what to do next, the courage to do it, and
the faith to trust You with whatever happens. In
Your Son's beautiful name, I pray. Amen.**

MASK WEARERS

Psychologists tell us we all wear masks. We put on false personas to keep people out to one degree or another. Some people feel guilty because of their sins, their (perceived) social status, their upbringing, their appearance. Any number of things can make us feel ashamed and want to hide.

While it's not inherently obvious, just as many others don their masks because of someone else's sin. They get hurt but don't confront it, choosing instead to put on a mask and pretend that everything is fine.

Regardless of which way we start, the inevitable effects of hiding behind a mask are blame, fear, denial, and anger, just to name a few. The shame that follows is like an undiagnosed infection spreading poison throughout our bodies.

Have you ever tried to put on a mask for a party and keep it on for the whole night? It's just about impossible to do. It's claustrophobic, smothering, and fake.

The same feeling comes when we put on a psychological mask—when we fake it till we make it. There's something inside that says, *Hey, this isn't real. This isn't true about me. I gotta take this thing off and come clean with myself. With her. With Him.*

For years, I had no peace from mask-wearing. "Mr. Up-and-Coming AT&T Guy" was never comfortable in his own skin. He wore so many different masks he didn't even *have* a face. Surrendering to Jesus brought authenticity and a new identity, birthed and sustained by an undeniable sense of being loved by a Heavenly Father. Everything changed for me. It can change for you.

QUESTION

If you knew you would be totally loved and completely forgiven, what mask could you take off and throw away?

7 STEPS TO SPIRITUAL MATURITY

A soul's journey through life passes through these stages:

1. **Blissful Ignorance**—Freedom. You are unconsciously incompetent. *I don't know, but I don't need to know.*

2. **Dissonance**—The world isn't safe after all. Now you are consciously incompetent . . . *I know I don't have what it takes.*

3. **Chasing Acceptance**—You are compelled to prove yourself. You relentlessly chase your version of enough, but it doesn't happen.

4. **Validation**—You find things that work for you, that validate you. Life is performance-based: *I can do this.* But down deep, there is a lingering fear of being seen through and found out.

5. **Disruption**—A health crisis, job loss, divorce, death of someone dear disrupts life. *This is the climax moment in your story.* How you respond here sets the trajectory and quality of your remaining life. There are two paths:

   Choose to keep on working, but harder. Divorce and find someone else. Become cynical. Or . . .

   Trust God. Believe you're loved. Forgiven. Accepted, unconditionally. That He actually *likes* you! You begin a new life entirely.

6. **Settle In**—The dissonance is resolved, or put to rest. People and relationships start to matter more. You flourish, becoming a lover of God and of people. The tension is gone.

7. **Elder**—You are at peace. You have a grateful heart, a selflessness birthed during the disruption stage when you couldn't solve your own problem and turned to Jesus. Gratitude becomes your theme. You've been blessed and want to be a blessing to others.

QUESTION

At which step are you? Did you miss it at disruption? Have you regretted it ever since? You will never regret accepting God's unconditional love and forgiveness. There's no other life that compares.

NOVEMBER 10

LIFE *WITH* GOD

The ideas that follow were inspired by and taken from With: Reimagining the Way You Relate to God, *by Skye Jethani, which I highly recommend.*

Here are four different identities. Check the one that *most* describes you in relation to God and your faith.

- ☐ I am a sinner.
- ☐ I am a manager.
- ☐ I am a consumer.
- ☐ I am a servant.

If you checked, "I am a sinner," then you likely live under the constant threat of God's wrath and punishment. You must appease His will through strict obedience to moral and spiritual commands. You live your life *under God*.

If you checked, "I am a manager," you're an autonomous being who has been given a divine manual for operating your life and world, and whose fate will ultimately rest upon how well you implement God's principles and instructions. This is life *over God*.

For those who checked, "I am a consumer," you're likely discontent inside because of unmet desires and longings. You want God to orbit around you and fulfill your expectations in life. This is life *from God*.

And if you checked, "I am a servant," you think you will get huge credit for being on mission from God. Your sense of value is inexorably tied to what you're able to accomplish and the magnitude of your impact on the world. This is life *for God*.

We want safety by appeasing God with our behavior. We turn our faith into a checklist of to-dos and to-don'ts, thinking we'll curry favor with the Creator through good behavior. Like a genie in a bottle, we want God to grant our wishes if we live out His principles. We insulate ourselves from the very God we seek by working ourselves to death building the Kingdom.

So where's the 5th box? I don't like the sound of any of these.

For most of us, one of these four descriptions hits us where we live and illustrates how we've (mis)interpreted the life God wants for us—a life *with God*. From Eden to Paradise, that's what He wants. That's all He's ever wanted.

But instead of embracing His love and leaning into a real relationship, we try to *use* Him instead of walking *with* Him and living consistently aware that He is *with us*.

When you saw the four identity boxes above, you probably thought, "Well, none of these are bad." And they aren't. But God has so much more for each of us. Somewhere out there in the future, after we've lived our life here, He's going to show us a white stone with His secret name for us on it (Revelation 2:17). It'll be a "just between you and me" kind of thing. Father-to-son. Father-to-daughter. That's how personal, intimate, intense His love is for us.

Can you wean yourself off the *for* God, *from* God, *under* God, and *over* God postures?

CHALLENGE

Will you change your narrative from, "I just want to do God's will," to "He is with me, and I am with Him?" Can you learn to walk and rest in His presence regardless of what's coming at you? Can you live it out knowing that He is here and He is enough?

KEEP WALKING

Every Jesus follower I know has hit a wall at some point. Their career brings them under the leadership of someone they don't respect. The family business stalls out; it won't die but won't grow. Their marriage is so-so, and their spouse is beginning to wear thin.

In *A Million Miles in a Thousand Years,* Donald Miller calls it "the long middle." The journey is underway. You've launched into the darkness and you're paddling in the direction you think is right, but you have no idea how long you're going to be in this just-keep-paddling mode.

It's frustrating when you're in the long middle and have no answers other than to keep moving.

Speaking of God, where is He in this?

Scripture says He's in you, and you are in Him. I get the reality of *His presence with me*—that I don't sit in the boat alone. Peace comes when I call out His name and sense Him saying, "You don't have to shout. I'm right here."

But there are times when God is silent, and He seems so still that your mind starts to wonder if He's actually there.

That's when we call on His promises: "I will *never* leave you." "I will *never* abandon you." "I will be with you *always.*" We have to move in faith and know He's there, even when there's no evidence to prove it.

CHALLENGE

Wherever you are in life right now, keep walking. Keep paddling. If you know Him, He's with you, no matter how it feels. And who is in the boat with you is more important than where the boat is going or what it's going through.

PREDICTING DIVORCE

Dr. John Gottman is a world-renowned researcher on marriage and relationships. He and his colleagues have probably done more up close and personal research on the dynamics of marriage than anybody. He and his team scientifically tracked how couples fight, and they identified four things that predict divorce.

1. **Contempt**—This is characterized by an air of superiority, often surfacing as mocking your spouse. Gottman says, "It erodes the immune system of the wife/husband."

2. **Criticism**—This personal attack at the other person starts as complaint, but it comes out much worse. It rapidly escalates the issues.

3. **Defensiveness**—When we operate from a defensive position, we feel under attack. And we are far less likely to work together towards a solution.

4. **Stonewalling**—Also known as the silent treatment. Eighty percent of the time it's men who stonewall.

Criticism, defensiveness, and stonewalling are behaviors we choose. They're habits—habits we can break through focused effort and self-discipline. We can even ask our spouses to help us recognize when we fall into them.

But contempt is different. It's deeper. Rolling your eyes when she talks, mocking her, making fun of her—these are deadly. Contempt is kryptonite for your marriage. If you feel contempt for your spouse, this is a big, big problem.

Take it to the Lord. Talk to a trusted Christian mentor, pastor, or friend. Get help to change your stinkin' thinkin' about your wife.

QUESTION

Does contempt, criticism, defensiveness, and stonewalling show up when you and your spouse disagree? Will you get out ahead and stop this stuff in its tracks? Will you lean into the "Jesus in you" and let more things go?

THE ROAD TO ORPHANHOOD

My dad was the last of my parents to die. After his funeral, we divided up a few treasures, sold the house, and it was over. I was an orphan.

I'd heard the command to "honor your father and mother," but it was at his funeral that Ephesians 6:3 hit me: "So that it may go well with you and that you may enjoy long life on the earth."

I hadn't grasped how long I'd live *after* they were both gone.

Here are a few things I tried to do before my parents passed. Don't get me wrong, I failed a lot. But at least consider these ideas for honoring your father and mother.

1. **Forgive**—Give them grace. Nothing good is going to come from holding a grudge. Drop it.

2. **Ask them the *really* question**—"How are you . . . *really*?" Be empathetic. You can't fix them or their situation, but they want to be known, loved, and understood. The last time I saw my dad before he passed, I asked him this question. His answer? "I'm lonely, son. I'm ready to go on and be with your Mama!"

3. **Praise them**—For their accomplishments, and specifically for their independence.

4. **Get answers while you can**—Ask them real questions about real stuff, and write down what they say.

5. **Pray for your parents daily**—Praying for someone regularly brings God in and keeps your heart soft.

My kids watched me as I fathered my elderly parents. Yours will be watching, too.

QUESTION

**Will you ask God to remind you to take
good care of your aging parents?**

SIX PRACTICES OF INTIMATE FRIENDS

Every year, I walk into a room with eight total strangers—new mentees grouped together by my church. These are future leaders who will grow in community together. Some will scatter when it's over. A few will become lifelong buds. But a couple of these guys will become intimate friends. How does that happen?

Here's my description of an intimate friend and some thoughts on the art of building and maintaining friendship at that level.

1. **Authentic love and acceptance**—This kind of love is natural, not forced. They enjoy each other's company.

2. **Common worldview and purpose**—Intimate friends usually see the world through similar eyes. They often share a big-picture purpose.

3. **Deals and destinations**—Intimate friends tend to know each other's priorities and locations, the goings and comings of each other.

4. **Put each other first**—It's hard to get an intimate friend to talk about himself. He's more interested in you, how you're doing and feeling.

5. **Purposeful memory**—Remembering what's going on with someone says they matter to you, not just when they're in your presence.

6. **Purposeless calls**—Intimate friends check in with each other. There's an art to intimate friendship. Too much attention and its unnatural, contrived, even smothering. Too little and you'll feel like you're a friend by-appointment-only.

John 15:13 says, "Greater love has no one than this: to lay down one's life for one's friends."

Intimate friendship costs something. But having lived over half my life without intimate friendship, I'll testify that the cost is absolutely worth it.

CHALLENGE

Are you willing to take friendship to another level? Ask God to lead you to the friend who will stick closer than a brother.

November 15

"100 PERCENT ALL NATURAL" MARRIAGE

We're buying 100 percent natural food these days. And lots of it. But what if someone offered you a 100 percent natural marriage? Would you want it? What would that look like?

Part of marriage *is* natural, especially the part that leads to children! That's instinct. It's natural to eat and sleep together, keep each other company, protect each other, and help with life's demands.

We've got genetics going on, too. I watch my adult children as they interact with their spouses, and sometimes I get a little nauseous. I hear my voice coming from their mouths and think, "Whoa! Did I really sound like that when I argued with their mom?

Most of what we husbands do comes from copying what we've seen others do, beginning with Daddy. Our defaults were set as we watched how Dad treated Mom. Whatever he did, we got permission to do when we got married. If he was unkind and demanding, it's predictable we'd be unkind and demanding. If he helped mom around the house, it feels natural when we do the same. And yes, we got some of our values from dads on TV and in the movies. We grew up watching *Father Knows Best, Leave It to Beaver,* and *The Andy Griffith Show.*

A 100 percent natural husband would be a compendium of all these—genetics, heroes, and role models. That's how many men learn to husband. Unintentionally, by osmosis. It just happened.

But we can do better. We don't have to settle for 100 percent natural. We have more resources, fewer traditions, and freer minds than any generation before. We can build marriages so far above 100 percent natural as to be called *supernatural*!

How?

By following Jesus as we love and lead our wives. Let's look at how a Christ-following husband might be different from the 100 percent natural package:

100 Percent Natural Husband	Jesus-following Husband
Self-centered	Considers others (especially his wife) better than himself
Selfish	Selfless (loves his wife as Christ loved the church *and gave Himself up for her.*)
Headstrong	Attentive, teachable
Proud	Gentle and humble in heart
Competitive	Collaborative
Unforgiving	Full of mercy and grace

Placing your minute-by-minute will under the control of Jesus brings God into your life and marriage. That means pausing to ask, "Lord, what would You have me know about this situation?" and then listening for His voice. It means asking, "Lord, what would You have me do with what You've shown me here?" and obeying His voice without question.

That's the foundation of a supernatural marriage. That's how we move from being a 100 percent natural husband to being a Jesus-following husband. Very few wives who call themselves Christians would turn away from a loyal husband who is moving from "100 percent natural" and toward Jesus. In fact, I've seen a bunch of wives fall madly in love with their husbands all over again. They say, "Who stole my husband and replaced him with this wonderful man?"

CHALLENGE

Don't settle for "100 percent natural." You can do better. And you'll feel so much better about yourself when you do.

THE FUTURE IS A *WHO*

I spend a lot of time thinking about the future. I always have! (I have that planner thing going on.) I'm constantly thinking, "What if we . . ." and, "I wonder what would happen if . . ." and, "if we don't, then . . ."

But in Matthew 6:34 Jesus said, "Therefore do not worry about tomorrow, for tomorrow will worry about itself. Each day has enough trouble of its own."

He knew our human tendency to worry. Heck, He walked around knowing the awful way His life was going to end, yet it didn't consume Him. How did He manage to do that? Well, the first answer is, "He was God," and that's true.

But He was also fully human. As a human being, Jesus stayed connected with His Heavenly Father through prayer. They were intimately connected.

His future wasn't wrapped around *what, when, where,* or *how much.* It was about *who.* Who is in charge of the future, not what was going to happen. Jesus' entire focus rested on the One who ruled it all, not the circumstances that lay ahead.

If we truly believe there's a God who is sovereign, omnipotent, and omniscient, then 100 percent of our future is in His hands. That means it's time to surrender it all to God the Father.

It's an act of faith, yes, but it's also an act of freedom. Worrying about the maybes of life will get us nowhere. We are connected to the Creator of it all, and He wants us to trust Him.

He is the Author of your story and mine. God is the *Who* of our future.

QUESTION

Will you trust Him?

November 17

WHEN TO QUIT

I'll never forget meeting with an entrepreneur who was looking for investment in his start-up company. His idea wasn't all that unique. In fact, it wasn't unique at all. I asked how long he'd been at it. He said, "A little over a year." I asked how he'd funded things so far. He said, "Credit cards."

I asked, "How much do you owe?"

He said, "$54,000." He should have quit long ago.

It's hard to quit stuff because we don't want to be wrong. It's embarrassing, especially when we look around for who got us into this mess and find the answer looking back at us in the bathroom mirror.

So how do we know what we need to quit? And when? A few questions to ponder:

- Is what I'm involved in wrong? Are people being hurt? If so, then *quit*.

- Is the thing I'm doing harmful to me or those around me? If so, then *quit*.

- Assuming they started where I am right now, has anyone ever been successful? If the answer is no, stop lying to yourself. *Quit*.

- Have I passed the point of reasonable risk? Is pride and fear of failure driving me to stupid tenacity and foolishness? If so, then *quit*.

I love Bob Goff's idea of quitting stuff to create bandwidth to do new things and engage with new people. It's one of the beauties of small group mentoring—of graduating eight guys each year to make room for eight new ones.

What do you need to quit? Is a secret porn habit sucking the life out of your marriage? Is alcohol quietly killing your liver and your relationships? Is a poor investment eating your assets and draining your energy?

QUESTION

Is it time to quit?

WHAT IT MEANS TO BE LOST

When someone is lost, the first thing that has to be determined is where they are. You can call for help, but unless you know where you are, help won't know how to find you.

That's where so many people are today. It's not just that they're lost, meaning they haven't accepted Jesus, it's that they don't really know where they are spiritually.

Without a moral compass, without a meaningful definer of right and wrong, good and bad, moral and immoral, wise and unwise, they're lost. They don't know where they are or where they are going.

Generally speaking, people have to hit rock-bottom before they realize they're lost, before they'll look up. When they run out of money, friends, drugs, booze, health, jobs, dates, or options—that's when they realize they're lost. That's when God presents Himself as an option.

We may be the only Jesus some people in our sphere of influence see. Living "found lives" has never been more important.

Truly found Jesus followers live loud just by living true. Through consistency, devotion, love, and acceptance, *the found* are God's most valuable instrument of redemption. By embodying Jesus in every moment, *the lost* may begin to see a better way of life.

As Jesus followers, we cannot get derailed. We must be the peculiar people referred to in Scripture. We cannot compromise. If we give in and simply do what everyone else does, the lost will have no one to show them what it looks like to be found.

PRAYER

**Lord, give me a constant awareness that lost
people are watching my every word and deed.
Their interest in the gospel may ride on my
willingness to be different and say "no" at times.**

THE STAIN OF SELF-RIGHTEOUSNESS

Perhaps nothing incites anger more than a religious person telling us we don't measure up like he does. Jesus followers are particularly at risk of sounding that way because we have a Lord who said, "I am the way and the truth and the life. No one comes to the Father except through me" (John 14:6). We believe Him. That's an *essential*.

But it's the peripheral things, the *nonessentials*, that stain our reputation and limit our influence. We're so confident of our answer that we sound closed-minded and closed-hearted. We end conversations rather than begin them, all over nonessentials that won't send anyone to heaven or hell.

Years ago, my friend Charlie looked at me and said, "Do you realize how self-righteous you are?" It was after a long conversation when I had vigorously defended what I thought to be right. I was thinking, *How in the world did he come to think that about me? We're having a conversation about ideas. This wasn't personal!*

But it was personal. Ideas are owned by people, and when you don't embrace their ideas—when you express *your* ideas as the right ones—you put *their* ideas down. And when you put down their ideas, you appear self-righteous.

So what can you do?

Make sure there's love in your heart.

Think through how the listener may hear what you are about to say.

Choose your words carefully . . . offer ideas but don't insist on them.

CHALLENGE

**Will you work to avoid communicating
"self-righteousness?"**

GOD RESPONDS TO EVIL, INITIATES LOVE

I read something profound the other day. It said that God's wrath is in response to evil. God's inherent nature isn't "wrath-ful." He's not performance-based. He didn't set up a pass/fail, win/lose world.

He created a perfect, loving, harmonious world. But when pride appeared in Lucifer, then in Adam and Eve, then in mankind as their descendants, God had no choice but to respond.

To be a just God, there have to consequences for evil. A perfect, holy God wouldn't be perfect and holy if He simply ignored evil. That would be the same as calling it good.

But wait a minute, does that mean God responds to the evil things I do or tolerate or turn a blind eye to? The answer is yes, He does. Or at least He did when Jesus went to the cross. All of our evil, all of our sins, past, present, and future were transferred to Jesus.

God released His wrath on His own Son, who had committed *no evil whatsoever*, so that we could be forgiven and restored to peace, innocence, and holiness. This is why it makes sense to live lives of gratitude for Jesus and what He did for us.

Unfathomable, self-sacrificing love.

God's heart—His true nature—is unconditional love, not wrath.

That's what He does, that's what He gives, that's who He is.

That's our Heavenly Father. Loving, good, kind, faithful.

PRAYER

Father, give me the courage to ask You the tough questions. Holy Spirit, inspire me to lean into my doubts, to study Your Word, ask for clarity, and receive Your truth. Lord Jesus, prepare me to be Your ambassador. In your beautiful, matchless name I pray, amen.

GOD AT HIS TYPEWRITER

Imagine God at His typewriter. He uses a typewriter because He loves it. There's no delete key because He never makes a mistake. No Wite-Out. No correction paper. When He writes our stories, they happen just as He envisions them.

But when does He write them?

No one knows.

God is timeless. He operates outside time and space. When we pray on any day of the year, God hears us. In our context, we're praying for things in the future, but because God is timeless, our prayers can be heard and applied to situations before *or after* they happen. It's mind-blowing!

So, because of the timelessness of God, all prayers are heard and considered before the story is continued or finished. *It is never too late to pray!* Isn't that comforting? To know that no prayer is unheard, no prayer is ever wasted, no prayer is irrelevant.

What happens when we're prayed for? Does prayer affect the outcome? I think so. James 5:16 says . . .

"The prayer of a righteous person is powerful and effective."

Often the outcome we desire isn't what we get in the short-term. But God is about long-term. All prayers are eventually answered one way or another. We may be in heaven before we know what He was thinking, but I believe whatever happens is always for our best and His glory.

PRAYER

Heavenly Father, please keep building my faith. I can't imagine living life without You. You are my awesome friend, Lord Jesus. It's in Your beautiful name I pray. Amen.

SALT LIFE

Ever notice how moms have to hide the candy and cookies but never the salt? They leave it out right there on the counter. You never find a kid stuffing salt in his mouth.

Salt is amazing stuff. It purifes and preserves. We can live (and are probably better off) without sugar and a bunch of other stuff, but salt is essential.

Jesus talked about salt. "You are the salt of the earth," He said in Matthew 5:13. I think it was His metaphor for grace. We also see it from Paul, who said in Colossians 4:6, "Let your conversation be always full of grace, seasoned with salt, so that you may know how to answer everyone."

Charles Spurgeon wrote about salt. As you read, substitute *grace* when he writes *salt*.

> "Believer, go to the throne for a large supply of heavenly salt. It will season thine afflictions, which are unsavoury without salt; it will preserve thy heart, which corrupts if salt be absent, and it will kill thy sins even as salt kills reptiles. Thou needest much; seek much, and have much."

Every time you see one of those Salt Life stickers or shirts, remember that Jesus wants us to live the "salt life"—a life aware of His grace and generous with grace for others.

Imagine a culture full of people spewing grace instead of anger, living grateful lives of peace instead of frantic lives of fear. Go to the throne, get a load of heavenly salt, and start sharing it today.

PRAYER

Give me an awareness of Your presence and nudge my soul to appreciate Your grace and to give it without measure to everyone I encounter. In Your beautiful name, amen.

SALT LIFE . . . LOST

Yesterday I mentioned what Jesus said about us being the "salt of the earth." But the rest of what He said can't go unnoticed.

> "But if the salt loses its saltiness, how can it be made salty again? It is no longer good for anything, except to be thrown out and trampled underfoot." (Matthew 5:13)

So how does our *salt* lose its saltiness? How does grace disappear from our lives? How do we end up sullen and sad, forgetting God's blessings and becoming unloving toward others, even our wives and kids?

I see three ways:

We perform—Sometimes we get caught up in doing good and being good. The harder we try, the more we think it's us instead of "Christ living within us." Grace is nowhere to be found in our lives.

We're lazy—The only love that's real is love that is demonstrated. Same with grace. Without action, it's just a concept. To give grace, you have to *initiate*. That's a lot harder.

We forget—We forget where we get grace, so we stop giving it. Giving grace requires selflessness, and our default state is one of self-interest, self-love, and self-protection. The only thing that sustains selfless behavior over time is *gratitude*.

Thankfully, we can recover when we lose our saltiness. All we have to do is stop, turn around, ask for help, and take a step toward being a little saltier.

PRAYER

Jesus, I don't want my salt to lose its savor. I understand that You want me to *use it* not *lose it*. Thank You for an unlimited supply of grace. Give me a grateful heart. You are the good and beautiful God of this life and the next. In the name of Jesus I pray, amen.

YOU'RE DEAD TO ME!

If you think Kevin on *Shark Tank* came up with the phrase, "you're dead to me," think again. The apostle Paul said it in Romans 6:11-13.

> "In the same way, count yourselves dead to sin but alive to God in Christ Jesus. Therefore do not let sin reign in your mortal body so that you obey its evil desires. Do not offer any part of yourself to sin as an instrument of wickedness, but rather offer yourselves to God as those who have been brought from death to life; and offer every part of yourself to him as an instrument of righteousness."

We are to remind sin that we're *dead* to it, that we're *alive* in Christ. We are no longer slaves to sin; we are free.

Here is what the contrast between "dead to sin" versus "alive in Christ" looks like from my personal experience.

Before Christ, I had to struggle not to sin to have a chance of being good.

Now, because I'm an adopted son of God Himself and have been completely forgiven, I know I'm good. I have to *go against His righteousness in me* to intentionally sin. The Holy Spirit pricks my conscience and reminds me who I am, making it easier to walk away from things that tempt me.

God will always do His part, but not your part. Resisting sin, however you do it, is your part. Deliverance is His. He will always come through when you call on Him.

PRAYER

Thank You for my new life in Christ, that You've made me new in You. Please give me courage quickly when I call out to You. I love You, Lord. In Jesus' beautiful name I pray, amen.

JUDGE NOT

We all have a picture of what should be said and done. When people don't say or do what we think they should, it's totally natural for us to think critical thoughts. To judge.

When judgmental thoughts turn into words that come streaming out of my mouth, they often start with the personal pronoun, "You." Nothing good hap-pens at my house when I start a sentence with "You." What follows is usually "*You* never . . ."; "*You* always . . ."; or "If only *you* would . . ."

Criticism happens when we look for reasons to think more highly of our-selves. Jesus leveled the playing field in Matthew 7:3-5, when He said that we look for a speck in someone else's eye and ignore the timber in our own. Paul carries it further in Romans 2:17-24, when he says that in condemning others, we are condemning ourselves.

A goal I've had for the last few years is to move from judging to perceiving. If I can watch someone, listen to what they say, and try to understand them rather than judging them, I will be a better mentor. You can't minister to someone you judge.

Are you more apt to *judge* someone and open your mouth about it? Or do you discipline yourself to *perceive* others with love, try to understand them better, and love them regardless of what they say or do?

Critical thoughts will come, no doubt. That's part of our flesh. But the Holy Spirit gives us the ability to exercise self-control, to perceive without judging, and most of all, to keep our mouths shut and our minds open.

Maturity is not saying everything you think.

QUESTION

**Will you move from judging to perceiving
and toward maturity?**

NOVEMBER 26

WHEN IS ADVICE TAKEN AS CRITICISM?

Unsolicited advice is (almost) always received as criticism. When someone offers unsolicited advice, it's usually received with suspicion. "Is there an element of accusation buried in here?" we wonder.

Key word? *Unsolicited*. Most of the time, friends and family members share what's going on in their lives to be known and understood. They want empathy, not advice.

It's a whole different thing *when they ask for your input*. In that moment, they're demonstrating openness. Humility. Teachability. Your advice is much more likely to land on fertile ground when it's sought after.

As I help men move into the role of mentor, I strongly suggest they be very careful about giving advice, even when it's solicited. Try to stay within these two guardrails:

1. **What does God say through Scripture?** You'll never go wrong pointing people to God's Word for advice.

2. **What's your story and *relevant* experience?** If you've been through a similar situation, sharing what you did and how it turned out can be extremely valuable to a younger person. You have to be honest, to be willing to share both good and bad decisions and outcomes. And you have to be disciplined enough to stop at the end of the story and *not* say, "So if I were you, I'd . . ."

Sometimes God leads us to challenge, and when He does, we have to step up. As long as we're obeying His clear instructions—as long as we're speaking the truth in love, leaning on Scripture and not our personal opinions—we'll be okay.

SCRIPTURE

"Instead, speaking the truth in love, we will grow to become in every respect the mature body of him who is the head, that is, Christ." (Ephesians 4:15)

SELF-REJECTING PEOPLE

Sometimes self-rejecting people can get so down on themselves that they become what I call "black-hole people." No matter how much praise is piled on, it leaks right out the bottom of their soul.

Pay them a genuine compliment and they won't actually accept it or believe it. Often they work themselves crazy trying to get praise they ultimately reject. On the other hand, self-accepting people take things in stride. They realize they're not perfect and never will be.

As I recovered from my lung transplant, I had more time alone than I can ever remember. But God was so present with me through that season.

One morning, my shaky hand knocked over a full glass of water. Out of my mouth came the words, "That was stupid!" Historically, I would have said, "You're an idiot!" Do you see the difference?

I didn't condemn myself! Without my realizing it, God moved me a little more away from self-rejection and toward self-acceptance.

When Jesus took your sin and paid the price of His life for it, He assigned the same worth to your life that He assigned to His own. Imagine that. An even trade—Jesus' life for yours.

We're clean in His eyes. A new creation. Sinless forever because of His sacrifice. Grasp that and you'll think differently about yourself. You and I are objects of His affection.

The next time you say something bad about yourself, remember that you're cursing someone Jesus loves personally. If He doesn't reject you, why would you continue to reject yourself?

CHALLENGE

**Ask God this question: "Lord, what do
You think of me? How do You see me,
Father?" and listen to what He says.**

HAVE YOU LOST YOUR JESUS?

"Tell me where you lost the company of Christ, and I will tell you the most likely place to find him," said Charles Spurgeon.

When I lose my awareness of Jesus in my life, I can often figure out where I lost it by looking first at my journal and then at my calendar. Almost without fail, that day and the days after were incredibly busy. Busyness is the enemy of intimacy. When I get busy, I leave Jesus behind.

Sometimes it's sin. The conversation when you intentionally spun the truth a little. That might be the place you left Jesus.

One subtle way of losing your Jesus is to forget about the Scriptures. Sometimes when I feel like I've lost my Jesus, I'll go back to the last place I have marked in my Bible. I start reading again, and before long I'm aware of His presence.

There *are* times when God just goes silent, times when you lose your Jesus through no fault of your own. Occasionally He just decides to be silent for a while. To go stealth and leave you unaware of His presence.

I've learned through these "desert times" to cling to my faith no matter what, to trust Him even when He's silent. I tell Him repeatedly, "I love You, Father. I trust You, Father." When His purposes are served, He comes back again. "I love you, Regi." *Whew! So glad that's over.*

Maybe the most important thing to know is that even when you lose your Jesus, whether through busyness, neglect, sin, or silence, Jesus *never* loses you.

PRAYER

Father, thanks for sticking "closer than a brother," and for the knowledge that even when You're silent, You're not still.

FINDING YOUR JESUS

When you realize you've lost your Jesus, turn around quickly. The further you go from the place you left Him, the harder it's going to be to get back. As soon as you realize He's missing, turn *all* your attention toward finding Him.

Why?

Because you need Him. Without Him, you're exposed. You're like a sheep without a shepherd. Your human conscience isn't as dependable as the Holy Spirit. You'll lie to yourself and try to get away with it.

When you lie to God, you know it almost instantly because the Holy Spirit brings it to your heart's attention. You're up against a stone wall—a holy wall of God's truth. If you've ever experienced His presence, His warm com-fort, His love and affection, you feel lost without it.

If you've lost your Jesus, seek Him with your whole heart. Examine yourself. Confess, repent, straighten things out.

Often we lose our Jesus after a tirade of anger against someone. If that's the case, go ask for forgiveness. Sometimes we lose our Jesus by telling a lie, or making a selfish decision, or deceiving someone. Go to the person you've hurt and make it right. Whatever He leads you to, surrender to His will, humble yourself, and do what you can to fix it.

Do you want to know how to keep from losing Jesus next time?

Fall more in love with Him. Make Him so preeminent in your life that you *can't* forget about Him.

PRAYER

Lord, I need You. Every hour I need You. Please make me so aware of Your presence that I can't leave You out, not even for one hour of my life.

NOVEMBER 30

SHEEP WITHOUT A SHEPHERD

Kids are like sheep. They're on their way to independence, but for now, they're powered by their youth and energy—and endangered by their lack of experience.

Like sheep, they need a shepherd. Someone to watch over them. They need a dad. A real father. Sadly, I know many kids who are growing up without a shepherd.

Hopefully you're one of the dads who take their shepherding job seriously. What does a shepherding father do?

1. **Tends**—Just as shepherds know where their sheep are, fathers know where their kids are physically, relationally, and spiritually.

2. **Herds**—Shepherds keep their flocks together. Dads have the same responsibility, and that starts with staying with his wife. You can't keep your little sheep together if you let the two big sheep drift apart.

3. **Feeds**—Shepherds are the prime providers for their sheep. Dads need to do this for their children. There should never be a deadbeat dad, especially not a Christian one. In addition to providing for their physical needs, Dads must provide unlimited, unconditional love for their kids, as well as providing their spiritual food.

4. **Guards**—Shepherds do whatever it takes to drive away anyone or anything that will hurt their sheep or lead them astray. Dads guard their kids from external threats and avoid hurting them through anger, thoughtlessness, or neglect.

Most dads would leave the herd of ninety-nine to go find their one lost sheep (Matthew 18:12). Will you also tend, herd, feed, and guard them?

QUESTION

Do you pay close enough attention to know when one of your sheep is drifting away?

DECEMBER 1

PROUD, SECRETIVE, OR HUMBLE

At the beginning of each of my mentoring groups, I meet one-on-one with each group member. I love going to a guy's office and picking him up for lunch. I've learned that the way I'm introduced can offer a clue to the guy's faith walk.

Three responses I've observed:

1. **Pride**—Some guys are really proud to introduce their "Christian mentor" around the office. As the year progresses, these are often the guys who turn out to be religious and somewhat self-righteous.

2. **Secretive**—A lot of guys are pretty nondescript about my visit. These men are quiet about their faith. A few have not yet connected with Jesus in such a way that they're all-in, ready to be identified as a Christian, church member, or serious Jesus follower.

3. **Humble**—When a guy takes me through his office and introduces me simply as his mentor, I get a sense this isn't news to anyone. He's not pushing his faith, but he's not ashamed, either. He knows he's a work in progress, but he also knows who he is in Christ.

Which of these three stereotypes fits you? When you go to work tomorrow, will you be talkative about your church and your faith? Will you be seeking affirmation for being a "good Christian"?

Will you be the "secret agent Christian" who never says a word about his faith?

Or will you be the humble but solid Jesus follower? The guy who lives it out. The guy who preaches a sermon every day with his actions, and when he has to, uses words?

QUESTION

Isn't that the kind of Christian Jesus wants us to be?

December 2

DOING GOOD FOR GOD

I believe God *values* us as His sons and daughters. When we obey His command to make disciples, we get great joy. I've watched a ton of guys light up as they've taken the Great Commission personally for the first time as mentors. I think it was Nate Larkin who said . . .

> "Something changes in a man when he first takes responsibility for the spiritual growth of another person."

That's totally true.

It's hard—no, it's impossible—to decide *prospectively* to be used of God. We can obey Him and make ourselves available, but we'll only be able to see how we were used *retrospectively.*

We rarely know when God uses us in the lives of others. We plant seeds, and occasionally, we see them bloom. It's His gift to us when we see the fruit of our lives and our labors. It's His encouragement for us, both to remind us how much He loves us *and* to build our faith in Him and His work of redemption.

Love is doing for God not because it's useful, or your duty, or because there's anything in it for you, but because you love Him. If what we call love doesn't take us beyond ourselves, it is not really love.

God wants us to give Him things that are *valuable*—things like our hearts, our desires, our future hopes and dreams, our personalities, and our souls. He'll take those things and make them *useful* as He chooses and when He chooses. But we'll only discover how He used us after the fact, maybe even after this life is over.

Do you want to do something good for God?

CHALLENGE

Surrender to Jesus, then He can use you all the time.

BALANCE

I hate the word "balance." Religious people live balanced lives. They don't let their faith get too invasive into their priorities, their lives, or their finances.

I'll never forget a former Chick-Fil-A executive standing in front of a group saying, "God is not a priority in my life." He repeated it a couple times, to everyone's chagrin. Then he paused and said, "God *is* my life!" That's not balance, that's passion!

Totally surrendered, all-in Jesus followers recognize that when we make God our ultimate priority, then He is responsible for all outcomes. It was Jesus Himself who said, "But seek first his kingdom and his righteousness, and all these things will be given to you as well" (Matthew 6:33).

God's Kingdom exists first in our hearts and minds. It's peace, love, and contentment (among other things). We can't have peace and worry at the same time. Contentment and ambition are like oil and water. Love and fear can't coexist. Jesus was saying, "Choose me. Put me first. Let me lead. You can trust me."

Instead of pursuing balance, pursue *obedience*. Pray "right now" prayers, in-the-moment conversations with your Heavenly Father. They're *collaborative* with God, issue-by-issue, person-by-person, decision-by-decision.

This is walking with God. This is abiding in Christ.

If we live our lives daily with this kind of interaction with the Father, balance will take care of itself. Most of the time, we *know* what He'd have us do. We simply need to slow down enough to seek His righteousness and obey it.

I don't want to be in *balance*. I want to be *passionate*, *available*, and *obedient*.

CHALLENGE

Live your life wildly out of balance.

December 4

LOVE STAYS

What makes a man godly? How does he demonstrate his love for God? By fulfilling the second commandment: "Love your neighbor as yourself" (Mark 12:31). Who are your closest neighbors? Your wife and your kids.

What's the first thing a husband and father does to demonstrate love for them?

He stays.

Godly men don't run off. They don't run away. John Lynch defines love as "meeting needs." Your wife's number-one need is security. That starts with you being committed. Staying. Regardless, you work it out.

Too many men are *moving away* instead of *staying*. We pursue selfish acts and ambitions that move us away from the good things God intends for us.

Love stays. Elder-type men stick with their Lord, the wife of their youth, their kids, their families, and the church. No matter what.

I'll never forget one of my mentees telling about how his dad would get up early to read his Bible and pray. He'd get down and kneel on the couch, and when the son got up later in the morning, he'd see the imprint of his dad's face in the couch. He knew his dad had been there before dawn, praying for him. He could see his face print.

If you're thinking about leaving, don't. Stay. If you're there in body but not in spirit, stay. Turn your heart to your family and get yourself together where it matters most. People are watching. Your kids are watching. Your grandchildren are (or will be) watching. People inside and outside the faith are watching.

SCRIPTURE

"To this end I strenuously contend with all the energy Christ so powerfully works in me." (Colossians 1:29)

DECEMBER 5

SILENCE THE DOGS—LISTEN TO HIM

It was my first silent retreat—two days without a word. As the retreat kicked off, we were asked to jot down our prayers for ourselves (e.g., "What do we want from God this weekend?").

We read them out loud. At first, they all sounded alike. "Get closer to God." "Get back on track." "Seek healing from a huge loss." Then someone turned it around. "What if this is God's retreat? Perhaps He's the one who invited you here. Suppose He has you at this place to tell you something He wants you to hear?"

Wow. Different ballgame. No way did I want to miss this one, but how could I make sure I heard His voice and what He had to say to me?

It required silence.

As I approached this extended period of silence, wishing only to hear God's voice, I quickly realized how many non-God voices there are. They're like dogs barking in my head—interrupting, irritating, demanding, and persistent. How could I focus on hearing God's voice with all this barking?

Just for fun, I named the dogs: Health, Calendar, Expectations, and Money, to name a few. Their barking brought an endless number of tasks, worries, and thoughts to mind.

All that barking can drown out God's voice.

When is the last time you were totally quiet? When did you last move into the room of silence, totally intent on having an intimate time with your Heavenly Father?

In Scripture, water is often synonymous with chaos. But in Psalm 23, it's different:

> "He leads me beside quiet waters, he refreshes my soul."

CHALLENGE

**Follow God to a quiet place. Let Him
refresh your soul. You'll be glad you did.**

DECEMBER 6

ENDING DOUBT ABOUT SALVATION

After coming to believe in Jesus at age twelve, I was baptized and that was about it. I lived like any other teenager, college student, husband, young professional, and finally, father. I went to church almost every Sunday, even took leadership roles. But I didn't know Jesus. Had I died in a fiery car crash at age seventeen, I honestly don't know where I would have gone.

On one hand, there's John 3:16: "For God so loved the world that he gave his one and only Son, that whoever believes in him shall not perish but have eternal life." God loved, God gave, I believe, I receive. Simple and clear. And I *did* believe at age twelve. In fact, I never stopped believing. So I was saved and secure, right?

Maybe.

There are a couple of haunting Scriptures that make it less clear. John 10:27 says, "My sheep listen to my voice; I know them, and they follow me." I didn't listen to God's voice until twenty-three years after I was "saved." And there was zero evidence of me following Him all those years. I was a "Christian" in label only, based solely on my belief in Jesus.

The other troubling verses are in Matthew 7:21-23.

> "Not everyone who says to me, 'Lord, Lord,' will enter the kingdom of heaven, but only the one who does the will of my Father who is in heaven. Many will say to me on that day, 'Lord, Lord, did we not prophesy in your name and in your name drive out demons and in your name perform many miracles?' Then I will tell them plainly, 'I never knew you. Away from me, you evildoers!'"

Up to this time in my life, I had made no effort to "do the will of the Father." I was all about *my will*, not His. The core question of salvation (or not) is in the heart. Spurgeon is tough and straightforward on this point. He says, "The man whose heart is unchanged is an unsaved man."

Wouldn't it be peace-giving to know for sure? Wouldn't it be good to put a date in your calendar that would, from this day forward, be the day when doubt was replaced by confidence? I asked those questions of men, while speaking at a conference. About sixty men ended their ambiguity and prayed this prayer. You can join them *right now*.

> "Heavenly Father, I'm ready to go all-in with You. I believe You love me. Yes, even me! I believe that You, Jesus, died on that cross to pay the debt for my sins, and I accept the gift of Your forgiveness. I'm ready to follow You now. I want to hear Your voice—to love, serve, and give. I know *about* You, Lord. Now I want to *know* You."

Next you have to *do something*. Tell someone of your decision. If that's a problem, you're not there yet; you're more afraid of what people will think than you are happy that your relationship with God is finally clear, established, and secure. There's probably someone who has been praying for you for a long time, or someone who, more than anyone else in the world, will be delighted to know what you've done. Call them. Go see them face-to-face. Confess your faith in Jesus, out loud, in real time.

QUESTION

Will you remove any doubt about your salvation?

CLIMBING, SLIDING, OR GLIDING

"In your faith walk, you're either climbing or sliding. There's no such thing as gliding!"–Brian Moore

I asked a good friend the other day, "How are you and God?" He said, "Just OK, nothing special." Isn't that what most of us would say if we answered that question honestly? We're *gliding*, or at least we think we are. Let's talk about what these words might mean.

If you're *climbing*, you're in love with Jesus and know He's in love with you. You make time for Him. You're in community with one or more guys, reading your Bible, serving your church, leading your family.

If you're *gliding*, you would say everything's OK. Church is OK; we make it to the worship service a good bit. There is no overt secret sin you're harboring. You're just coasting through the Christian life.

If you're flying solo, it's inevitable you're going to start *sliding*. The busyness of life, the requirements of work, marriage, kids, even church, all of these good things pull us into thoughtless activity and away from intimacy with God. Busyness is the enemy of intimacy with God, with our wives, with our friends.

If you can't remember the last time you sat down and truly talked with God, listened to His voice, and read His Word in a thoughtful, intentional way, you're probably sliding.

"It may be hard for an egg to turn into a bird: it would be a jolly sight harder for it to learn to fly while remaining an egg. We are like eggs at present. And you cannot go on indefinitely being just an ordinary, decent egg. We must be hatched or go bad."–C.S. Lewis, *Mere Christianity*

CHALLENGE

**Decide today to slide no more. It's a
new day. Begin to climb again.**

OBEDIENCE

Exactly what *is* obedience? "Compliance with an order, request, or law or submission to another's authority," says the Oxford Dictionary. Obedience says there's a commander, a command, and a "commandee." Someone with authority tells us what we're to do (or not do).

But what are God's commands? How do we know they're really from Him? And what are the consequences for obedience (or disobedience)?

I think there are three kinds of commands, three levels of direction God gives to help us, protect us, and bring glory to Him when we obey.

> **Macro-commands**—The commands of Scripture are macro-commands. They're universal—for everyone.

> **Micro-commands**—This is when God lets us know what to do in a situation not specifically covered by Scripture. These are the kinds of commands that come when we ask, "What would Jesus have me do?"

> **Nano-commands**—This is the specific guidance God gives only to *you* in a specific situation. Sometimes God will initiate these commands, but more often they come in response to your asking for help.

My pastor says, "God's blessing waits on the other side of obedience." Macro-commands are clear; they take more discipline than faith. Micro-commands get a little more personal because we ask God what we're to do.

Nano-commands are particularly high risk. They're specific, real-time, and generally not verifiable. That's why they take faith to act upon. We're trusting that it's God who is speaking, that we've heard what He's telling us to do, and that we'll be OK if we just do it.

Few things are more faith building than obeying one of God's whispers and seeing Him do something amazing in someone's life as a result.

CHALLENGE

**Will you listen for God's whisper
and obey what He says?**

December 9

BE HAPPY!

Everybody wants to be happy. But before some self-righteous ascetic tries to make you feel guilty for it, remember that Scripture mentions a lot of happy people.

Genesis 30:13: Leah is *happy* at the birth of her second child, Asher.

Psalm 137:8: The Israelites are *happy* because Babylon is being judged.

Psalm 113:9: A barren woman is *happy* because she becomes a mother.

2 Corinthians 7:9: Paul is *happy* as he watches the sorrow of the Corinthian believers lead to repentance.

What do these situations have in common? Happiness shows up when circumstances are good.

But what about times when things are just okay? When there's nothing to fire you up?

I believe Jesus followers should be the happiest people on earth. We have faith in a loving Heavenly Father who's providing for our long-term safety, security, and, yes, happiness.

We can believe God and relax in His love or we can kill (or at least postpone) happiness by thinking, *If I could just . . .* or, *If I only had . . .*

There will always be something you don't have or can't do, but you won't have this day *ever again!* Happiness rides on contentment with where you are and what you have right now.

QUESTION

Are people drawn to your faith because they're curious about the source of your happiness?

SPIRITUAL CANCER

A recent report says 41 percent of Americans will have cancer and 21 percent will die from it. We know certain things make cancer more likely, but nobody knows who will or who won't get it.

But 100 percent of Americans will get *spiritual cancer*. Here are some of the symptoms:

- Self-confidence and self-righteousness (from pride) that lead to a loss of God's presence in our lives.
- Quiet but pervasive focus on money, the places it can take you, and things it will buy.
- Drifting from regular prayer, which brings more anxiety, less gratitude, and a decreased focus on God.
- Constant distraction from our faith walk due to busyness.
- Unabated passion for screens—apps, texts, emails, sports, movies, TV shows, and music.
- Disappointment and/or anger toward someone or something.
- False beliefs that get in our heads and grow into paralyzing roadblocks between us and our Heavenly Father.

Spiritual cancer is more sneaky than physical cancer. There isn't a test for it. We wake up and realize things aren't right. We're exhausted, we have no peace, we feel disconnected from God, and we don't know how to get back.

We've just lost it. We've lost Him.

Charles Spurgeon once described it this way:

> "The heart has been occupied with something else, more than with God: the affections have been set on the things of earth, instead of the things of heaven. A jealous God will not be content with a divided heart; He must be loved first and best. He will withdraw the sunshine of His presence from a cold, wandering heart."

QUESTION

Does that sound like where you are?

SPIRITUAL CHEMOTHERAPY

The scenario is all too familiar. Cancer shows up and tests show it has spread. It can't be cut out, so the doctors try to eliminate it with chemotherapy.

We all know somebody who has been through chemo, usually administered through a long series of IVs. As patients, we know very little about how the chemicals work. We have to trust the medicines and doctors and do what we're told. We give up a lot of life in the short-term. We feel bad, our hair comes out, our immune system is weakened, and we can't be around other people. But over time we feel better, life returns, and our time on earth is extended. Sometimes, when the cancer is caught early, we're healed completely.

If you've come down with *spiritual cancer*, you've got to do something.

The good news is that God hasn't lost you, and He's got a spiritual chemo regimen that can get you back on track and heal you. There are four treatments we need for recovery—treatments that are healing for us now and helpful in preventing spiritual cancer from returning. Take a look . . .

1. Read and study your Bible daily. Let God's Word pour into you.
2. Tell somebody you're spiritually sick. The Christian life isn't meant to be lived alone.
3. Pray every day. Really talk to your Heavenly Father.
4. Do something for someone else once a week.

Physical cancer patients almost never miss a treatment.

If you're experiencing spiritual cancer right now, will you commit to this treatment plan for the next thirty days?

PRAYER

**Please give me the faith and the discipline
to follow this regimen, and please meet me
there. In Your beautiful name, amen.**

WHAT MAKES A GREAT LEADER?

Leaders are people who have influence and use it for a purpose. Leaders are always leading, in one direction or the other.

In truth, leadership is more about the *who* than the *what*. It's about the people leading and being led more than what's happening under someone's leadership.

As I think about the qualities of leaders I've followed and learned from, I see five key attributes.

1. **Curiosity**—Leaders have an insatiable hunger to learn and be more.

2. **Humility**—The greatest leader of all time, Jesus, used only two words to describe Himself: "I am gentle and humble in heart" (Matthew 11:29).

3. **Intentionality**—The leaders I've followed knew where they were going and consistently motivated themselves and others in that direction.

4. **Purposeful**—Strong leaders know *why* they're doing what they're doing.

5. **Secure**—They are not about themselves, their egos, or proving anything to anyone. They're comfortable in their own skin.

The best leader knows who he is, where he's going, and why. He uses his God-given intellect to learn and grow. And in humility, he never forgets the two fundamental facts of human enlightenment:

1. There is a God.
2. I am not Him.

PRAYER

Jesus, remind me that I am a leader and You want me to be a leader worth following. Help me be the man who will be given influence that can be used for Your Kingdom. Give me the wisdom to make solid decisions and the courage to act. Above all, let my life and all that I become bring Glory to Your name. Amen.

DECEMBER 13

THE CURSE OF CRITICISM

There's a huge difference between *correction* and *criticism*. The word "criticize" isn't found in the Bible. In fact, most of the verses about criticism use words like "correction," "reproof," "discipline," and "instruction."

Verses like Proverbs 15:1, "A gentle answer turns away wrath, but a harsh word stirs up anger." And Matthew 18:15, "If your brother or sister sins, go and point out their fault, just between the two of you. If they listen to you, you have won them over."

Over and over, God's Word warns us against being harsh, stirring up anger, and judging people. Over and over, He tells us to be edifying and uplifting.

Criticism is "the expression of disapproval of someone or something based on perceived faults or mistakes." *Disapproval of someone* is the problem! As parents, mentors, and leaders, we need to disapprove of sinful behavior but not of sinful people.

It takes patience and care to correct the behavior without criticizing the person. I'm afraid parents today are messing up on this. In the hurry of life, they're criticizing instead of correcting. In a busy moment, it's easy to get the two mixed up and revert to a critical spirit and harsh tone.

Over time, that will lead to low self-esteem, which is a curse that haunts us throughout life. It shows up as defensiveness, perfectionism, and depression. Other parents are so into positivity and so want their children to be happy that their kids rarely receive correction. Over time, that will lead to entitlement, arrogance, a critical spirit, and, ultimately, to low self-esteem.

CHALLENGE

**Correct, don't criticize. Be fully committed
to truth and graciously lead others to live
as they are called in that truth.**

DECEMBER 14

THROWING SHADE

The term "throwing shade" has seeped into mainstream culture over the last few years. It means to talk trash about a friend or acquaintance, to publicly denounce or disrespect.

The term comes from the way a cloud slips between the sun and what it's shining on. The cloud *throws shade*. It doesn't shine as brightly in the shade as it did in the sun.

If I want someone not to shine so brightly, I throw shade on them by subtly cutting them down in public. I become the cloud that makes them dimmer and less brilliant.

I think a lot of us throw shade on our spouses and don't have a clue we're doing it. When I used to do this, I honestly thought I was being funny. I finally figured out that it wasn't funny and stopped.

Now I catch myself before it comes out. One definition of maturity is "not saying everything you think." Maybe I'm finally maturing.

Your wife is a daughter of the King of kings. When I explain this concept to my mentees, I share this vision: "Imagine you live in the castle of your father-in-law, the King. He lives on the top floor, while you and your wife (his daughter) live on the middle floor. All his armed guards and troops live on the floors below. They have lots of swords, knives, and guns, and they're *very loyal* to the king."

Would you throw shade in that situation?

I don't think so.

CHALLENGE
Never throw shade on your wife. Ever.

RADICAL EMPATHY

My friend Reggie Joiner gives a great talk about *empathy*. He has the most useful definition I've heard.

> Empathy: to pause your thoughts and feelings long enough to engage with the thoughts and feelings of another person.

It's simple to say, harder to do. For starters, we live in our own world. We're constantly thinking and feeling things about ourselves. We can't help it. We're naturally "me-focused," looking out for ourselves and making plans for our next meeting, snack, phone call, whatever.

Our focus is fleeting, and after the first few seconds of a conversation, we're done. Our minds slip back to *our* agenda, to *our* thoughts and *our* feelings. The other person felt cared about for a second, but it left as quickly as it came.

An empathetic person *pauses*. Stops. Focuses. Actually pays attention. Fully engages. Listens to the other person and connects with what they're saying and feeling.

This requires *selflessness* and *patience*. It requires *love*.

In our ultra-busy lives, *listening is loving*.

When we pause and truly listen to another person—when we take the time to care by engaging—they feel that love and the relationship gets stronger.

Try it! With every person and in every conversation this week, put the other person first. When you feel the urge to talk about you, ask a follow-up question about something they said. Stay with *their* thoughts and feelings rather than switching back to yourself! This is moment-by-moment loving your neighbor.

SCRIPTURE

**"The second is this: 'Love your neighbor as yourself.'
There is no commandment greater than these." (Mark 12:31)**

5 KEYS TO PATIENCE

I'm a work in progress when it comes to patience. For years, I had almost none. I was always in a hurry, impatient with everything and everybody. Slowly but surely, I'm making some progress. Here's how:

1. **Control the controllables**–Then set aside what you can't control. Once I've done all I can do to affect the controllables, I can relax and trust God for the outcome, if I choose to!

2. **Think about the worst-case scenario**–I learned this one from my wife while sitting in an awful traffic jam. She saw my frustration and said, "Hey, what if God has allowed us to be right here to protect us from something awful?"

3. **Look for more information**–I hate putting things off. I'm a "build it, try it, fix it," kind of guy. But if I wait just a little bit, if I let the situation unfold and the facts reveal themselves to me, I end up with more data and a better decision.

4. **Patience is respect**–Not everyone thinks, decides, or moves at the same speed. Impatience can communicate disrespect.

5. **Lean on your faith**–Our faith in our sovereign, loving God enables us to choose patience. If I choose to trust God with the outcome *of everything,* I grow in patience. James 1:3 says,

> "Because you know that the testing of your faith produces perseverance."

And then there's verse 4 . . .

> "Let perseverance finish its work so that you may be mature and complete, not lacking anything."

To paraphrase, patience grows as you exercise your faith.

QUESTION

Do you want to be mature and complete? Practice trusting God, and along the way, He'll grow your patience.

DECEMBER 17

UNEXPRESSED GRATITUDE

"Thank you very much!"

It slides off our tongues like butter. But have you noticed your reaction when you do something for someone and they say nothing?

Gratitude carries weight. Watch your reaction when you do something for someone and they don't acknowledge it. Andy Stanley teaches this principle:

> Unexpressed gratitude feels like ingratitude.

Nothing chaps us like ingratitude. Even though we might not have expected a thank you, there's a vacuum when gratitude isn't expressed. We feel unappreciated, taken for granted, and even angry when our efforts toward kindness aren't acknowledged.

One of my young friends just surrendered to Jesus. He's brand-new at this walking with God stuff. "What do I do?" "What do I say?" he asks. "You tell me God in my daily life is more than a fifteen-minute quiet time in the morning. Help me out here."

My advice? Say, "Thank You, Lord!" All day long. Over and over. "Thank You, God, for loving me. Thank You for saving me. Thank You for adopting me into Your family. Thank You for sending Jesus to pay for my sins. Thank You for giving me peace about death and confidence about heaven. Thank You, Lord, for everything You give me."

Gratitude is the only sure cure for anxiety, and nothing develops an attitude of gratitude like thanking God for everything. Big things. Little things. Hard things. Easy things. Everything.

CHALLENGE

Starting today, see how many opportunities you can find to say an authentic thank you. If there's someone you've been meaning to send a note to or call, do it now. Make this the beginning of a more grateful heart, one that doesn't just think it but expresses it.

December 18

SCARS OR MERIT BADGES

I love the conversations I have with my friend Rocky. One of the most thoughtful men I know, he came out with this one the other day:

"I teach from my scars, not my merit badges."

For years now, I've been trying to inspire men to become mentors to younger men. I tell them they don't need a vest full of merit badges, just a willingness to "go there" about the crap in their lives before Jesus forgave them and the good stuff that's happened since. Good mentors don't give advice, they point guys to Scripture and share their stories. *They show their scars.*

When I share my life story with men, they yawn when I talk about my accomplishments—about my merit badges. But when I open up about my scars, I have their undivided attention!

Why? Because it's real, genuine, and authentic. Yeah, they can read stories about people who made the same mistakes, but they don't *know* those people.

Do you get a merit badge for sharing the evil stuff God redeemed you from? Not at all.

But two things happen when a guy opens up about his dark corners with the men he's trying to influence.

First, God gets the glory, not just for forgiving all that stuff, but for creating a clean heart in him.

The second thing is that a bond forms between transparent people. Mutual respect comes from mutual humility. Instead of counting each other's merit badges, we're seeing each other as peers, as equals before God, as sinners saved by grace.

QUESTION

**Are you willing to share your scars and your story
to help younger men avoid the mistakes you made?**

DECEMBER 19

PREOCCUPIED

If your mind is *preoccupied*, it's taken. It's off the grid. It's uninhabitable by any other meaningful thought. I see drivers who are preoccupied, swerving gently down the road, talking on the phone or reading texts and emails. I see husbands in restaurants with their wives and kids, preoccupied with their smartphones, sports scores, fantasy leagues, business stuff, whatever.

Here's how being preoccupied impacts my life . . .

1. I can't focus on the *current thing* because I'm thinking about the *next thing*.

2. I know I'll feel free when I'm *caught up*, but I'm never caught up, so I'm never totally free.

3. I'm constantly preoccupied with the future. It's hard to stay focused on the *here and now*.

4. Being preoccupied leads me to put things off, especially when I'm facing things I don't particularly want to do.

5. Being preoccupied keeps me constantly busy. There's never a break for rest. I'm more tired throughout my day and especially at the day's end.

The Lord reminds us we'll "be transformed by the renewing of our minds" (Romans 12:2), not the refreshing of our calendar. It's what (or who) we think about that matters.

One of my favorite (and most convicting) words is *deliberate*. I set out to be more *deliberate*. I also love the word *intentional*, but intentionality without thoughtfulness can be exhausting.

I love getting out one of my older Bibles and reading everything printed in red ink—just the stuff Jesus said. It always strikes me that *Jesus was never in a hurry*!

QUESTION

Will you be more deliberate today?

LIKE-HEARTED VS. LIKE-MINDED

The other day I was trying to describe the kind of people I want to be close friends with. I rarely struggle to find words, but I was stumped. Then these words came out of my mouth:

"I want to do life with people who are like-hearted."

I had to think about what that really means.

Most of my friends are like-minded. So are yours. It's much easier to live as a Christian in the presence of other Christians, just like it's easier to have conversations with groups of people of the same sex, or race, or political persuasion. Like-mindedness says we think alike, believe alike, watch a lot of the same shows, and are appalled by the same evils. It's a lot about what's in our heads.

But like-heartedness is different. The Scriptures often interchange the word "desire" for the word "heart." Like-hearted people *desire* the same things. In creating characters, screenwriters always start with, "Who is he and what does he want?"

In the real-world, what we want flows from who we are, from our character. Like-minded people usually believe the same things are wrong or bad, but may *want* very different things. Like-hearted people want the same things, have similar hopes and dreams, and are active in pursuing them.

I can choose to spend my life sitting around talking about things with like-minded people, or I can *do something* with people who are like-hearted.

There is nothing like being on-mission for Jesus with people who have a heart for God similar to yours. We need more people in our lives who are like-hearted, ready to work, serve, and lead together in order to impact others for eternity.

QUESTION

Will you seek like-hearted people to do life with?

WHY IMAGINATION MATTERS

My friend Reggie Joiner says, "Encouraging imaginative thinking in your kids can help them be more empathetic when they grow up."

There's an important connection between imagination and empathy. How can we foster this in ourselves and others? Let me illustrate.

I heard a speaker tell about being in the car with some of his mentees when they came upon a police officer directing traffic. The cop was scowling and being mean to everyone. One of his guys said, "Man, is he having a bad day, I hope my wife never runs across him."

The mentor said, "Oh, I know him. He lost *his* wife to cancer recently. His daughter is struggling with accepting the loss of her mother and has turned to drugs to hide her pain. The cop asked for a leave of absence, but his boss told him to 'get over it,' and to add insult to injury, because of his personal anger and instability, his boss took him off regular patrol and relegated him to directing traffic."

"Is that really true?" asked the mentee.

"No, I totally made it up," the mentor said. "But it might be. We're called to love him, right?"

When I interact with someone personally and I'm pausing my thoughts and feelings so I can pay attention to *their* thoughts and feelings, I have to *imagine* what they're facing, the environment they're living in, the dynamics of their relationships, and how they really must feel in that moment. Imagining can give us a head start on empathy, help us be motivated to stay in the conversation, and enable us to *truly listen* to learn what they're facing.

QUESTION

Will you take time to empathize and imagine the other person's world? It's the first step toward showing them the love of Jesus and building a stronger relationship.

"I KNOW"

I reconnected with an old friend recently, and as we talked, I was totally distracted by something he was doing. No matter what I said, his response was, "I know!"

I wanted to say, "No, you *don't* know. I haven't even finished my thought!" It felt like he wasn't interested in what I said, or he was so arrogant he thought he knew everything. The conversation ended, and I moved on with my day. We're still friends, and I didn't try to fix him.

But then I started catching myself saying the same thing to my wife. I heard my voice saying those words and realized how it must make her feel. "I know" doesn't invite more conversation, it shuts it down. When we're talking to our wives, we must *train ourselves to listen*.

There are other words we sometimes use to punt the conversation and move forward—"Yeah, yeah, yeah," "Uh huh, I get it," "Sure," or simply speaking over the person with your next thought as your get-this-over-with getaway strategy.

The Bible doesn't include a lot of the dialogue before and after Jesus spoke what's recorded in Scripture. But if there was ever a guy who could have said, "I know," and be telling the truth, it was Him!

Yet I can't imagine Jesus saying, "I know," in conversation. He was full of love, joy, peace, patience, kindness, goodness, gentleness, faithfulness, and self-control. And He listened. Really listened.

CHALLENGE

**Let's replace, "I know," with eye contact
and genuine interest.**

FIGHTING FEAR

One of my favorite Scriptures is 2 Timothy 1:7: "For God has not given us a spirit of fear and timidity, but of power, love, and self-discipline" (NLT). The spirit of fear that grips us is not from God. It's coming from the other source—from the evil one.

We can argue all day about who or what Satan is, but almost everyone will go along with the idea that evil is at least the absence of God. So we could rephrase the verse this way: "The spirit of fear shows up when God is absent."

God's presence and the presence of evil are mutually exclusive. If we remember to call out to Jesus the instant we feel fear, the *spirit of fear* will back off.

The next phrase of the verse says that instead of fear, God gives us a *spirit of power*. He's reminding us that He's powerful. That He has the ability to protect us from whatever people or circumstances we're facing.

Then He tells us He's given us His *spirit of love*.

God is love—perfect love. Scripture says, "Perfect love drives out fear" (1 John 4:18). Now we've taken a double dose of calm pills. We've realized the fear we're feeling isn't from God, we've called out to Jesus, who has replaced the darkness of fear with light, and we know His perfect love will cast out fear when it comes back.

Lastly, God gives us a *spirit of self-discipline*. It's an inner confidence to make hard choices now that reap rewards later. It creates an unwavering strength in the words of God to face the world and all of its unknowns.

QUESTION

Will you call on God and His Word to fight fear?

DECEMBER 24

PROCESSING GRACE

At age twenty-three, I got my first promotion with AT&T. I was placed in charge of an administrative office and was responsible for managing Betty, Mary, and Janie.

Not long after I started, my boss called me to his office. It seemed important. He handed me an envelope with Betty's name on it.

He said her job had been reclassified and the company was giving her back pay for several years. The check was for over $12,000. . . more than half her annual pay. How would she respond?

"I'm not going to take this check. I didn't really earn it." Or maybe, "It's about time someone took note of how hard I work and made things right." Or, "I guess this is just my lucky day. I'm going to book a cruise and have myself a good time!" Or maybe, "I'm really grateful for this check, but I'm torn. I don't feel like I *should have this!*" Or, "I'm so grateful for this. Thank you, thank you, thank you!"

Believers in Jesus have the same decision to make. When we think about God's grace towards us, there's a response in our hearts. It's automatic. Some try to earn it by being good. Some say, "This is too good to be true." Some accept grace with their words, but fail to grasp it in their hearts.

God's grace, when we accept it, gives us the freedom to live our lives *forward facing* and with a heart full of *gratitude*.

Thank You, Jesus!

(Oh, and she cashed the check!)

SCRIPTURE

**"For it is by grace you have been saved,
through faith– and this is not from yourselves,
it is the gift of God." (Ephesians 2:8)**

SUNBALLOUSA

I often think about Jesus' mother at this time of year. I imagine Mary standing there watching all these people bowing down and worshiping her baby. From kings to shepherds, they brought gifts and stared at her newborn.

Scripture says she "treasured all these things in her heart" (Luke 2:51). Other versions use the word "held" or "pondered." The original Greek text used the word *sunballousa*, which means "placing together for comparison."

What things could she have been comparing?

Mary was human. There was a *flesh narrative* running through her head that told about her future life, marriage, and family. Her life had changed in a way she could never have imagined. Far from home, cast out of her community, now an unwed mother with a baby and a boyfriend.

But then she had the *God narrative*. Watching men honor baby Jesus would surely have been humbling, gratifying, and fulfilling if she could ignore the flesh narrative and totally embrace the God story.

Mary pondered which narrative she would believe, own, and live out of. Maybe that's the beauty of Mary and the lesson God has for us from her experience. Mary had a choice as to which story she would tell herself—the flesh version or God's.

We face this same dilemma every day. We all have two stories going on at the same time. The flesh narrative explains everything in human terms (i.e., without God), and the God narrative sees God's hand in all the happenings of life.

We're free to choose which narrative to believe. As for me, I'm believing the God version. And Scripture implies that Mary did too.

QUESTION

Which version of *your* story will you believe?

KNOWING ALL YOU'RE SUPPOSED TO

Occasionally we get hung up on something and struggle to get by it. A theological question, like if God is all good where did evil come from? Or why do bad things happen to good people? How can we ask God so many questions but get so few answers?

Sometimes, we want more of God, but it doesn't seem God is ready to show us more. Apparently, this isn't a new problem. Here's what Catherine of Genoa wrote back in the fourteenth century:

> "Therefore I will not weary myself with seeking beyond what God wants me to know. Instead I will abide in peace with the understanding God has given me, and I will let this occupy my mind. If we are to see properly, we must pluck out of our eyes our own presumption. If we gaze too long at the sun, we go blind; in this manner, I think, does pride blind many of us who want to know too much."

If pride *is* the enemy of humility, it makes sense that pride may be driving our need to know. It is not natural for us to say, "This is all I need to know for now. I will 'abide in peace with the understanding God has given me,' and I will let *that* occupy my mind."

Life is a journey. We can't know what's ahead, but our best life is lived knowing God is *with* us. A life of faith lived in rhythm with God, not getting ahead nor behind.

SCRIPTURE

**"Trust God from the bottom of your heart
don't try to figure out everything on
your own." (Proverbs 3:5 MSG)**

December 27

RENEWING YOUR MIND

I've been trying to renew my mind by replacing negative thoughts with good, positive ones. My words with better words.

I started with the list of adjectives from Philippians 4:8 where we are told to choose . . .

True thoughts	Noble thoughts
Right thoughts	Pure thoughts
Lovely thoughts	Admirable thoughts
Excellent or praiseworthy thoughts	

Think about whatever you're most grateful for and turn that thought into a prayer, "Lord, I am so grateful You adopted me into Your family." "Jesus, thank You for letting me be born in such a great country." "Father, thank You for giving me such a healthy, caring wife."

Before I know it, the negative stuff is gone from my mind, and I've been lifted up.

Can you see how important *words* are? The words we think usually come out in what we say. I love the verse where Jesus explains how important our words are: "What goes into someone's mouth does not defile them, but what comes out of their mouth, that is what defiles them" (Matthew 15:11).

How cool would it be if in *every* relationship, conversation, and writing, we used words that communicated truth, purity, and excellence in thought and deed?

SCRIPTURE

"A good man brings good things out of the good stored up in his heart, and an evil man brings evil things out of the evil stored up in his heart. For the mouth speaks what the heart is full of." (Luke 6:45)

DAYS OF DOUBT, SEASONS OF PEACE

Years ago, a close friend faced a big decision. He wrangled with it for months, leaning one way, then the other. One day, he walked out by the water to think and pray.

A friend saw him and strolled out to chat. Once the man shared his dilemma, his friend asked, "Do you have days of doubt and seasons of peace? Or days of peace with seasons of doubt?" It was a game-changing question. Soon my friend knew what to do.

My favorite verse about this says to "let the peace of Christ rule in your hearts" (Colossians 3:15). The word "rule" comes from *brabeúō*, which means to "act as an umpire." Christ is an arbitrator. He looks at the facts and rules one way or the other—in this context, peace or not peace. If we let the *peace of Christ* lead us in our decisions, we'll either have peace or we won't, depending on how He leads us.

Sometimes we don't have a clear peace in our hearts. We're torn. We need time to just sit in the decision for a while and wait to see how God moves in our heart, giving Him room to send the *season of peace* and dial down the *days of doubt*.

Are you wrestling with a big decision? Does either option conflict with Scripture? Sometimes that can narrow the options. Does either option create strife with your wife and family? That might make it simpler. Of the remaining options, which offers *seasons of peace*?

SCRIPTURE

**"Let the peace of Christ rule in your hearts,
since as members of one body you were called
to peace. And be thankful." (Colossians 3:15)**

DECEMBER 29

IN LIGHT OF THE FACTS

"Just give me the facts." We men say it all the time. But sometimes our biggest problems stem from not accepting the facts, from deceiving ourselves and believing something other than the truth. Here's a painful principle:

A problem without a solution is a fact.

This is particularly true of optimists like me. I tell myself all kinds of lies to keep hope alive, to see "a pony in the pile," to think a certain problem can be solved.

Suppose my problem is that I want to dunk a basketball. Now, I'm about 5'10" and I can't jump. At all. I can lose weight, work out, hire a personal trainer who works with the vertically challenged, practice jumping eight hours a day, but this side of heaven, I'll never dunk a basketball. There is no solution to this problem. So failing to dunk a basketball is no longer a problem, it's a fact. I cannot dunk. Period.

Think about how much time and effort we spend on unsolvable problems. To call it a fact seems so final. So hopeless. That's why we call them cold, hard facts. But wouldn't it be smarter to accept the facts and live in light of them?

What's bothering you these days? Are you stuck, trying to solve a problem that has no solution? Will you accept the facts and set yourself free?

God is with you. He might not take away the problem, but He'll help you deal with it. He won't change the facts, but He'll be with you as you live in light of the facts, no matter how hard they are to accept.

SCRIPTURE

"Then you will know the truth, and the truth will set you free." (John 8:32)

CURRICULUM HELPS US DODGE COMMUNITY

Over the years I've observed that people, especially men, often avoid opening up and truly connecting with others. Having a book to read and discuss or homework to do and share is a surrogate for getting together, listening to each other, and truly knowing and being known.

I've come to this realization slowly—like glacier speed. We were once in a small group with John Maxwell and his wife, Margaret. Everyone just wanted to be social and talk. Guess who was always pushing for a curriculum? Yep, yours truly. A disciple is a learner and follower of Jesus Christ, right? So, if I wasn't learning something, why bother?

What I missed was that life is primarily about relationships. It began with the Trinity—relationships between God the Father, Jesus the Son, and the Holy Spirit. Through Christ's death on the cross, we were added to this circle, kindred spirits on a journey hand-in-hand with the members of the Trinity and with each other.

I'm not busting on curriculum. We do need to keep learning about God and His Word. But we also need men to slow down and engage with other men, sometimes without a curriculum and even without a specific purpose. We just need the connection. We need to know and be known.

QUESTION

Will you get out of your self-imposed isolation and push yourself to get connected with other men who want to follow Jesus?

LEADERS GO FIRST

Drive through any small town and you'll see buildings crammed side by side. First there was a store, then a cafe, then a bank, then a barbershop. Before you know it, there's a little town with sidewalks, churches, and schools.

It struck me that someone had to go first. The first building had to be built with four walls before anyone else could come beside and attach one with only three. Whether it's a town, school, business, or church, someone has to go first if anything new is going to happen.

Is there something you've been thinking about starting? How do you know if you should? Here are a few questions to ponder.

- Is there something you feel could and should be done?
- Is it a burden? Does it weigh on you?
- Have you thought and prayed about it for a long time?
- Do you have experience or expertise that can make it happen?

You've heard the saying, "God doesn't call the prepared, He prepares the called." That is sometimes true. The wisdom of Proverbs points to seeking many counselors. And Jesus talked about counting the cost before launching into things.

While experience is the best teacher, it's often expensive training (sometimes called the school of hard knocks). If we're following Jesus' model for life, we're in community with others, hopefully including wise and discerning folks who would be glad to help you think through your idea.

But thinking through the idea isn't enough. Just like someone had to build the first building, you must act. Leaders do things. They don't get stuck thinking endlessly.

You won't know unless you go.

QUESTION

What would you start next year if there was a zero percent chance it would fail?

It's our hope that your daily journey through Radical Wisdom was helpful. We want you to know that 100% of the profits from this book will be used to grow the relational disciple-making movement through Radical Mentoring.

About Radical Mentoring

Radical Mentoring is a 501(c)(3) organization focused on equipping and encouraging churches and mentors to build leaders and disciple-makers through intentional men's small group mentoring.If your church is ready to activate its men or if you're ready to take your leadership to the next level and make "the outward turn" by investing your life experience in the next generation, visit radicalmentoring.com.

About Regi Campbell

Regi Campbell is the husband of Miriam, the father of two adult children and grandfather of five. He was CEO of five startup companies, twice served as an Elder at North Point Community Church and is the Founder and Chairman of Radical Mentoring. His previous books include *About My Fathers Business, Mentor Like Jesus,* and *What Radical Husbands Do*. He and Miriam reside near Atlanta, Georgia. For more info, visit regicampbell.com.